OTHERWHERE

Also by Kurt Leland

Menus for Impulsive Living:
  A Revolutionary Approach to
  Organizing and Energizing Your Life

OTHERWHERE

A Field Guide to Nonphysical
Reality for the Out-of-Body Traveler

KURT LELAND

HAMPTON ROADS
PUBLISHING COMPANY, INC.

Cover design by Marjoram Productions
Cover art from the *Dream Series*,
by Carolyn Callahan/Moon Island Studio
copyright©1998 Carolyn Callahan

For information write:

Hampton Roads Publishing Company, Inc.
1125 Stoney Ridge Road
Charlottesville, VA 22902

434-296-2772
fax: 434-296-5096
e-mail: hrpc@hrpub.com
www.hrpub.com

If you are unable to order this book from your local
bookseller, you may order directly from the publisher.
Call 1-800-766-8009, toll-free.

Library of Congress Catalog Card Number: 2001094078
ISBN 1-57174-241-7
10 9 8 7 6 5 4 3 2 1
Printed on acid-free paper in Canada

To the memory of
Robert A. Monroe,
pioneer in the exploration of nonphysical reality,
with thanks for having shown me how to get there
and what to do once I'd arrived.

Darest thou now O soul,
Walk out with me toward the unknown region,
Where neither ground is for the feet nor any path to
follow?

No map there, nor guide,
Nor voice sounding, nor touch of human hand,
Nor face with blooming flesh, nor lips, nor eyes are in
that land.

I know it not, O soul . . .

—Walt Whitman, *Leaves of Grass*

Acknowledgments

I'm deeply appreciative of Eleanor Friede's expert advice on the shaping of books, so helpful in the earlier stages of this one. Thanks also go to Rita Warren for monitoring several of my lab sessions at The Monroe Institute and for providing helpful suggestions at an early stage of writing; to Teena Anderson and Skip Atwater, also of The Monroe Institute, for technical support during lab sessions; and to The Monroe Institute itself for permission to quote from transcripts of these sessions.

I owe the greatest debt of gratitude, perhaps, to Alan Goodwin, Brian and Judy Galford, Andrea Isaacs, Steve Katz, George Corbett, Mark Douglas, Kevin Johnson, and the Boston Charles group for encouraging me to share my adventures, believing in them, and providing an unlimited supply of hugs—one of the best antidotes I know for fear of the unknown.

Contents

Preface

Books on astral projection or out-of-body experiences may be divided into three general categories: the first-person accounts of people who are skilled in inducing such altered states of consciousness; how-to manuals for those who wish to acquire these skills; and surveys of scientific and parapsychological studies of the phenomenon. All three types seem to have an unusually long staying power in the book market.

The late Robert Monroe's groundbreaking classic *Journeys Out of the Body,* for example, has been continuously in print for nearly thirty years. Oliver Fox's accounts of experiments undertaken in the earlier part of this century are never out of print for long. The more scholarly studies often refer to these classics, and the how-to manuals refer to both.

I've often had the feeling that, with the exception of the rare personal accounts, books on out-of-body experiences are more or less interchangeable. They serve up the same or similar statistics, anecdotes, and induction techniques—even the same conclusions. Monroe stands alone in the range and novelty of his adventures.

My out-of-body adventures began when I was fourteen. I had no idea what was happening to me and tried to make it stop. Years later I came across *Journeys Out of the Body* and after reading it, summoned the courage to explore the strange world that's accessible only through such experiences. Monroe the pioneer demonstrated that it was possible not only to visit distant locales on Earth while out of body and to see what was happening there, to return and verify the accuracy of what was perceived, but also to venture into a reality completely different from the one we're familiar with: a nonphysical reality that I call *Otherwhere.*

I've spent many years exploring Otherwhere. These explorations—some conducted at The Monroe Institute, a research organization in Faber, Virginia, dedicated to the scientific study of altered states of consciousness—have allowed me to answer for myself some of the questions that have excited the curiosity of humankind since the beginning of time: how our universe came to be; what God is; the nature of ordinary versus altered realities; the origin and ultimate purpose of humankind; the existence of the soul; survival after death; and the sense of individual purpose in living. I call these the *eternal questions.* I've written this book to share with my readers the answers I've discovered through exploring nonphysical reality. I also wish to spur them on to undertake such explorations themselves—not to take my word on these matters, but to satisfy their own curiosity about them.

It's my firm belief that what prevents people from having out-of-body experiences and exploring nonphysical reality on their own is fear of the unknown. In my experience, the best way to overcome fear of the unknown is to familiarize oneself with the personal accounts of people who have overcome that fear themselves. I believe that personal accounts of out-of-body experiences are far superior to how-to manuals in stimulating people to venture into the unknown. Reading such accounts makes the unknown less unfamiliar, and therefore less frightening. Furthermore, personal accounts do what no scientific study can—they stimulate in the reader an intense yearning to have adventures similar to those of the author.

In my explorations, I've benefited little from how-to manuals. The exercises contained in them have rarely worked for me, and I know many others for whom the same thing has been true. It was the yearning stimulated by reading *Journeys Out of the Body* that helped me overcome my fear of the unknown. By presenting the scenes, dwellers, and phenomena one is likely to encounter in Otherwhere, I intend my field guide to nonphysical reality to help others do the same.

Dr. Raymond A. Moody, Jr.'s best-selling book *Life After Life* and its several equally best-selling sequels began a spate of first-person accounts of near-death experiences—for example, Betty Eadie's best-seller, *Embraced by the Light.* Such books describe cases in which people have died under traumatic conditions yet were resuscitated. While unconscious, these people have often visited a nonphysical reality that they assume was the Afterlife. Their visits are usually cut short by the return to life of their physical bodies. Such tantalizing glimpses of what happens after we die clearly have a great fascination for the public.

Many of my own out-of-body adventures have taken place in what I call the *Afterdeath Zone,* an area of Otherwhere in which the spirits of the deceased may be encountered. Thus, I've had near-death experiences of my own—without the requisite close brush with death. My adventures weren't cut short by resuscitation, so I've been able to get a more complete view of what happens after death than many people who have had near-death experiences. In the hope of answering the questions left open by the fragmentary nature of their accounts, I've made descriptions of what goes on after death a central theme of this book.

Although I've left the summarization of scientific research on out-of-body experiences to others better qualified—indeed, I've been the subject of such researches myself on several occasions—I have provided discussions of the advantages and drawbacks of a number of means of accessing nonphysical reality, including meditation, hypnosis, drugs, shamanism, out-of-body experiences, near-death experiences, and lucid dreaming.

The focus of *Otherwhere,* however, is my adventures—this is not the usual how-to book. Even so, on numerous occasions, I was given instruction in how to achieve the states of consciousness necessary to explore Otherwhere—usually by one of its denizens—so I've passed along this information in the hopes that others may be able to use it as well.

PART I

ORIENTATION

1

A Visit to Nonphysical Reality

"Are you completely comfortable?" Rita asked.

I did a quick check of my environment. The waterbed on which I was lying beneath a light blanket seemed warm enough. The slightly restraining pressure of the electrodes attached to my fingers to monitor my heart rate and galvanic skin response would take some getting used to. But the headphones through which Rita was speaking to me were well-adjusted—they wouldn't crush my ears. The room was so dark that it was impossible to see the microphone dangling above my mouth.

I'd been told that "the Booth," as it was called by the staff of The Monroe Institute, was totally sound- and lightproof. Lined on the outside with copper sheets and oriented toward magnetic north, the Booth was supposed to be the ideal setup for producing altered states of consciousness, including out-of-body experiences. Only one ingredient was missing: the patented Hemi-Sync sounds invented by the late Robert Monroe, author of the well-known book *Journeys Out of the Body*.

Monroe believed that altered states of consciousness could be facilitated by subtle manipulations of sound waves. He founded The Monroe Institute, located in the foothills of the Blue Ridge Mountains of Virginia, as a laboratory in which to test his theories. It was here that he hit upon the idea of feeding slightly different sound signals to each ear through a pair of headphones. The two hemispheres of the brain would act in concert to produce a third signal that existed within the brain alone. The resulting hemispheric synchronization made it possible to achieve a variety of altered states of consciousness, each with a different set of properties.

Subsequent research at the Institute focused on how to use these distinctive brain-wave states to enable out-of-body experiences. After many successful experiments along these lines, The Monroe Institute began offering outreach programs to the public. People could come to a week-long program, experience the Hemi-Sync sounds for themselves, and share their adventures and questions with Monroe—while he was still living—and his excellent training staff.

I'd come to the Institute by a different route. My former literary agent, Eleanor Friede, was a neighbor of Bob Monroe. She arranged for me to spend some time in the lab when I was visiting her in the fall of 1988. Having read *Journeys Out of the Body* some years earlier, I'd experimented more recently with the Hemi-Sync tapes manufactured and distributed by The Monroe Institute. I was already familiar with several of the altered states produced by these sounds. The advantage of spending time in the Booth, however, was that the monitor in charge could generate Hemi-Sync sounds that were custom-tailored to one's needs in an environment free of distractions.

"Everything seems fine," I told Rita, who was sitting some distance away from the Booth at a console that allowed her to produce and mix the Hemi-Sync sounds. Rita was a former university professor of criminal psychology who came to The Monroe Institute after she and her husband had retired. Fascinated with the work of the Institute, they bought property and built a house nearby. Rita, I was told, was one of the best of the lab's monitors. She too was wired with headphones and a mike so that we could communicate easily as the session progressed.

Before going into the Booth, I'd been informed that one of the unique properties of the Hemi-Sync sounds and the Booth setup is the creation of a split consciousness: one can report on what's happening in an altered state without disrupting one's participation in that state. I would be expected to give a detailed description of what I was going through at every moment. Meanwhile, Rita would be on standby to provide assurance, ask for clarification of my observations, or to bring me back to ordinary waking consciousness if I became frightened or was otherwise unable to proceed.

Rita began to feed Hemi-Sync sounds into my headphones. At a certain point I alerted her to the fact that I was in an altered state.

"Very good," Rita replied. "When you're ready, I'd like you to continue to expand your consciousness. Relax and let the energy flow, and go to a comfortable place for you to report from."

After a while, I described a sensation of floating, of being gently pulled or led somewhere. When I no longer seemed to be moving, I found myself in a cave. I was surrounded by ragged, semi-human creatures who were moaning in unspeakable pain. Some were tearing their hair out and beating their breasts, others were gnashing their teeth and gouging themselves with their fingernails.

I noticed an intense light far away. I made my way toward it. It turned out to be an exit from the cave. When I emerged from this exit, I found myself in the midst of a brilliance so dazzling that I was stunned, unable to move. As I got used to the brightness, I began to make out the features of a landscape. Everything was bathed in golden light.

The surface I was standing on was like a plain that extended a considerable distance before it ran up against a series of rounded terraces. Each terrace was about the same height as the last, but not as wide, like a sequence of low steps that ascended to a dais in the center. On the dais was an object so bright that it could have been the Sun. It was the source of the light that pervaded the plain. It seemed to be beating like a vast heart, and every pulse sent waves of light that somehow also seemed like waves of love throughout the entire region.

I began to drift across the plain, irresistibly drawn toward the Sun/heart. At a certain point, I came across a being made of the same light that emanated from the Sun/heart. This being was like an eddy in the stream of light, a place where the light curled in on itself, creating a localized variation in density. I realized then that a diffuse awareness permeated the entire region, and that the being I had just encountered was like a condensation of that awareness into a more focused form.

I greeted the being and asked where I was.

"This is the Afterdeath Zone," it replied. "And you are currently in the region called Heaven by most of the world's religions."

"Does that mean the cave I just passed through is Hell?"

The being was puzzled. "Hell?" it said. "I don't know what you mean. Over there is someone who should be able to answer your question." The being directed my attention toward a larger vortex of energy nearby and moved on.

My curiosity about the cave seemed to draw me away from the first being and toward the second. As I approached the larger being, I felt that I was coming into the presence of a holy man, a saint, some highly developed soul. I wondered if I should kneel or bow. The first being had a businesslike air. No doubt it was fulfilling some kind of duty when I interrupted it with my question. The larger one, however, radiated an overwhelming sense of compassion.

"Can I be of service, little one?" it said. Somehow I didn't mind being called "little" by a presence so immense. There was nothing condescending about the being's tone: it was all gentleness and humor. Since it seemed to be towering over me, the being was clearly just stating a fact.

"I was wondering if you could tell me about the cave I

passed through on the way here—the one where everyone seems to be suffering so intensely. Is that Hell?"

The being laughed, a musical sound like the shimmer of tiny bells. "No, little one. There's no such thing as Hell here—except for the private hells people create for themselves from anger, fear, regret, guilt, shame, lust, and self-pity.

"You see, the Afterdeath Zone is a part of nonphysical reality—or Otherwhere, as we call it. Thought creates experience over here. When people who have repressed such emotions die, they experience a kind of hell until the emotions have been discharged. We do our best to help them release themselves from their private hells. But some are more stubborn about punishing themselves than others.

"As for the cave you mentioned, call it an insane asylum for existentialists. Their problem is they don't believe they're here. They remain in that place for as long as it takes them to accept that there's an Afterlife. Their self-immolation is an expression of how their consciences tormented them while alive. They had dispensed with the idea of a Higher Power that insists that all action must contribute to the greater good, and so there was no basis for them to determine which of their actions were appropriate and which were not.

"This Higher Power doesn't judge them for having performed inappropriate actions. Sometimes it's necessary to work against the greater good in order to understand that obstructing someone else's growth merely obstructs one's own. And ignoring the greater good can be just as obstructive as actively working against it.

"They're in that cave because they're still blind to the existence of this Higher Power. They *can't* see what they *won't* see. Even their torment is purely their own invention."

"The Higher Power of which you speak—is that the Sun/heart I see way off in the distance?" I asked.

"In a manner of speaking, yes. But don't confuse that being with the omnipotent presence you call God. There are more comprehensive powers than that one in Otherwhere! You could call this being the god of humanity. It represents the essence and highest realization of what humans can be, toward which all of us are evolving. As long as there are humans to participate in the cycle of birth and rebirth, that being will pulse its light and love through their veins."

Shortly after this adventure, I returned to ordinary waking consciousness in the Booth. A lab technician entered and removed the electrodes attached to my fingers and I joined Rita in the console room for a debriefing. Aside from a feeling of weariness, I was more amazed and puzzled by this experience than frightened.

I'd heard of near-death experiences in which people who had been pronounced clinically dead had somehow been revived. Often such people reported that they'd been sucked into a dark tunnel and carried into a region of light. While there, they may have engaged in conversation with an entity made of light or love who asked them questions about their lives. This entity may then have pointed out reasons why they should resume these lives and sent them back to their physical bodies. As far as I could tell, I hadn't died while in the Booth. Yet I'd visited a similar region of light, had spoken to a similar entity—and had received answers to some questions of my own. Could I have truly stumbled into "the region called Heaven by most of the world's religions," as the first being I encountered had said?

Sometime later, I read that many people who've had near-death experiences go back to their lives on Earth with reluctance. They often feel an intense desire to return to this region of light and love—but without dying. Had I somehow stumbled upon a way to do so?

2

The Out-of-Body
Training Program

My adventure at The Monroe Institute wasn't the first time
I'd had an unusual experience in an altered state of consciousness. Such experiences had by that time been a part of my life
for almost twenty years. They began when I was fourteen years
old. I remember the night well. Something odd happened as I
was falling asleep. In the midst of a dream that was just beginning to form, I saw myself fainting. A loud noise like the sound
of an airplane taking off filled my ears. A tingling electrical
surge ran from my head to my toes. I thought I was dying.
Terrified, I forced myself to wake up.

Something similar occurred a few weeks later. In the middle
of the night I seemed to awaken from sleep into a totally black
space. I could see, hear, and feel nothing anywhere around me.
All I had was a sense of being gently pulled along, as if on my way
somewhere. I resisted the pull and fought my way back to waking consciousness. When I was fully awake, I found that I'd broken out in a cold sweat. I even felt nauseous from the exertion of
freeing myself from the grip of that frighteningly persistent tug.

For the next several years, as I was falling asleep, I would sometimes hear a rushing noise and feel an electrical surge, which I had come to recognize as the preliminaries of such "nightmares." I trained myself to block these sensations, believing that doing so was a matter of life and death.

At the start of my junior year in college, where I majored in music, I told these experiences to a freshman trumpet player I'd met in the symphonic wind ensemble we both played in. He said that they represented the initial stages of an out-of-body experience. My soul had been in the process of separating itself from my body when I'd heard the rushing noise and felt that electrical tingle. My new friend claimed that ever since his mother had nearly died on an operating table a few years earlier, she'd had frequent out-of-body experiences. He lent me Robert Monroe's first book, *Journeys Out of the Body*, which convinced me that there was nothing dangerous about experiences like the ones I'd had in high school. I began to experiment with altering my consciousness, using Monroe's exercises. I had little luck at first, possibly because the mental block I'd created in high school was so strong.

About this time I began to take a twenty-minute nap each afternoon to recharge myself between classes. That nap became the focal point for my experiments. Just after lying down, I would give myself the suggestion that I might have an out-of-body experience. Sometimes I would just fall asleep. Other times I drifted into an odd state, half awake and half asleep. It was in these "twilight states," as they're sometimes called, that unusual things would happen.

Often I would feel as if I'd passed through some kind of interface, such as that between air and water. I seemed to be slowly sinking in a current of energy that was rushing past me. Everything was blurred, as if I were watching a movie at high speed. I got the sense that I needed to make a mental adjustment so that I would be moving as fast as the energy stream. Only then would I be able to see things clearly. But I was unable to discover just what adjustment was required. Sometimes I passed through another interface into an even faster energy stream. More often than not, however, when I came to that second interface, I seemed to bounce off of it, without passing through, and would awaken immediately.

Sometimes I would dream during my naps. These dreams often took the following form. I would be lying on my bed in my room sleeping. I would hear a rushing sound and feel an electrical surge. These sensations would pass, and I would find myself rolling out of my body, standing up or floating, and looking around the room. At this point I would realize that there was something peculiar about my room. It would be on the wrong wing or floor of my dormitory, or the head of my bed would be oriented in a direction different from its actual one. Sometimes the furniture had been rearranged, or there were things on the dresser that weren't there in real life. I was never sure what to make of these incidents: Were they dreams or out-of-body experiences?

Once, when I awakened in the middle of the night, I sat up and looked around. I felt an odd sensation in the area of my waist. It reminded me of the feeling of immersing my hand in a pool of water: the greater density of the water below the point of immersion, the lightness of the air above it. Suddenly, I realized I was partially out of my body. My torso was completely out, but my legs were still attached. This explained the feeling of lightness in my upper body and that of greater density in my legs. It felt as if I'd waded into a swimming pool, but the lower half of my body was immersed in physical matter rather than water.

I continued experimenting. A year or so after reading Monroe's book, I had my first out-of-body adventure. After lying down for a nap, I felt as if my consciousness were shooting violently out of my head. Instantly, I was several miles away, in a subdivision where one of my high-school friends used to live. I found myself in the kitchen of a house I didn't recognize. As I wandered into the living room, wondering where I was, a dog noticed me and began to bark. A toddler also seemed to be able to see me and began to approach me with curiosity, just as a second, somewhat larger dog rounded the corner of the sofa to see what the commotion was about. The child's mother wasn't within my line of vision. Before I could decide what to do, I felt as if a giant rubber band had stretched as far as it could, and then snapped back. In a rush, I reentered my body and woke up.

A second adventure occurred shortly after that one. While lying down for an afternoon nap, I imagined myself driving on a perfectly straight country road that undulated over steep hills, each of which was exactly the same height as the last. Because some of Monroe's out-of-body experiences began from a feeling of riding gently undulating waves, I figured that if I could imagine that sensation as vividly as possible, using my memory of driving down a country road, I might be able to stimulate an out-of-body experience. My assumption was correct.

Tingling vibrations began to run the length of my body in wavelike rhythmic pulses. But just as I started to rise above my body, the waves became rougher. I began to feel seasick, so I somersaulted back into my body, hitting it with such an impact that I thought I'd knocked myself off the bed. After reorienting myself within my body, I drifted into a state of deep relaxation. A disembodied voice began providing me with nonverbal instruction that went something like this:

"In order to get out of body there are four functions that need to be brought to the same degree of openness," the voice said. "The first is *thinking*. It's best that the mind be relatively clear of worries and concerns. Meditation can be useful in learning how to empty yourself of such mental static.

"The second function is *feeling*. Strong emotions can propel you into unpleasant realities, once you're out of body. Try to conduct your life in such a way that fear, frustration, anger, and so forth are kept to a minimum. And, by all means, do everything you can to eradicate your fear of the unknown.

"The third function is *sensing*. If your body isn't comfortable, its needs may become so insistent that you'll be unable to maintain the altered state that makes out-of-body experiences possible. Thus, it's best to prepare your environment so that you'll be neither too warm nor too cold. The environment should be free of distractions. Use as little light and sound as possible, and make sure there's no chance of disturbance by others. The bladder should be empty when you lie down, since the pressure to urinate can cut short your adventure. Also, it's important for the stomach to be neither too empty nor too full. Both hunger and the feeling of being stuffed will prevent out-of-body experiences.

"The fourth function is *intuiting*. Different senses and mental faculties operate when you're out of body. For example, communication with other beings is largely telepathic. Intuition is the word you use to describe these faculties when they operate in physical reality. The more you can develop intuition while in the body, the easier it will be for you to understand what's happening when you're out.

"If you're having problems managing any of these functions, it's unlikely that you'll be able to get out of your body. However, the following visualization can be useful in preparing yourself for an out-of-body adventure. Imagine a control panel with four levers, one for each of the four functions. Thinking will be on the far left, with feeling, sensing, and intuiting to the right of it, in that order. The levers may be pushed up or down along a scale of intensities. The ideal position is the halfway point between the top and bottom of the scale. As you prepare yourself to go out of body, check the positions of these levers in your mind's eye. If any of them are above the halfway point, then the corresponding function is overstimulated.

"For example, if thinking is too high, then you're too full of worries and concerns about other matters for an out-of-body experience to occur. If feeling is too high, then there's some strong emotion dominating your consciousness. If sensing is too high, then the body is uncomfortable. If intuiting is too high, then you're trying too hard to achieve an altered state. Try to remedy any of these situations.

"If the body is uncomfortable, do whatever may be necessary to eliminate the problem. If you're trying too hard, see yourself gently pulling the intuiting lever down to the halfway point, while telling yourself to relax.

"If any of the levers are below the halfway point, then the corresponding function is understimulated. You're too mentally, emotionally, or physically exhausted for an out-of-body adventure to occur. You'll probably just fall asleep. Go ahead and let yourself do that. You can always try again later, after you've gotten some rest. If the intuition lever is too low, then your fear of the unknown is blocking this function. The only way to get rid of your fear of the unknown is to confront what you're afraid of. So keep on trying.

"After you've made any of these adjustments, see yourself moving the appropriate lever to the halfway point. If it doesn't budge, doesn't move far enough, or springs back to its original position, then you've still got some work to do.

"Once you've gotten the four levers into position, you may try an induction technique for getting out of body. Any technique you feel comfortable with will do."

After I'd received these instructions, it became clear to me that I'd been unable to sustain my earlier out-of-body state because one function was overstimulated and another understimulated. I tried to get out of body again but was unable to maneuver all four levers into the proper positions.

Despite the difficulty I had in applying what I learned from this adventure, I seemed to be making progress with my experiments. But then I ran into a major hurdle, one which Monroe had warned about in his book: sexual desire.

The state of consciousness that allows out-of-body experiences to occur seems in some way to be connected with the libido, at least in men. Perhaps the connection is physiological. Just as men often experience erections during REM sleep—the period when dream activity peaks—so can they have them during an out-of-body experience. As Monroe so tactfully puts it, the sometimes overwhelming desire that can accompany an out-of-body experience may lead to thoughts of "sexual contact (at first with a loved one, then at a strictly sensory level)" (Monroe 1977, 223).

For the next five years, nearly every attempt I made to get out of body would degenerate into sexual fantasy. Only after I recalled what Monroe had done to overcome this hurdle was I able to continue my exploration of the out-of-body state. Monroe discovered that if he were to become distracted by desire, instead of "fighting the idea of sex, ignoring it, or denying its existence," the best thing he could do was to think, "yes, the idea of sex is a very good one, and we (I) must do something about it. I will in just a little while, but first, I want to go somewhere else" (ibid., 192). The technique worked as well for me as it had for Monroe. I was able to resume my experiments.

The next phase of exploration involved becoming familiar with the peculiar characteristics of the out-of-body state. I discovered that the so-called astral body—the part of oneself that seems to separate itself from the physical body—appears to be weightless: it can float and fly. When it encounters physical objects, it usually passes right through them. I found that the wood of a wall, the glass of a window, the metal of a fire door all had different densities. A peculiar and indescribable mental adjustment would allow me to attenuate the substance of my astral body. I could then penetrate such objects as if I were somehow fitting the particles of my own being between the atoms of wood, glass, or metal. The sensation that accompanied my passage through a wall, window, or door was thrilling—an electrical tingle that resembled a sexual orgasm.

I also learned that the astral body is as elastic as a rubber band. On one occasion, I was able to reach my arm from where my body lay on my bed up to the overhead light—a distance of about ten feet. Walking while out of body was awkward until I realized that it wasn't necessary for me to will my feet to take one step at a time. It was far more efficient merely to think of where I wanted to go, near or far. My vision would blur for a moment as I passed through the intervening space, and I would find myself there in short order.

As speedy as this method of locomotion was, it could sometimes be unreliable. I found that the slightest whim could throw it off. Once, when I was returning from an out-of-body visit to my folks, who lived in Dayton, Ohio, roughly a thousand miles from my home in Boston, I found myself flying above the state of Ohio, which was laid out like a relief map below me. Earlier that week an auto mechanic had noticed my Ohio license plate and commented that his wife was from Marion, Ohio. Simply recalling this remark during my out-of-body flight was enough to land me in someone's backyard in Marion, where I found a cat sleeping on a sun-drenched patio.

I couldn't help but wonder what it felt like to reach my hand through organic matter, now that I had mastered wood, glass, and metal. Somewhat mischievously, I reached my hand into the cat's belly. What I encountered felt like tightly twisted sheets coiled up in a pail of warm water. The cat woke up with a start and dashed away, frightened but unharmed.

It was difficult to break myself of certain deeply-ingrained habits. When I approached a door while out of body, I automatically reached for the doorknob. While I might make contact with it, I would be unable to turn the knob and walk through the door—until I remembered that I could simply pass through it if I wished.

My sense of sight was radically affected when I was out of body. Sometimes I could see nothing at all. If I told myself that all I had to do was open my eyes, my *physical* eyes would obey, and that would be the end of the experiment—I'd wake up. So I learned instead to will myself to *see*. My astral vision did not require ambient light as does its physical counterpart. My room could be pitch black, yet I would still be able to see things clearly. Everything appeared in tones of sepia, as in a daguerreotype.

As if to compensate for the frequent lack of color, my astral vision substituted richness of another order. Not only could I see what was in front of me, I could also see what was behind me without turning around. Furthermore, I could perceive both the near and the far sides of things simultaneously, as if I were diffused throughout the room, like a mist, and all of me was capable of sight.

An odd series of dreams paralleled these experiments. The dreams resembled out-of-body experiences, in that I would usually feel myself leaving my body and traveling somewhere. But what occurred after I got there would seem highly improbable. For example, in one of these dreams I traveled to what I believed to be a local art school. I'd stayed in bed quite late that morning because conditions seemed right for practicing the process of getting out of body. I'd already gone out from and come back to my body several times before I arrived at the college, just as classes were changing.

Although I was unaware of the exact time of my visit, it was so late in the morning that the situation seemed plausible. In the midst of a group of girls who were laughing and talking as they walked through a lobby carrying notebooks and backpacks, one seemed to notice me. I was sleeping in the nude. The astral body often appears as a replica of the physical body. That might explain why the girl seemed shocked by what she saw. Still plausible.

Even though I've noticed that animals and very young children seem more able than adults to see someone who's out of body, I've heard of people who are able to sense, and sometimes actually perceive, such a presence. The girl looked as if she'd seen a ghost. I enjoyed her fright, and proceeded to chase other frightened girls through the halls. At one point, I found a grand piano and began to improvise wildly. To an observer it might have seemed as if the keys were moving by themselves. Some people were fascinated, others scared out of their wits. Eventually, I was written up in the school newspaper as a haunting. Hardly had I finished playing the role of ghost when I found myself witnessing a drug deal on a nearby street corner. I wanted to tell someone about the illegal proceedings, and drifted to the nearest police station. No one would pay attention to me.

I was unsure of whether to call this unlikely set of events an out-of-body adventure somehow corrupted by dream elements, or merely a dream of such an adventure. Similar experiences occurred on a regular basis for over a year. After a while, I noticed a pattern. Each of these apparent dreams allowed me either to practice a specific technique for getting out of body or for moving from one location to another, or to set up a situation I might encounter during an out-of-body adventure so that I could figure out the most appropriate way to behave.

These dreams seemed to serve an educational purpose, so I began to call them *out-of-body simulations*. Just as weight-training equipment can isolate a particular muscle group and exercise it alone, so my out-of-body simulations helped me to isolate certain components of the out-of-body experience and rehearse them—without the distraction of all the unfamiliar ways of perceiving and moving that would accompany a full-fledged out-of-body experience.

In retrospect, it seemed clear that the experience described above was a simulation dealing with the philosophical problem of how present I am in my out-of-body image. Am I present enough to be visible to others? To influence matter and thus draw attention to myself? To communicate an urgent message? In later experiences, I learned that, while I may be visible to a few psychically gifted individuals when I'm out of body, I'm otherwise unable to influence my environment, draw attention to myself, or communicate with others—unless they also are out of body.

There seems to be plenty of room for self-indulgence in an out-of-body simulation—terrifying art students or playing mad improvisations on the piano, for example. I've come to believe that such self-indulgence is just a part of the learning process. What would *you* do if you suddenly found that you could make yourself as insubstantial as a ghost? In Woody

Allen's movie *Alice*, one of the male characters takes a special formula of Chinese herbs and becomes invisible. In short order, we find him in a chic New York boutique—in the women's dressing room.

I think that many of us, upon discovering ourselves to be capable of the apparently supernatural powers bestowed by an out-of-body experience—the ability to visit remote locations as if invisible—would want to take advantage of them. My own out-of-body simulations allowed me to do so with no harm done. Such self-indulgence, though enjoyable at first, eventually became boring. Then I was ready to move on to another set of lessons.

Looking back on this series of explorations of the properties of the astral body and of the various problems posed by out-of-body simulations, I've often wondered whether I might have been participating in some kind of training process. If so, my teachers kept a low profile. With the exception of the disembodied voice that offered me instruction in how to get out of body, I rarely had the sense of being guided. Yet the progression of my experiences seemed to have a certain order.

Perhaps the climax of this training period was the point when I allowed my out-of-body self to observe my physical body lying on my bed without believing that I'd died. A few weeks after this experience, during a nap, I found myself looking at a computer screen. Someone I couldn't see was typing at the keyboard. I noticed the following prompt at the bottom of the screen: "COMMAND = ." The invisible typist entered the words "out of body," thus: "COMMAND = OUT OF BODY."

Immediately a set of diagrams and some pages of text appeared on the screen, almost like a dossier. I had trouble reading what was written there and didn't understand the diagrams. But one phrase stuck out: "Most Americans believe they are dying." The invisible typist moved the cursor to that line of the dossier, pressed a couple of keys, and caused it to vanish from the screen. Immediately, a shock of energy ran from the top of my head to my toes and woke me up. It seemed as if the fear that causes many people to misidentify an out-of-body experience as death had been removed from my belief system. From that point forward, my experiences became both more frequent and more involved.

Naturally, the question about whether any of this was real—in the sense that the everyday reality that surrounds us is real—often came up during my experiments. Three incidents allowed me to set the question aside. In one, I found myself hovering near the top of Boston's Bunker Hill Monument—a tall obelisk, like the Washington Monument, which I'd often seen from the highway that passes near it but had never visited. Many months later, while showing my parents around the town, we stopped at the monument and I climbed the stairs to the top. I looked out of each of the four windows, enjoying the sight of the city spread out below me. From the last window, I saw the same view of Massachusetts Bay and the North Shore that I'd remembered from my out-of-body visit.

On another occasion, I found myself in an unfamiliar part of town, standing—or, more properly, floating, since I was out of body—by a wrought-iron grillwork gate to a garden-level apartment in a townhouse that abutted a park with an old-fashioned fountain in its center. I looked for the place for a couple of years until an errand happened to take me down an unfamiliar street in Boston's South End and I saw the townhouse, gate, and fountain, just as I'd remembered them.

The third incident involved travel to the city of Worcester, Massachusetts, which is about fifty miles west of Boston. I had never been there before, although I'd driven along its outskirts on Route 20. There I was, flying over Route 20 late at night. I saw a strip joint that I'd noticed from my car on that earlier occasion—that's how I knew where I was. The place seemed to be closing for the night. The patrons were leaving the building and getting into their cars, or standing around in the parking lot talking to each other. During the next part of my adventure,

I took in the following impressions, which seemed oddly jumbled: an old city-hall-like building; a grassy park with concrete walkways radiating in various directions; a sign made up of large, red plastic letters, which I took to belong to a Woolworth's store; and a couple in a glass-enclosed lobby getting some money from an ATM.

Two years later, a friend and I drove out to Worcester to see the art museum. We passed by Worcester Common, which contained an old city-hall-like building and a grassy park with concrete walkways. We looked for the ATM machine and found it in a high-rise that abutted the common. The red sign, however, was on a different side of the common, much higher up on the building it was attached to than a Woolworth's sign would have been. It said, simply, "NEWS." Even though I'd misread the sign, the correspondence between the elements I remembered from my out-of-body visit and those I discovered upon my real-life visit left me with little doubt that I really had traveled to Worcester on that earlier occasion. If that adventure was real, what about the later ones that, like my visit to the cave of the existentialists, took place in environments so different from those I was familiar with—in what the great being of light called "Otherwhere"? Could they have been real as well?

3

Nonphysical Reality and the Fear of the Unknown

Since 1985, I've recorded nearly two hundred of what I call adventures in consciousness. Some were out-of-body experiences, like those already described. Others involved altered states for which I have no name. Most occurred in the middle of the night, while I was sleeping, or during daytime naps. I couldn't predict when my adventures would occur or induce them at will. I would simply awaken in the morning with memories of a few dreams that referred to mundane matters, along with a residue of something else. When examined, this residue would unfold into one of the adventures recorded here. Sometimes several hours were required to turn these experiences into words.

I've kept a dream log since 1982. Almost every night I recall from one to five dreams—sometimes as many as a dozen. I've taught myself to interpret these dreams and have often received helpful guidance from them. After so many years of paying close attention to my dreams, I'm quite familiar with their emotional flavor. The adventures have a different flavor. They don't seem to yield themselves to interpretation in the same way that dreams do. Sometimes they contain their own interpretations—that is, one of the characters in the adventure may explain the meaning of something I haven't understood.

The ostensible subjects of these adventures are far removed from the usual messages that I receive from my dreams, such as "This is why you're mad at so-and-so" or "You need to cook more often for yourself." The adventures appear to deal with much larger issues: where we came from, why we're here, our place in the cosmos, and what happens after death.

For most people, including myself, the dream world is unstable. Dream objects, locales, and people mix, merge, and transform themselves before our eyes. We rarely return to the same location or meet with the same people on later nights, nor do we have any sense that information gathered in one dream builds on what we already knew from a previous one. My adventures, on the other hand, have an internal consistency. The environments in which I've found myself are usually stable. Information gained during one experience is often confirmed and elaborated by another. I've even encountered the same personae in later adventures—and they and I remember each other and sometimes make reference to our earlier encounters. It's hard for me to dismiss such experiences as mere dreams.

A common thread that has run through all of my adventures is fear of the unknown. With the exception of nightmares, which I have only rarely, this fear is yet another factor that isn't present in my dreams.

I'm not the person I was before the adventures began. My initial excitement gave way to fear as I realized that what I was learning conflicted with my root assumptions about our world. Consistencies kept piling up, however. After a while I could no longer ignore their implications. I began to adjust my beliefs accordingly. But then I became afraid that my new beliefs made me so different from everyone else that people might find me strange, and that I might be rejected or ostracized.

The result of this fear was that the adventures, which had been occurring at the rate of one or two per month, nearly ceased for almost two years. I began to miss them. They had added a dimension of wonder to my life that I eventually came to crave. After a period of soul-searching, I realized that I had lost no friends as a result of telling them about my adventures—and that I was continuing to make new friends. Not only that, but some of the people I'd confided in seemed to respect and appreciate me more deeply for what I'd experienced. In retrospect, it seems that my fear of the unknown was really a fear of having to live the rest of my life alone and unloved—because of what I'd experienced in these adventures. Once I figured this out, and had demonstrated to myself that the fear was unfounded, my adventures resumed.

In order to differentiate between those adventures that seemed to take place in the so-called real world and those whose stable, undream-like, yet often strange or alien environments couldn't be easily located there, I refer to our everyday world as physical reality and the other as nonphysical reality, or Otherwhere. I'm convinced after much shuttling back and forth between these two realities that the latter has some sort of concrete, though immaterial existence. For the sake of this book, however, let's call the idea of nonphysical reality a working hypothesis—an as-if-true or provisional belief. I won't persuade you to accept it. Instead, I'll invite you to consider some of the consequences that such a belief has had on my life, in particular on my inner life.

You've probably heard the phrase "irresistible force meets immovable object." When it comes to exploring nonphysical reality, few truer words were ever spoken. For those who believe that such exploration is possible, the irresistible force is their yearning to undertake it; the immovable object is their fear of the unknown. Somehow, quite unintentionally, many such people have balanced their yearning and their fear so perfectly that their consciousness rarely travels beyond our familiar, everyday environs. But what would happen if they were to reduce their fear of the unknown? The irresistible force of their yearning might begin to gain some ground, perhaps enough to propel them into the nonphysical adventures that they're seeking.

In my opinion, there are three ways to reduce one's fear of the unknown: orientation, familiarization, and communication.

By *orientation*, I mean getting a sense of what nonphysical reality is like. One of the best ways to do this is to read accounts by people who've been there. Such accounts may also stimulate your yearning to explore nonphysical reality.

By *familiarization*, I mean exploring nonphysical reality on your own. Unfamiliar things are often perceived as dangerous. The more exposure you have to them, the less threatening they'll seem.

By *communication*, I mean talking about your experiences to others. Making an attempt to turn these experiences into words not only furthers your own process of familiarization, but also helps to provide others with some idea of what they might encounter in nonphysical reality. They may then become less afraid to undertake their own adventures there.

After-the-fact communication to others of what you've experienced can be one of the more challenging aspects of exploring nonphysical reality. Describing a piece of classical music is similarly difficult. Saying that it was beautiful or exciting doesn't convey much of the experience to someone else. Because I've been trained as a musician, I could tell someone that the violins played a soaring melody and then the flute came in on a trill. I could talk about themes and cadences. That person's idea of what went on still won't come close to what I experienced.

Our language is rich in opportunities to describe things seen. When it comes to the other senses, however, it seems woefully inadequate. We can say that something tastes good, bad, sweet, salty, tart, bitter, spicy, or bland—and that's about it. When we try to describe nonphysical reality, we're even worse off. Language seems to have been invented primarily for referring to visual experiences in physical reality. If there are few words to describe sounds, smells, textures, and tastes, there are practically none for the sense impressions characteristic of nonphysical reality. In either case, when we run out of words, we either give up and say, "You had to be there," or we use an analogy.

Analogies describe something unknown in terms of something known. For example, in a wild-foods class at summer camp years ago, I sampled the fruit of a mayapple plant. One of my fellow campers, more squeamish than I, asked how it tasted. I replied that it had the texture of an apple but the flavor of a pear and a banana mixed together. Obviously, my explanation would make sense only to someone who had already experienced the taste of apples, pears, and bananas.

Everyone alive has had extensive experience in physical reality. Nonphysical reality is much less familiar. Perhaps the best way to talk about what goes on in the latter is in terms of the former. In other words, one may have to describe the mayapple of nonphysical reality in terms of the apples, pears, and bananas of physical reality. Actually, it's a bit more complicated than that. Even though the flavor of the mayapple is an unknown quantity, mayapples are just as physical as apples, pears, and bananas. Because there's nothing physical in nonphysical reality, that environment can seem completely alien to us.

The ocean might provide a useful analogy for understanding the nature of nonphysical reality. Diving in is like entering nonphysical reality: there's no doubt that you've come into an alien environment. Your senses of vision and hearing are distorted. Familiar means of getting from place to place, such as walking or running, are no longer feasible. You swim through areas in which the water temperature changes suddenly, constantly aware of the push and pull of powerful currents. You're surrounded by strange kinds of life that seem to be much better adapted to the environment—and they become increasingly bizarre as you go deeper.

In the out-of-body states that sometimes precede my adventures in nonphysical reality, my sense of vision is distorted. I've already mentioned that I'm able to see the fronts and backs of things simultaneously. Communication doesn't enter my ears, as in speech, but directly penetrates my mind, as a kind of telepathy. Walking is a much less efficient means of getting somewhere than merely thinking about a place, which often transports me there with an unsettling abruptness. In nonphysical reality, I sometimes feel myself passing through variations in intensity that seem to correspond to the ocean's temperature changes. Occasionally, I've been carried along by powerful currents like waves. The deeper I've penetrated into this alien environment, the more unusual have been the beings I've encountered.

Yet because nonphysical reality is as immaterial as music, the ocean analogy may be no more effective in putting across what that reality is like than attempts to describe a Beethoven symphony to someone who has never heard it. Even though the only person who will understand such a description completely may be someone else who has visited nonphysical reality, the act of telling your story to a sympathetic ear can be therapeutic.

In my opinion, our fear of the unknown is really just anxiety about becoming unlovable as a result of having had unfamiliar experiences and being changed by them. If we attempt to explore nonphysical reality and succeed, we're afraid that we'll be rejected, disbelieved, or thought to be crazy.

Having a sense of purpose in exploring nonphysical reality seems to me to be as essential as overcoming one's fear of the unknown. I believe that it's possible to answer a number of questions that have puzzled humanity throughout the ages by means of visits to nonphysical reality—questions about how our universe came to be, what God is, the origin and ultimate purpose of humankind, the existence of the soul, survival after death, and the sense of individual purpose in living. I call these the eternal questions and have found that my curiosity about them is a type of yearning, often sufficiently strong to propel me into journeys of discovery.

Although the eternal questions have been answered in various ways by science, religion, psychology, philosophy, and metaphysics, the answers in one field often contradict those in another. Even within the fields themselves there are conflicts between theories.

Science says that mankind has no ultimate purpose, that we're simply the accidental outcome of random chemical reactions that happened billions of years ago. The Christian religion tells us that our goal is to redeem ourselves for the sins of our ancestors, Adam and Eve, who somehow violated the will of God. Behavioral psychology says that our ultimate purpose is sheer physical survival. Humanistic psychology argues that it's to achieve self-realization. Some branches of philosophy suggest that we're to develop ourselves as moral and social beings. Metaphysics explains that spiritual evolution is what we should all be striving for.

The proliferation of attempts to answer the eternal questions certainly demonstrates how important they are to us. Yet, unless we're actively involved in furthering our knowledge in any of the fields mentioned above, these answers are all hearsay. I believe that each of us can answer the eternal questions for ourselves, through personal experience instead of hearsay. Shamans and medicine people have been doing so for centuries through visits to nonphysical reality. Because we live in completely different circumstances, the ancient shamans' answers may not be of much use to us. But perhaps we could follow their example and come up with relevant answers of our own. If there's a God, why not go see where he/she/it lives? If there's an Afterlife, why not take a tour of it?

The object of this field guide is to describe the characteristics of nonphysical reality as I understand them and the entities I've encountered there. On occasion, I've merged aspects of several adventures for greater clarity. For the most part, however, I've described them exactly as they happened to me.

I've used journeys into nonphysical reality as a means of answering the eternal questions for myself. In the process of doing so, I've visited what I believe to be the Land of the Dead and had a glimpse of something that could easily be called God. But that doesn't mean I have the final answers to such questions. Everything in this book is just hearsay, as far as you are concerned.

It's entirely possible that this is "merely" a book of dreams written by someone who has an unusual capacity to remember them and bring them to life in words. If so, I may not have been the first writer to base a work dealing with the eternal questions on answers received in dreams, while believing that what he has written is true.

Dante, for example, claims that his *Divine Comedy* recounts a visionary experience that took place between Good Friday and Easter Sunday in the year 1300. We may never know whether he really believed in what he wrote, although he presents himself in the poem as a deeply religious man. As a writer, however, Dante believed enough in the *project* of mapping Hell, Purgatory, and Heaven to work on his 14,000-line epic from 1306 until his death, some fifteen years later.

Few of us have the literary and spiritual stature of Dante. Maybe we *are* fooling ourselves when we try to attach any sort of spiritual meaning to life. Perhaps science is right—we're nothing more than a cosmic accident, and our tragedy is that this accident has gifted us with an absurd desire to believe it isn't so. Yet that desire persists, not only in myself, but also in many of my friends and acquaintances, and many of the poets and writers of fiction I enjoy reading. There's something characteristically human about it.

I'd like to think of this book as a celebration of what it means to be human, although in what many might consider to be unusual ways. It's up to you to decide whether I've answered any of the eternal questions to *your* satisfaction, or whether my answers spur you on to have adventures in consciousness of your own.

In my own skeptical moments, I wonder whether what I've written here is a work that demonstrates only the mind's need for answers, the power of the imagination, or our capacity for making life's difficulties and challenges more bearable through belief. But most of the time, in thinking about or rereading passages from this book, I find that my mind becomes quiet, calm—as if, for a little while, I could free myself from the nagging compulsion to wonder about why I'm here or what purpose life serves. How wonderful it would be if with these words I could pass a little of that inner peace along to you.

4

The Art of Translation: Describing Things Unseen

Imagine what it would be like to find yourself suddenly transported to ancient China. You don't know the language, the alphabet, or the customs. Once culture shock has worn off, you may begin to notice that ancient Chinese society has a highly sophisticated, though alien, structure. Through comparing this structure with the one you're used to, you can make deductions about appropriate behavior. You're setting up a mental *translation table*. For example, you may suddenly realize that a formerly obscure gesture functions as a ritual form of greeting and necessitates a certain response—just as the offer of a hand leads to a handshake today.

As a prospective explorer of nonphysical reality, you'll be in much the same position. Unless you make a translation table by comparing your experiences in nonphysical reality with your experiences in physical reality, there's little hope that you'll ever make sense of what you perceive there. Luckily, we practice making such translation tables every day of our lives—when we dream.

I believe that dreams are translations of things we've experienced in nonphysical reality into images from physical reality. For example, the image of a rapidly flowing river is familiar to almost anyone. If, in the nonphysical reality of a dream, I find myself immersed in a stream of energy that sweeps me up and takes me somewhere, I might translate that experience into being carried along by powerful river currents.

I also believe that dreams contain symbolic messages. Upon arising each day, I translate my dream images yet again—into verbal descriptions. Then I'll attempt to derive a message from them. This action involves a third kind of translation: from verbal description to the interpretation of symbols. In a dream, the sense of being carried along by a river might indicate a need to "go with the flow."

Any experience in nonphysical reality needs to go through several stages of translation in order to make sense. First there's *immersion* in the experience. Without translation, it's impossible to recall what happened during this immersion, except perhaps as a feeling of indescribable intensity. People who have had near-death experiences sometimes return from visits to the Afterlife unable to put into words what happened, especially if they found themselves in what they call a "region of light and love." The fact that they refer to light and love, however, indicates that some degree of translation has occurred. Beyond that, words fail them. What they're describing is the intensity of immersion.

After immersion comes *representation*. In this phase, the individual seeks to understand what's going on in nonphysical reality *in situ* by imposing on it images from physical reality. People who have had near-death experiences may encounter the spirits of deceased loved ones during visits to the Afterlife. Since there are no physical bodies in nonphysical reality, there has to be some way for the near-death experiencer to recognize the identity of a deceased relative. So the nonphysical expression of that person's identity will be translated into a representation of his former physical form. Clearly, such representation will rely heavily on the near-death experiencer's memories of the deceased relative.

No matter the experience in nonphysical reality, representation can use only what already exists in memory. If what's being experienced during immersion bears little resemblance to anything in memory, the translation will proceed by analogy.

Following representation, there are two more phases of translation: *description* and *interpretation*. By description, I mean turning one's *in situ* representation of an adventure in non-physical reality into words. This act of translation always occurs after the fact, in ordinary waking consciousness: one either writes down the experience or tries to tell someone about it.

Just as there can be a wide variation in quality between translations of a work of literature into English, depending on the translator, so can there be wide variations in quality between one individual's description of an adventure in consciousness and another's. The ability to describe such adventures is a skill that requires both patience and practice. Traditionally, this has been the domain of poets, who are constantly seeking to communicate to others emotional states for which there are no exact verbal equivalents. I've written poetry for years. My familiarity with the use of metaphors has often proved valuable in the process of describing nonphysical reality. Short of becoming a poet yourself, I would recommend keeping a dream journal as a means of practicing the description aspect of translation.[1]

Not every poet makes the leap from describing emotional states to states of consciousness, however. As Dante put it in his *Divine Comedy*:

---

[1]The chapter called "Keeping a Dream Diary" in *The Dream Game*, by Ann Faraday, Ph.D. (1976, 37–48), provides a useful set of guidelines for beginning to keep a dream journal.

> *I have been in that Heaven of His most light,*
> *and what I saw, those who descend from there*
> *lack both the knowledge and the power to write.*
>
> (Dante 1970, 24)

Should we take Dante literally? What if the *Divine Comedy* was his attempt to describe visits to nonphysical reality—specifically the regions to which the soul migrates after death? Part III, the *Paradiso*, abounds with references to the process of translation. For example, here is what Dante has to say about immersion:

> *As one who sees in dreams and wakes to find*
> *the emotional impression of his vision*
> *still powerful while all its parts fade from his mind—*
>
> *just such am I, having lost nearly all*
> *the vision itself, while in my heart I feel*
> *the sweetness of it yet distill and fall.*
>
> (ibid., 362)

A wholly satisfying description of any event in nonphysical reality may be impossible. As I've already pointed out, language just can't do it. Dante may also have felt this to be so:

> *O power divine, but lend to my high strain*
> *so much as will make clear even the shadow*
> *of that High Kingdom stamped upon my brain . . .*
>
> (ibid., 24)

The idea of a shadow stamped on his brain suggests that Dante may have understood the nature of representation. At a certain point, his heavenly guide, Beatrice, even critiques one of his representations:

"The river and the jewels you see
dart in and out of it, and the smiling flowers
are dim foretastes of their reality.

Not that these fruits are in their natures tart
and unformed, but that you still lack the vision
of such high things. The defect is on your part."

(ibid., 330)

At another point, Dante articulates the problem I've often encountered in trying to describe events in nonphysical reality:

How speak trans-human change to human sense?
Let the example speak until God's grace
grants the pure spirit the experience.

(ibid., 26)

The example, of course, is the *Divine Comedy*. Dante must have known that language would fail to communicate what he experienced in a fully satisfying way. The best that he could do was to provide an example, so that anyone who ventured into the same regions of nonphysical reality (if adventures of this sort were indeed the source of his writings), would have an easier time representing it—using this example's imagery.

In my experience, entities encountered in nonphysical reality communicate with each other nonverbally, using a kind of telepathy. In this method of communication, thoughts are not transmitted or received sequentially, as in ordinary speech, but all at once.

Comic-strip artists often use balloons to contain the speech of their characters. Each balloon contains a number of words which must be read sequentially in order for the meaning to become clear. Yet all the information the character wishes to communicate is contained within the balloon. In a similar way, an entity in nonphysical reality projects all thought pertaining to the topic of a conversation simultaneously—it's as if a balloon containing this information had suddenly appeared in the receiver's mind. I'm often able to catch enough of the meaning of such a message to respond with questions. But only when I'm back in physical reality am I able to figure out exactly what was said—by translating it into English, one word at a time.

Despite the problem of describing nonphysical reality in a satisfying way, not to mention that of rendering nonverbal communications intelligibly, it's nevertheless possible to communicate the essence of an experience so that anyone who has had a similar experience—or who finds himself in the midst of one—can recognize it. Because of the difficulties involved, many people give up before they reach this point, calling their experiences indescribable. Yet in taking the time to find serviceable images, analogies, and words—no matter how approximate they may seem in light of the experience itself—many details that were obscure during immersion can suddenly become clear.

Memory apparently stores the whole experience, no matter how undigested some parts of it may have been by the process of representation. While verbalizing it, you may discover that analogies for the undigested portions of it suggest themselves, leading to *ex post facto* representations. It may seem as if you're remembering forgotten details. In reality, you're merely clothing the immersion experience in imagery that will allow ordinary waking consciousness to make sense of it, even if after the fact.

I'm not talking about elaboration or exaggeration here. There's an inner sense of rightness that emerges from a description when somehow the information conveyed in words corresponds with that contained within the experience itself, no matter how wordless it may have been. That sense of rightness is what I mean when I refer to a *satisfying* description of events in nonphysical reality.

I've found that the more work I put into creating a translation table for my experiences in nonphysical reality, the richer my experiences become. Not only am I able to recall more of the immersion phase through verbalizing my experiences, I'm also able to carry each new analogy I invent for this purpose into future adventures. These analogies are of inestimable value in the representation phase of translation. And since representation takes place *in situ*, as my personal translation table becomes more sophisticated through the addition of new analogies, my experiences in nonphysical reality become more elaborate and my level of involvement more profound.

The last phase of translation is *interpretation*. By interpretation, I mean figuring out what an experience means with reference to the eternal questions: how our universe came to be, what God is, the origin and ultimate purpose of humankind, the existence of the soul, survival after death, and the sense of individual purpose in living.

Even though I place interpretation at the end of the translation process, it can actually occur simultaneously with representation and/or description. It's very easy to misinterpret what goes on in nonphysical reality—just as it's easy to misunderstand idiomatic or slang expressions in another language. Think of the perplexity of a foreigner who hears the phrase "hang loose" for the first time and translates it literally.

Attempting to interpret an adventure in consciousness while it's happening will often lead to erroneous conclusions. The best approach to interpretation is to avoid coming to conclusions about what one's adventures in nonphysical reality mean for as long as possible. Because of our fear of the unknown, we seem inclined to interpret any new and unfamiliar experience in the scariest way possible. Perhaps this tendency is an heirloom from our jungle days, when our minds were largely occupied with the problem of staying alive, and anything unknown to us might pose an imminent physical danger.

Regardless of its source, I've found that the best way to prevent fear of the unknown from leading to misinterpretation of experiences in nonphysical reality is to determine how their components function with respect to one another. I look for consistencies within the experience itself, between the experience and others of my own that seem related, and between my own and those of explorers whose judgment I've learned to trust. Patterns often emerge from the contemplation of such consistencies—patterns that may teach me more about what my adventure means than anything I may have thought while in the midst of it.

Recognizing consistencies is a vital part of the process of creating a translation table. Every consistency I've discovered has made the tasks of representing and describing my experiences easier. The more fluent I become in translating nonphysical adventures into physical terms, the less likely I am to misinterpret them. Or so I hope.

5

Aliens and Angels: The Making of Translation Tables

Translation tables come in two forms: public and private. A private translation table is based on one's own adventures in consciousness. Often it will involve invented words or familiar words used in unfamiliar ways. For example, in *Far Journeys*, Robert Monroe's second book, the author creates a special vocabulary to describe some of the ways nonphysical entities interact with one another. The infinitive *to flicker* indicates that an entity is uncertain about something; whereas *to blank* means a lack of understanding. Such entities *light up* when they show enthusiasm and *dull* when they lose interest.

Clearly, Monroe is using an analogy to light or fire in order to describe nonphysical phenomena.[1] Dante does the same thing in the *Paradiso*, in which the souls of the blessed

---

[1] See Monroe (1985, 77–78) for the rest of this special vocabulary for describing the ways nonphysical entities interact with each other and their environment.

are perceived as envelopes of light surrounding a human form:

> *And lo! another of those splendors now*
> *draws near me, and his wish to give me pleasure*
> *shows in the brightening of his outward glow.*
>
> (Dante 1970, 106)

To construct his translation table, Monroe confined himself to existing English words, which he redefined to suit his purposes. His intention was to give the reader a sense of what goes on in nonphysical reality while still maintaining intelligibility. One could equally well make up new words as redefined old ones for such a purpose.

Anyone who invents a vocabulary to describe adventures in consciousness runs the risk of isolation. Only people who are willing to learn this vocabulary would understand him. Furthermore, psychologists define the tendency to create private languages as one of the symptoms of schizophrenia. No matter how sanely someone manages his everyday life, people will probably think he's crazy if he attempts to describe such adventures exclusively in made-up or redefined words. Public translation tables can help bridge this communication gap.

Public translation tables are made up of the myths and folklore from which one may borrow to describe experiences in nonphysical reality. Here's an example of a public translation table in action. During my freshman year in college, I had a hard time adjusting to the new social milieu. On weekends, I often wandered from one party to another, desperately trying to fit in. One night, after a particularly lonely evening of such wandering, I awoke to find that my head was at the foot of my bed. I seemed to be floating. All around me were strange gray creatures, like gargoyles, who were commanding me to twist my body into impossible positions. I was powerless to resist their orders. The gargoyles laughed and taunted, pinching, pushing, and prodding me. Suddenly, a shining presence appeared in the middle of the room—powerful and serene, so bright that I couldn't look at it directly.

Cowering, I averted my eyes. The gargoyles fled and the bright apparition vanished. Emotionally exhausted, I fell back asleep. Upon awakening in the morning, it was easy to perceive the gargoyles as demons, since they seemed to have tortured me, and the radiant entity as an angel, since it seemed to rescue me. Demons and angels are part of a public translation table associated with the Christian religion, in which I was raised. I believe that I borrowed these images in order to represent the presence of two kinds of nonphysical entities.

There are a variety of public translation tables from which to draw representations of events and entities in nonphysical reality. The Christian translation table is a common one. Many people who have had near-death experiences encounter a being of light who helps them review their lives and asks them what they've learned before sending them back to the world. Often this being is described as Christ or a saint because of the intensity of love emanating from it.[2]

Christian tradition speaks of St. Peter, who determines who should be admitted to Heaven. Note the similarity in function between the life-review entity described above and St. Peter. To my mind, someone, somewhere—who knows how long ago—may have had a spontaneous vision of the Afterlife, perhaps in the form of a near-death experience, in which he encountered the life-review entity and represented it to himself as St. Peter. Other people may have heard about it. If any of them then had a similar experience, the image of St. Peter may have come up again. This would seem to confirm the first person's report, whereas it may actually have derived from it. As St. Peter continued to appear to others as the life-review entity, his role in Heaven would eventually become a part of the Christian translation table.

---

[2]See *Life After Life* by Dr. Raymond A. Moody, Jr., (1976, 58–73) for descriptions of the being of light and life reviews.

If someone confronting the life-review entity had never heard of St. Peter, he might represent this entity differently. Comparing his account with that of a Christian who had seen St. Peter, we might assume that there's no relation between them. In Egyptian mythology, however, the jackal-headed god Anubis weighs the heart of the deceased. If the heart is lighter than a feather (which symbolizes the truth), then the soul is allowed to pass on to the Afterlife. If the heart is heavier than the feather, it's thrown to a monster who devours it (Grof and Grof 1980, 48).

Clearly, the function of Anubis and that of St. Peter are analogous. In my view, Anubis and St. Peter are alternative representations of the same class of nonphysical entity. Cultural differences are responsible for the choice of imagery, but the underlying function of the entity is the same in both translation tables.

In the Christian tradition, Dante's *Divine Comedy* is perhaps the most thorough exposition of the stages through which the soul passes after death. The Tibetan Book of the Dead (Fremantle and Trungpa 1987) provides an alternative set of images to describe the same experiences. Another public translation table available to Westerners, but less well-known than the Christian one, can be found in the writings of occultists. Such writings seem to be less concerned with the various stages in one's progress through the Afterlife than with the layout of nonphysical reality. The occultists' term for the latter is the astral plane.

I became aware of the occultists' translation table through a book found in my grandfather's library after he died: *The Astral World: Its Scenes, Dwellers, and Phenomena,* by Swami Panchadasi (1915). The Swami (whom I suspect to be a Westerner writing under a pseudonym) claims that the astral plane is allegedly the third of seven planes of being, of which physical reality is the first. Each of these planes is divided into seven subplanes, each of which itself has seven subdivisions. The book describes the environments and entities one is likely to encounter in each subdivision of the astral plane.

For some reason, perhaps deeply rooted in the structure of the human psyche, the number seven is often associated with mystical endeavors. I don't believe that there are just seven subdivisions or planes of anything in nonphysical reality. But superimposing such subdivisions on this largely unexplored territory might have helped the good Swami orient himself within it.

In order to determine a location in nonphysical reality, we would need at least one point of reference. If we were to draw a set of coordinate axes on a blank piece of paper, for example, arbitrarily calling the point where they meet *zero*; and if we were then to determine a unit of measurement and mark the axes accordingly, we would be able to describe the location of any other point on the page. We could then say that the coordinate (2, 3) describes a point that's two units to the right of the vertical axis and three units up from the horizontal axis.

The idea of planes, divisions, and subdivisions is a set of coordinate axes placed over nonphysical reality, separating it into seven times seven times seven (or 343) regions. Even the most ardent adventurer might have trouble filling that many slots on his map of nonphysical reality with "scenes, dwellers, and phenomena" encountered during a lifetime of exploring the unknown!

The urge to map nonphysical reality is not limited to the occultists. In fact, just as there are translation tables that help to identify the various entities one is likely to encounter in nonphysical reality, there are others whose purpose is to provide some orientation within that great unknown. Dante describes the scenes, dwellers, and phenomena of nine spheres of Heaven, seven levels of Purgatory, and nine circles of Hell—the latter with a multitude of subdivisions. At the end of *Far Journeys*, Monroe (1985, 243–46) lists a number of nonphysical regions surrounding our planet like rings. The major ring, for example, has four subdivisions. In the outer quarter, according to

Monroe, one is likely to encounter the souls of deceased "contemplatives, philosophers, certain religious groups, service-to-humanity devotees, helpers, guides, rescue workers, and others" (244). Similarly, Panchadasi (1915, 72) declares that: "On the highest of the sub-planes of the Astral we find many regions inhabited by the philosophers, scientists, metaphysicians, and higher theologians of the race." In Dante, the fourth sphere of Heaven contains the great theologians of Christendom.

We could argue over which of these three maps of non-physical reality is more accurate—but accuracy isn't the point. Once again we come back to the idea of function. It seems that there's a "place" in nonphysical reality where one is likely to encounter the souls of great thinkers. The differences between where these souls are located with respect to others is more a matter of how Monroe, Dante, and Panchadasi drew their coordinate axes.

Rather than in terms of their probable accuracy, I prefer to evaluate translation tables in terms of their possible usefulness. If a translation table helps me identify an entity or environment I've encountered in a way that encourages my continuing exploration of nonphysical reality, then it's useful. On the other hand, a translation table that causes me to abandon my exploration of nonphysical reality out of fear is not useful—and I reject it.

On several occasions I've been awakened in the middle of the night by a nonphysical entity standing at the foot of my bed. This being appears to be shrouded entirely in black. A hood obscures its face. A bright light surrounds the entity, like the Sun's corona during a total eclipse. The entity grasps my big toe and gently shakes my foot until I awaken. It then takes me on a journey into nonphysical reality.

If I were to use the Christian translation table to interpret the entity's presence, I might see it as a "dark angel"—one of the company of angels thrown out of Heaven with Lucifer—or as the Angel of Death. Terrified by such a visitation, I would resist going with the entity.

On one of this entity's visits, its robe was slightly open. Beneath it I could see a kind of breastplate, which made me think of a space suit. I've read that a commonly reported type of space-alien abduction is called "the bedroom scenario": an individual is awakened from sleep and taken somewhere by an extraterrestrial being. Sometimes these beings are perceived as wearing space suits, occasionally with breastplates. Perhaps I would be equally justified in calling my visitation an alien-abduction experience. Such an interpretation might also lead to terror and resistance. Yet on neither occasion did the entity give me any cause for alarm, other than the understandable surprise of my perceiving it in the first place.

I believe that alien abductions are real experiences, but that most if not all of them (especially the bedroom scenario) take place in altered states of consciousness. The aliens are actually entities from nonphysical reality who are represented, during translation, as extraterrestrials. Since the word "extra-terrestrial" means "from beyond the Earth," there's a certain validity to its being used in this way. It seems that a new pub-lic translation table is in the process of emerging, and it bor-rows elements from science fiction—just as the Christian translation table borrowed religious elements.

So what *was* the entity in my bedroom? If I'd called it a dark angel or a space alien, I would have been too terrified to accompany it. Since I believe that any translation table that prevents me from exploring nonphysical reality isn't useful for me, I had to come up with another interpretation of these vis-its. The best way to do this was to analyze them in terms of their function.

For me, the word "function" has an emotionally neutral valence. The fact that, in a car engine, the carburetor serves a certain function is hardly terrifying. The same thing should be true of adventures in consciousness. When I break them down into their various components and have determined the func-tion of each, I want to deal with neutral valences instead of a potentially overwhelming fear of the unknown.

First, the entity awakened me from sleep into an altered state, in which I would be able to leave my body and travel with it into nonphysical reality. The way it woke me up, by gently shaking my foot, reminded me of how my mother would get me out of bed for school. The entity seems to have chosen this action (or I had represented the entity's telepathically projected command to awaken in this way) so that I would realize that its intentions were as loving and supportive as my mother's. Furthermore, I was being awakened for a kind of schooling—the exploration of nonphysical reality.

The radiance surrounding the entity's robe and hood made me think of a total eclipse of the Sun. An eclipse is one of the few times when it's possible to look directly at the Sun. Perhaps the function of the robe and hood was to cloak the radiance that surrounded the entity so that I could look at it. The entity's radiance might otherwise have terrified me, as did that of the being who routed the gargoyles. The breastplate may have served a similar shielding function. Apparently, I had the sense that some sort of shielding was going on, and interpreted it as a hooded robe on one occasion and a breastplate on another.

Many of the currently available public translation tables may not be useful to a would-be explorer of nonphysical reality, since they may make the unfamiliar aspect of the unknown more terrifying (as in the case of dark angels or alien encounters). They could also set us up for possible rejection by those we may try to communicate our experiences to. If we fumble around with traditional descriptions of unusual, perhaps mystical experiences, such as seeing God, talking to angels, fighting off demons, we're more or less certain to be scoffed at, to have our sanity called into question. The more recent idea of being abducted by extraterrestrials won't serve us much better.

For this reason, I've sought to develop a new translation table for prospective explorers of nonphysical reality. It's based entirely on function. Since the terms have little or no emotional charge, they're less likely to invoke the fear of the unknown. Thus, I call the hooded-and-robed entity a *Guide*, because its function is to guide me in exploring nonphysical reality.

6

Mapping Nonphysical Reality

The idea of mapping a nonphysical reality may seem to contradict itself. The kind of mapping I have in mind is not much different from composing a translation table. We've already seen that such a table may be necessary in order to represent to oneself what one has experienced in nonphysical reality. Both Monroe's rings and the occultist's planes and subplanes are maps of a sort. Such terms as rings and planes function not only as labels for certain kinds of experience, but also as structures for organizing particular experiences relative to one another.

Nonphysical reality has no spatial dimension as we understand it. Nevertheless, we must have some way of differentiating the environments in which we find ourselves from one another. A map would not only allow us to do so, but also could help us recognize a particular environment, if we should happen upon it more than once, or intentionally return to it for further exploration.

Maps of nonphysical reality, just as any other kind of translation table, seem to be highly personal in nature. Monroe believes that his rings surround the physical planet Earth with environments that become increasingly nonphysical as one gets farther away from their center. The occultists believe that planes and subplanes exist in hierarchical relationships—some higher, some lower than others, according to their degree of spiritual purity.

I prefer to use the term *zones* to identify nonphysical environments. Because such environments *are* nonphysical, I prefer not to place them in a relationship with the physical Earth, as Monroe does. Furthermore, it's difficult for me to gauge how physical or nonphysical such environments may be. I only know that they differ from one another, usually in terms of function. The word "zone" also avoids a pitfall inherent in the idea of planes and subplanes—that is, the implied value judgement in calling them higher or lower.

The following adventure provides some idea of how I've constructed my own map of nonphysical reality. It began from a dream in which I found myself in a subway station waiting for a train. I intended to get on an outbound train, which I knew would take me home. It had been a long night, and *home* meant physical reality. I was ready to leave the dream environment behind. But I accidentally got on the wrong train—one marked *inbound*.

The train took me to another station, much larger than the first. I got off, wondering where I was, feeling sleepy and confused. It occurred to me that the trains in Boston stop running at 1:00 A.M. I knew it was later than that, because my roommate had come back to our apartment at 2:30 A.M. His stomping up and down the hall had briefly awakened me. I quickly glanced around the station, worried that I might have to wait until the morning trains began running again at 5:30 A.M. to get home.

The station seemed to be the hub of several different transportation lines. People of all ages and descriptions—housewives, old men, young children—were waiting on a central platform. The size of the crowd surprised me. The hour seemed late for so many people to be about.

A trolley came flying past on a track abutting the platform. Only two or three people were on it. I wondered why it didn't stop. There was more than enough room on board for the people on the platform.

I began exploring the station. It was carved out of solid rock, like a cavern. The walls were rough, not covered with a tile mosaic like the one in Park Street Station, the hub of Boston's transportation lines. Three tunnels radiated outward from the central platform. If the platform were the face of a clock, with the middle tunnel representing the number twelve, then the tunnel on the left would have been at eleven, and the one on the right at one o'clock. The trolley had come into the station through yet another tunnel, located at three o'clock. It had curved around the circular platform and then exited through a fifth tunnel at nine o'clock. A sixth tunnel, at six o'clock, had its own platform—the final stopping point of the monorail train I'd ridden in on. After letting me off, that train had reversed its direction, presumably on its way back to the station where I'd boarded it—and who knows where beyond that.

I walked down a short flight of stairs, located at eight o'clock. It led to another platform, at one end of which was a dock. A canal began from that point, its black waters curving to cross beneath the trolley tracks. Because of the curve, I was unable to see what angle the canal took as it exited the station.

As I speculated about what might lie beyond the curve, a pitch-black gondola came around it. The gondolier seemed very solemn, even morose. I couldn't see his face. It was hidden beneath the hood of a black cape. His oar was topped with a miniature human skull. There was no one else in the boat.

The gondolier's formidable appearance brought me out of my stupor. He pushed back his hood and looked up at me, standing above him on the dock.

"Where am I?" I asked respectfully, wondering if the being's cadaverous face meant that I was in the realm of the dead.

"No, this is not the Afterdeath Zone," the being said with some amusement, "although I have recently come from there. It's my duty to take the dead back to physical reality to visit their still-living relatives. How do I appear to you?"

I described his bulging and bloodshot eyes, his disfigured face, the skull on the tip of his oar. "I see you've represented me as Charon," he said, "the ferryman of the dead in Greek mythology. How poetic."

"I take it that's not how you perceive yourself?" I asked.

"The function is the same: I facilitate travel between physical reality and the Afterdeath Zone. The other attributes are your own invention.

"As to where you are," the being continued, "you could call it Grand Central Station, if you wish. A transportation system of sorts connects all points in Otherwhere. Grand Central is a major hub, linking the Human Zone with all the other zones of Otherwhere. A number of lines intersect here, each with different origins, destinations, and functions. You came in on the *EO Line*—Earth to Otherwhere—which you perceived as a monorail train running through the Dream Zone.

"The trolley line provides service to zones of Otherwhere beyond the human. You could call it the *NZ Line*, short for *Nonhuman Zones*. That line doesn't get much use, which is why you rarely see more than a few individuals riding it—and why it almost never stops at this station. Humans currently have problems enough accepting those of their own kind who have different skin colors, languages, or beliefs. They're not ready to confront the radically different consciousnesses of nonhuman species.

"I run the *AF Line*, short for *Afterdeath Ferry*. You've represented this line as a system of canals, by analogy with the rivers of Hades in Greek myths. At this stop, I pick up individuals such as yourself, who have left their bodies behind—temporarily—in order to explore the Afterdeath Zone. As you can see, I have a thriving business."

I looked around, eager to befriend any fellow travelers who might have been waiting on the dock with me. No one else was there. I turned back to the ferryman, realizing that his remark had been ironic.

"Most people are afraid they'll never come back from such a journey," he explained. "But the occasional exception, such as yourself, makes my work worthwhile. From this point I could take you to any portion of the Afterdeath Zone you might wish to visit."

I was about to ask the ferryman whether I should board his gondola, and if he had any particular destination in mind for me. But then I remembered the three tunnels on the upper platform. The ferryman anticipated my question.

"The tunnels you're wondering about lead to what we call *Shadow Worlds*. There are three types of Shadow World: *Alternate Was, Alternate Is,* and *Alternate Will-Be*. Bus lines run to each of them.

"Most of the people on the platform above are deceased. They came from the Afterdeath Zone on ferries run by my colleagues. They're waiting for a bus to the Alternate Was worlds, where they'll experience what things would have been like had they made other choices at major turning points in their lives on Earth. The other two lines are of benefit to the living rather than the dead. The Alternate Is worlds may be visited by people who want to see what the present would be like if they had made a different decision at some point in the past. Alternate Will-Be worlds give them the chance to see what consequences might develop from a decision currently under consideration.

"The Alternate Was system is the only one of the three Shadow World lines that gets much use these days. People have forgotten that they can travel to the Shadow Worlds to help themselves make decisions about how to lead their lives."

My adventure continued with visits to each of the three Shadow Worlds, which I'll describe in later chapters. What happened there will only make sense after you've been introduced to some of the "scenes, dwellers, and phenomena" you're likely to encounter on your own adventures in Otherwhere.

PART II

FIELD GUIDE

7

Guides

Most field guides contain pictures of the flora and fauna they describe. Since the entities I'll be identifying are immaterial, the best I can do is provide verbal descriptions. Because of the personal nature of the translation process, my representations may be different from those of other explorers. In natural history, identifications are based on similarities in size, shape, and coloration. In this field guide, the *function* of the entity is the key to its identity, not how it appears.

Guides are among the most useful entities to be encountered in nonphysical reality. Their function is to facilitate travel from one area to another and to answer questions about what you experience there. We've already met two such Guides—the dark-robed being who stood at the foot of my bed, trying to wake me up, and the ferryman of the previous chapter. In the *Divine Comedy*, Dante meets three Guides of his own. The first is the Roman poet Virgil, who died almost thirteen hundred years before Dante was born. Dante was a great admirer of Virgil's work, particularly his epic poem the *Aeneid*. In his capacity as Guide, Virgil led Dante through the nine circles of Hell and the seven levels of Purgatory. Having been born before the time of Christ, however, Virgil was largely unfamiliar with the layout of Purgatory, which had been created for the exclusive use of Christian souls.

If we accept the idea that the *Divine Comedy* is Dante's translation of experiences in nonphysical reality, then several questions concerning Virgil's identity arise: Is Dante's Guide the soul of the deceased poet? Or is he some kind of nonphysical entity whom Dante has represented as Virgil?

In the *Aeneid*, Virgil describes the meeting of Aeneas and his father, Anchises, in the Elysian Fields—one of the regions of the Afterlife in Greek and Roman literature. Anchises functions as kind of a Guide, explaining the processes whereby souls prepare themselves for reincarnation. Because Virgil demonstrates some familiarity with the Afterlife in the *Aeneid*, it seems natural for Dante to trust him as a Guide. Because the two of them often discuss poetics as they pass from region to region, we might assume that Virgil really is Virgil. Laying aside the question of whether Virgil was a purely imaginative invention of Dante's, we—and Dante himself—might be wrong in making this assumption. We've seen that one way to avoid misinterpreting experiences in nonphysical reality is to perceive them in terms of function. Virgil *functions* as a Guide—and that's all we know for sure.

The same thing can be said of Beatrice, who guides Dante through the nine spheres of Heaven. She was a woman of Florence who died young, beloved of Dante for her enlightenment and spiritual purity—qualities which made her an ideal Guide in Heaven. In the Empyrean, the final goal of Dante's journey, Beatrice's role is taken over by St. Bernard. As a contemplative mystic, the latter is well suited to the task of leading Dante to a vision of God.

My own Guide, though imposing in his dark robe and halo of light, has none of the earthly credentials of Dante's. Here's an account of one of our journeys together:

One morning I decided to see if I could get out of body. I began by relaxing on my bed and quickly drifted into a light sleep. As if in a dream, I found myself on the floor of a completely empty, totally white room with no doors or windows. I hadn't really gone anywhere: the room represented a mental space within which there would be no distractions.

An intense dot of light was orbiting above the middle of my chest. It would pass clockwise across my torso, vanish into the floor, and then reappear on the other side for another sweep. Somehow I had to reach out with my mind while the dot was visible and pull it toward me. I tried to do this several times before I succeeded. When the dot of light hit my chest, it set off tremors that ran through my entire body. I heard that familiar rushing in my ears, as if I were a few feet away from a jet engine—the sensation that has often preceded my out-of-body experiences. Once this sensation had passed, I was able to unhook the immaterial arms of my astral body from their physical counterparts, but I couldn't get the rest of me to follow suit.

"Twist time to the north," a voice said. I could see no speaker.

"What is that supposed to mean?" I replied.

"Time is related to gravity," the voice continued. "The lines of force emanating from magnetic north create what you call 'now' anywhere on the planet. When you're out of body, these lines of force become tangible."

My head had been oriented toward the north when I fell asleep. In my altered state, I noticed what seemed like a spike driven from the top of my head through my torso, exiting at the crotch. Although I could still move the arms of my astral body, the rest of me remained transfixed by the spike.

A second voice piped in. "He can use that technique to go back a hundred years, you know."

The first responded quickly. "Don't tell him that! He's not ready!"

I pondered what it might mean to "twist time to the north." All at once, I knew. With my nonphysical hands I grasped the spike above my head, pulled my legs up over my chest, and swept them to the right, picking up momentum. I vaulted over the force line that had transfixed me as if it were a piece of gymnastics equipment. I was completely out of body now.

"As you can see, magnetic lines of force also keep you focused in the physical body—although you can use them to release yourself," the first voice said.

My vault over the force line had carried me into a standing position. I looked around the bare room: there was no sign of the two entities I'd overheard. I saw no way out of the room. I called for help, but nothing happened. Suddenly, I found myself back in my body again.

I recalled the dark-robed figure of the earlier-described Guide who had recently introduced himself to me. Perhaps I could summon him. Focusing on everything that I could remember having felt in his presence, I vaulted over the force line again.

"Beautiful," the Guide said. He was now beside me in the otherwise empty room. This time he looked more human: no robe, no corona, just a pair of sunglasses. It later struck me that the shades were another variation on the theme of shielding that I associate with Guides.

"What is our mission?" I asked, melodramatically.

"We're going to the Serenus Sor system," the Guide replied.

"Where's that?" I was wondering if we were about to depart for the planets of some faraway star.

"It's also called the Sirius Thot system," said my Guide. "But first we have to find a qualifying line."

The Guide grasped me by the arm and hustled me through the wall of the room. We were instantly in the real world, about a half mile from where I live, in the woods by Jamaica Pond.

As I tried to figure out what my Guide meant by the term *qualifying line*, he interrupted my thoughts.

"Qualifying lines link power points. Power points are the pegs upon which the illusion of physical reality is hung. They also act as points of entry and exit for alternate realities, or as a means of rapid transit between distant places in your universe. Power points are like the dots in a child's coloring book. Connect them and you have qualifying lines. I call them that because they ameliorate, or *qualify*, the restrictions imposed by magnetic force lines—which can keep you in the vicinity of your physical body, or prevent you from leaving Earth. There's a power point at this end of Jamaica Pond."

We took a leap from the woods to a shimmering globe of energy about eighteen inches in diameter, hovering above the pond. Instantly we were drawn upward, so quickly that I caught my breath and closed my eyes, clutching the Guide for dear life.

"What's the matter with you?" he said.

"Nothing. I just forgot what this was like." When had I experienced this sensation before? I couldn't remember.

I made myself open my eyes and look down. The Guide slowed our progress. Now I could identify objects that had blurred together with the speed of our ascent. It was raining. Despite our height, I could see the surface of the pond clearly: small waves from the breeze, interconnecting ripples from the raindrops, large rings made by fish coming to the surface. I could also see the bare trees, the carpet of brown oak leaves on the ground, patches of grass just beginning to green, gray and purple storm clouds in the background. Everything had a peculiar intensity of color.

I had been holding onto the Guide's back with a desperate grip. He began poking me, telling me to relax, while at the same time pulling me onto his shoulders. We proceeded to climb a little higher—and then I abruptly found myself back in bed, no longer out of body.

All morning I puzzled over what "Serenus Sor" and "Sirius Thot" might have meant. It occurred to me that since this adventure involved acclimating myself to a form of rapid transit while out of body, I was learning to *soar serenely*. When I mistook this message for the name of a star system, my Guide must have been amused. He teased me with the name of the dog star, Sirius. Punning on the words *serious* and *thought*, he let me know that I was taking things too seriously.

I remember reading in *Journeys Out of the Body* that Monroe seemed to have out-of-body experiences more often when he was lying with his head oriented toward magnetic north (Monroe 1977, 244). Even though my bed remained oriented in that direction for a number of years, most of the elements of the above adventure have yet to be duplicated in later ones. I've never again used magnetic lines of force to vault out of my body, or traveled between power points along qualifying lines, or attempted to twist time to the north in order to go back a hundred years. The only thing that has carried forward into later adventures is the dark figure of the Guide.

8

Creatures

The gargoyles I encountered in my dorm room years ago represent another kind of nonphysical being, which I call *Creatures*. The word has a humorous connotation for me when used to describe monsters—perhaps because I grew up as a member of the Saturday-morning cartoon generation, for which creepy creatures were a staple. I like the word for another reason: it implies something created.

One of the peculiarities of nonphysical reality is that thought seems to manifest itself more or less instantly as experience there. Anything I may conceive will immediately appear. Powerful emotional states can affect nonphysical reality in the same way, although unconsciously. If I enter nonphysical reality feeling a lot of fear, that emotion can manifest itself as a frightening monster: a Creature.

Robert Monroe describes several Creatures in *Journeys Out of the Body:* a rubbery, humanoid entity of subhuman intelligence who likes to climb onto his back once he has gotten out of body; fishlike suckers that will sometimes attach themselves to parts of his astral body; a large doglike entity with which he fought a desperate battle for survival; and an invisible attacker, without personality, but acutely aware of

Monroe's weak spots. He speculates that such beings may have been the basis for folkloric accounts of demons, goblins, and gremlins (Monroe 1977, 136–44).

If we look at each of these descriptions in terms of function, we may be able to interpret them. The fish suck like parasites, for example. In much the same way, worries and fears can drain one of energy. Thus the parasitic fish could perhaps have been Monroe's apt representation of entering nonphysical reality with a lot of niggling (or nibbling!) worries on his mind.

I've encountered the rubbery Creatures myself. Their function seems to be that of clinging. When people are overly concerned about the well-being of loved ones, we say that they're clinging. Monroe recalls that the rubbery entities transformed themselves at one point into images of his daughters. Perhaps the rubbery entities were a representation of his clinging to them—or of theirs to him. The rubbery entities used to appear for me when I had a crush on someone and couldn't seem to let go of it—another type of clinging. In his last book, *Ultimate Journey*, Robert Monroe provides an alternative perspective on these clinging, rubbery entities. He claims to have visited his *past* self, ridden by rubbery entities and thrashing in terror, in a more recent out-of-body state. His present self plucked the Creatures that so terrified his past self off of the latter's back. After removing them, his present self saw that they were not children, as he'd originally believed, but the playful out-of-body doubles of his pet cats.

I've never encountered the out-of-body doubles of animals in my own adventures. This fact, along with my opinion that at times Monroe takes aspects of his adventures literally that to me seem symbolic, makes me suspicious of his claim that the childlike Creatures tormenting his past self were merely pets.

Once again I have to ask myself, what is the function of this experience? Whether actual out-of-body cats were involved or not, I see the function of Monroe's new perspective in *Ultimate Journey* as one of reassurance: the rubbery entities that had so frightened him were no more harmful than pet cats. If they were actual out-of-body cats, their clinging to the younger Monroe's back could have represented their dependence on him for food and shelter. Children of course are dependent on their parents in the same way.

My own experiences in nonphysical reality, in which thoughts and emotions can manifest themselves instantly, incline me to believe that the rubbery beings Monroe describes were neither children nor cats, but feelings of his that had taken on forms separate from himself so that he could confront and release them. In that case, whether they appeared to be cats or children, they were actually what I call Creatures— creations of the mind. See Monroe (1994, 115–16).

Similarly, the two attackers described above call Monroe's survival into question. He may have been doing battle with survival fears brought about by his exposure to the alien environment of nonphysical reality. Or there may have been some physically or emotionally challenging event going on in his life at the time of these encounters. It seemed to threaten his survival and resulted in the representation of his fears as apparently life-threatening Creatures.

As for the gargoyles, their function was to twist my astral body into impossible shapes. In much the same way, I was trying to contort my personality in order to fit into the social groups on campus.

During my senior year in college, I lived in a room by myself in one of the older dormitories. I loved the wood floors and high ceilings, but the walls were too thin to block the sound of other people's stereo systems. Perhaps because I was a musician, it was difficult for me to tune out even the softest music. If anyone was playing records down the hall after midnight, I had trouble falling asleep.

Several times that year I exchanged heated words with a roomful of guys who seemed to be more interested in partying than studying. Often their music kept me awake until the wee hours of the morning. One night, when I could no longer stand the noise, I tried to concentrate all of my anger and frustration into a powerful mental command for silence. Could such a thought force the guys down the hall to quiet down? Moments later, a lit firecracker came flying through the open transom window above the door of my room.

I wasn't hurt by the ensuing explosion, but the adrenaline rush that followed it seemed to put me into an altered state. I felt that my room was filled with an ominous presence that made it difficult for me to sleep. I ended up experiencing one of those nights when the body shuts down but the mind stays active, when dreams are replaced by a continuous stream of accelerated thoughts.

While I was in this twilight state, a point not far from my bed seemed to glow like a luminous hallway into some other reality. A dark shape at the entrance of this hallway—the ominous presence I had felt earlier—was beckoning me to enter. I resisted. Hours later, however, I found myself locked in combat with this being. We wrestled until I awoke at dawn, a blood-red sun rising behind the enormous oak outside my window. I was exhausted.

The dark shape, like one of Monroe's attackers, had no personality. It too seemed to know my every weak spot. I believe it to have been the embodiment of my anger and frustration. Somehow the shock of the firecracker's explosion had separated these feelings from me and they'd taken on a quasi-independent form. Then, having slipped into nonphysical reality, I had to come to grips with this anger, to wrestle with it until I had purged myself of it.

There are a variety of ways to deal with Creatures when one comes across them. Monroe's response was to return to his body. Once he was back in physical reality, they could no longer bother him. Direct confrontation is another method. Wrestling to the point of exhaustion can indicate that the troublesome emotion that created the Creature has been purged.

The literature of lucid dreaming includes techniques for dealing with nightmares that are equally valid when applied to

Creatures. In fact, some nightmares may be translations of encounters with such beings. Because nonphysical reality responds to one's thoughts, one can will the Creatures to vanish, or transform them into something else. However, recognition of what they represent may be necessary before such changes can occur.[1]

After returning to physical reality from an encounter with a Creature, one's description and interpretation of the experience may help one figure out what emotions the Creature embodied. The function of the Creature will provide clues: whether it clings, drains one's energy, pursues, torments, or attacks. If possible, one should identify the real-life source of these emotions and find some way to release them.

I've learned that any unexpressed emotion can appear to me as a Creature in nonphysical reality. The only way I can avoid encounters with such creatures is to avoid repressing what I feel in physical reality.

---

[1] *Lucid Dreaming*, by Stephen LaBerge (1985), and *Exploring the World of Lucid Dreaming*, by Stephen LaBerge and Howard Rheingold (1990), both contain information on how lucid dreamers can deal with nightmares.

9

Rescuers, Helpers, and Healers

Monroe reports that a dark-robed entity with tonsured hair and a serious expression once responded to his call for help when he was beset by Creatures. The entity cradled the rubbery things in his arms and they immediately went limp.[1] Similarly, the gargoyles in my dorm room were dispelled by the appearance of a radiant being. These beings each served a similar function—that of rescuing. The differences in appearance of such *Rescuers* reflect how my own and Monroe's temperaments may have influenced the translation process.

---

[1] In Monroe's reassessment of this experience in *Ultimate Journey* (1994, 115–116), a future version of himself appears as the tonsured Rescuer, and he sees the whole scene from this vantage point. I'm more inclined to accept this reassessment than that of the rubbery entities that were terrifying his past self as cats—in part because some of my own experiences have involved reliving past events as if they were still happening. Whatever the astral dynamics of such experiences might be (I can think

People who have had near-death experiences sometimes recall encounters with Rescuers—especially if their brush with death occurred in dangerous surroundings. Some years ago, Dr. Raymond Moody published several accounts of this type in *Reflections on Life After Life*. In one of them, a man was trapped in a vat of hot acid. As the vat filled and the acid burned through his clothing, he cowered in a corner, unable to open his eyes because of the heat. A bright glow seemed to light up the area and a voice began speaking to him. He followed the voice, which came from the one direction that led to safety. Later, he concluded that the presence who had rescued him was Jesus (Moody, 1978, 24–26). Similar stories have appeared in print in recent years in books about the intervention of guardian angels in the lives of people in great need or danger.

I have no trouble believing in the historical Christ. He was certainly a great spiritual teacher—whether or not, as church dogma states, he was the Son of God. But when a supernatural rescue has been attributed to him, or to a guardian angel, I suspect that the Christian translation table has been at work.

---

of several possible scenarios: a memory of Monroe's past replayed in an altered state, with the observer's perspective changed; a situation in which Monroe rescues someone in a similarly terrified state in the present and is then reminded of a past self; a demonstration of the simultaneity of time when viewed from the timelessness of nonphysical reality, in which the terms past and present have no relevance), my identification of Monroe's tonsured being in terms of its function as a Rescuer may still hold.

One purpose of identifying entities encountered in Otherwhere in terms of their function is to keep the options for interpretation open until one has gathered enough information about them that one can be reasonably certain of who and what they are. It may be to the advantage of anyone who wishes to explore nonphysical reality on his or her own to keep these options open as long as possible. All identifications based on the terms I've employed in this field guide are perhaps best considered to be provisional—as open to revision, in other words, as the experiences described by Monroe in *Journeys Out of the Body* were by the time he'd published *Ultimate Journey* nearly twenty-five years later.

After all, for want of a better word, I'd called my own Rescuer an angel.

I've only met that one Rescuer, and I wasn't in a position to question him about how he perceived himself. If I were ever to encounter another, I would be sure to ask about his other roles and activities. It's certainly possible that Rescuers, Guides, and some of the other nonphysical species I'll describe later, may be the same kind of being in a variety of roles. In the *Divine Comedy*, for example, there are nine orders of angels. Some have been assigned the task of worshipping God, others are in charge of maintaining various aspects of creation, and still others guide and protect the lives of mortals. There's nothing wrong with using such a classification system to represent nonphysical entities. Because each angelic order is defined in terms of function, this system resembles my field guide in approach.

The only problem I see with the idea of angelic orders is that the Christian translation table assumes that there are only a few types of nonphysical entities: deceased humans, saints, angels, Satan and his ilk, Jesus, and God. If there are others, they'll be translated into one of these categories, possibly resulting in misinterpretation. For example, if a person steeped in Christian tradition were to encounter an alien intelligence—one organized along quite different lines from ours—fear could cause him to classify the experience as demonic. A valuable opportunity for learning might then be lost.

When it comes to the taxonomy of nonphysical species, I prefer having too many categories to having too few. Having too few can lead to misinterpretation, whereas a larger number can always be narrowed down when new information becomes available.

In a chapter of *Journeys Out of the Body* entitled "Angels and Archetypes," Monroe (1977, 127–35) recounts a number of incidents in which he received help from nonphysical beings. This help usually appeared in response to Monroe's desire to accomplish something in nonphysical reality. Unseen hands would sometimes propel him from one location to another. Occasionally, such hands would take him to visit the spirit of a deceased friend. Several times they held a book before his eyes, riffled the pages, showed him the spine, and then opened it for him to read.

In the first two cases, the unseen hands could be identified as those of a Guide. But I've come to associate Guides with explanatory tours of nonphysical reality in which I'm able to ask questions. Monroe's *Helpers* are often silent. Their function seems to be nothing more than to enable him to carry out some task that he may be incapable of performing on his own.

It can be difficult sometimes to maintain the altered states of consciousness that allow one to visit nonphysical reality. I suspect that the firm grip of these "helping hands" is a representation of support in keeping one's state of consciousness firmly focused on some task.

On numerous occasions when I've made attempts to get out of body, I've felt the unseen hands of Helpers. Ironically, they often seem to be *hindering* my process of getting out rather than helping it. The hands will push me back into my body once I've released myself, and will hold me down if I try to resist them. I feel no malice on the part of the hands when they prevent me from getting out of body, only a sense of duty. I've since come to the conclusion that there are times when, for some reason, going out of body may not be an appropriate or beneficial activity. The hands are simply making that fact clear. I have yet to figure out why.

In *Far Journeys*, Monroe (1985, 65–69) describes some lab sessions with people who had volunteered to explore nonphysical reality. Several of these reports refer to nonphysical entities in healing capacities. In one case, whirling disks of energy were used to help the subject rid himself of a pain in his side. In another, the nonphysical entities gave the subject a foot massage.

I experienced a similar massage by unseen hands one night as I fell asleep. Relaxing into the soothing touch, I awakened suddenly when I realized that I didn't know who—or what—was responsible for it.

The accounts of shamans are full of references to healing spirits—nonphysical entities whom the shamans have contacted for information on healing, and sometimes for direct intervention in a cure. One typically shamanic scenario is called "death and dismemberment." It usually occurs before a shaman has recognized himself as such. During a serious illness, he's visited by spirits who seem to kill him, chop him up into little pieces, strip the flesh from his bones, and sometimes even devour him. The spirits then spit him out in a new form, or reassemble the bones and clothe them in new flesh. When he awakens from the ordeal, the illness is gone. In tribal societies, such an experience usually indicates that one has been chosen by the spirits to become a shamanic healer.

I believe that many illnesses are psychosomatic—the result of stress generated by acting from negative beliefs and attitudes. Thus physical symptoms may point to dysfunctions within a person's belief system. They'll vanish only when the dysfunction has been dealt with. I like to think of our beliefs as the skeleton upon which we drape the flesh of our personalities. Thus the death-and-dismemberment scenario could symbolically portray the restructuring of a belief system (represented by the body) under the guidance of nonphysical entities (or spirits). In shamanic societies, the result of such a restructuring is a cure. The ability to perceive spirits might then indicate a talent for translating nonphysical experiences into physical terms—a prerequisite for shamanic exploration of nonphysical reality.[2]

The literature of alien abductions often describes operations in which something is put into or taken out of the body of an abductee. I can't help but see a resemblance between

---

[2]See *Shamanism: Archaic Techniques of Ecstasy* by Mircea Eliade (1964, 33–66) for a more complete discussion of the death-and-dismemberment scenario and its role for determining one's talent for shamanism.

such reports and the accounts of death and dismemberment by shamans. Perhaps both scenarios represent the same nonphysical experience: the addition or subtraction of beliefs from one's belief system.

I once encountered a team of *Healers* in the following out-of-body experience:

One morning, after I'd practiced releasing myself from the body several times, I found myself in a structure of girders that rose very high, like the framework of a skyscraper. There were no walls, but the different levels were clearly defined. I stepped onto a kind of elevator. It took me up through several levels, but without permitting me to see what was happening on any of them. Instead, I sensed changing energy intensities, as if my motion were progressing through greater or lesser degrees of density. Sometimes my progress felt as if it were being impeded or accelerated by such fluctuations in density. On some levels I felt as if several G's of gravity were compressing me. On others I felt light and expansive. I stopped at level seven and got off.

I seemed to be in a workshop area. A group of people—two men and three women—were repairing a complex machine. They tinkered and debated about what to do next, totally absorbed in the project. Finally, one of them saw me and approached.

"Have you been: a) sent to monitor; b) registered for retraining; c) other?" he asked.

I was confused. With the first choice there came a psychic impression of awe, as if I might have been from a higher level of development, on a tour of inspection. With the second choice there came an impression of contempt, as if I might have failed at some important learning and had been returned to an earlier phase to start over. With the last option came a simple question mark.

I considered for a moment and answered: "'C'—I'm a dreamer," by which I meant someone still alive in physical reality but presently out of body.

The man's jaw dropped open in disbelief. He muttered that he'd heard rumors about such people but had never encountered one himself. He started to turn back to the contraption.

"Wait!" I cried. "You have to tell me everything about what's happening here! Let's sit down and talk!"

Before he had a chance to tell me anything, however, I began to flicker, unable to sustain my focus in this reality.

"I guess I have to leave now," I explained. "We'll talk some other time."

I have yet to encounter him or his associates again.

Of course there are no girders, elevators, or complex machines in nonphysical reality. Each of these things represented something else. Girders create a kind of framework—in this case, perhaps, a means of structuring my perceptions of nonphysical reality. Because there's no up or down in nonphysical reality, the idea of an elevator moving through various levels symbolized my traveling through a certain *psychological* distance to arrive at level seven. We've already seen that nonphysical reality can be arbitrarily divided into a multitude of divisions and subdivisions. I never found out what was on levels one through six. As I mentioned earlier, I don't like the idea of levels as a framework for describing experiences in nonphysical reality because of the value judgments implicit in the concepts of higher and lower. So I don't ascribe any special significance to my presence on level seven.

The reason I call the entities I encountered Healers is that their function was to repair—a kind of healing. The machine may have been my representation of someone's belief system, which was undergoing adjustments while he slept.

10

Gatekeepers, Sleepers, and Rangers

As I've already pointed out, nonphysical reality seems to consist of a number of regions or zones. When we dream, I believe we visit the *Dream Zone*, for example. The instability of our dream environments suggests to me that, as in the rest of nonphysical reality, thought instantly creates experience there. Except in lucid dreams, when we actually become conscious that we're dreaming and can affect the dream reality at will, most of the time we're unaware of the relationship between our thoughts and what we experience in our dreams. And of course when we die, we enter the Afterdeath Zone.

Between zones are nonphysical boundaries that keep them distinct. I often represent such boundaries to myself as walls. Passages between zones—*gateways*—may be guarded by entities whose function is to determine who may enter and who may not.

We've already met one of these *Gatekeepers* in the guise of St. Peter, the Christian representation of an entity who guards the entryway to Heaven, itself a representation of the

Afterdeath Zone. Dante describes several Gatekeepers in the *Divine Comedy*. One guards the gate to Purgatory—an angel with a blazing sword and an unbearably radiant face. Other angels are stationed at the passages between the seven levels of Purgatory and at the entrance to the Earthly Paradise. Dante must fulfill certain conditions before he is permitted to pass through each of these gateways. The act of imposing conditions on those who wish to pass through a gateway seems to be a characteristic of Gatekeepers, as the following encounter demonstrates.

During an out-of-body experience, I found myself on a great barren plain. Abruptly rising in what seemed to me like "the middle of nowhere" (an apt metaphor for nonphysical reality's immateriality) was a gate. The gate appeared to be made of ancient stone: an arch, just tall and wide enough for a single person to pass through. There was no wall on either side of it. In that barren plain it was the only distinguishable feature. As I approached the gate, a grizzled old prospector—the spitting image of a nineteenth-century gold miner—arrived ahead of me, carrying a bundle under his arm. The Gatekeeper asked him a question, and, apparently satisfied with the answer, allowed him to pass through. Then the Gatekeeper, an old man in robes, addressed me.

"What is your mission in Otherwhere?"

"I don't know what you mean," I replied.

"This is the *Barrier Zone*. Otherwhere lies beyond the Gate. Only individuals with missions in Otherwhere may pass."

Hoping not to seem obtuse, I asked about the Barrier Zone. The Gatekeeper told me that it's the border between the Dream Zone and the rest of nonphysical reality.

"You humans are notorious for your distractibility," he continued. "Since thought manifests itself instantly as experience out here, we can't have minds wandering all over the place. In Otherwhere, randomness of thought creates a kind of pollution—very unpleasant for the inhabitants to wade through. So we've confined most of you to the Dream Zone, where you'll have plenty of opportunity to experience the results of that randomness of thought—your dreams—and perhaps to learn how to free yourselves from it."

The Gatekeeper went on to explain that randomness of thought consists of uncentering emotions stirred up while we're awake. All we have to do is enter the Dream Zone and these emotions will instantly begin to shape our experience there. For example, if we repress our rage at an event that has occurred in physical reality, our feelings may be converted into dreams of fighting or killing people. We're not permitted to pass beyond the Dream Zone until we've learned to exercise some control over randomness of thought—either by not allowing ourselves to get emotionally stirred up in the first place, or by quickly getting rid of uncentering emotions whenever we're distracted by them.

By "getting rid of" these emotions, the Gatekeeper didn't mean pretending we're not experiencing them. Rather, he meant tracing them back to their origins, recognizing that they were a reaction to the event that seemed to cause them, and realizing that we could have chosen another more balanced or wholesome reaction to that event. Processing such emotions in this way, provided one has properly understood what caused them, allows their intensity to diminish until they're completely out of our systems.

I asked if the Gatekeeper would let me pass through the gate.

"The fact that you're in the Barrier Zone means that you've made it farther than most," he says. "Unfortunately, you're still contaminated enough with uncentering emotions to cause a problem once you're on the other side."

I argued, pleaded, cajoled. But the Gatekeeper remained unbending. Frustrated, I pushed my way through the gate. Just on the other side a force knocked me to my knees, blocking further progress. The Gatekeeper shrugged his shoulders and said, "You can only pass through when you have a mission in Otherwhere and can complete it without distraction."

75

Who was the grizzled old prospector who arrived at the gate just before I did? If I were to take his nineteenth-century garb literally, I would have to assume that he was either a long-dead miner or someone alive today who reenacts events from history in period dress. Later experience has taught me that the Afterdeath Zone is on the other side of the Otherwhere Gate and that the souls of the dead are only rarely allowed to visit physical reality.

It's possible to encounter the souls of the dead while one is out of body, but I doubt that the prospector was such a soul. Furthermore, anything I perceive in nonphysical reality is more likely the result of representation—for which I must assume full responsibility—than of some intention on the part of the being I've perceived. The prospector may have been a living human being, himself out of body. Although he could have used his own thoughts to create the nineteenth-century outfit, it's more likely that his appearance was completely in the eye of the beholder. Perhaps I was telepathically aware of his intentions and represented them in symbolic form.

We sometimes say that we've "struck gold" when we come across a rich and valuable information source. Maybe the prospector was mining nonphysical reality for information. The bundle under his arm could have represented the questions he was taking with him into Otherwhere. His mission would then have been to "prospect" his experiences there until he'd "struck the gold" of answers that satisfied him.

I believe that the miner's garb was a clue to his function as a prospector of information. If I'd interpreted his presence more literally, assuming that he was someone from the nineteenth century or from a modern-day historical pageant, I may never have arrived at this conclusion. I may also have missed a more subtle point: my desire to explore nonphysical reality was not enough to grant me access to it. If my journeys were motivated by questions that could perhaps be answered in Otherwhere, however, the Gatekeeper might let me pass. I would then have a genuine mission on the other side of the Barrier Zone.

The first time I found myself in an area of nonphysical reality beyond the Dream Zone, I had no memory of passing through the Otherwhere Gate. In fact, I rarely recall the transition between dreaming and venturing into other areas of nonphysical reality. Presently, I'm working on becoming more conscious while dreaming so that I'll be able to monitor this transition more closely, including passing through the Barrier Zone and the Otherwhere Gate.

I believe it's possible to encounter other living human beings while visiting nonphysical reality. They come in two varieties: *Sleepers* and *Rangers*. Sleepers are unaware of their presence in nonphysical reality. Their outlines may appear fuzzy or indistinct, and they move in slow motion. Attempts to interact with them are usually frustrating. Sleepers don't receive nonverbal communications clearly, and their responses may be incoherent. They behave as if drugged.

Rangers, on the other hand, are fully aware of their presence in nonphysical reality and are able to move through it at will. This ability to move freely is why I call them Rangers. Their function is to range widely through nonphysical reality, exploring and gathering information. I believe that the prospector mentioned above was a Ranger. In contradistinction to the Sleepers I've seen, his outlines were quite clear and he moved quickly and resolutely. However, he was too involved with his mission to chat with me, so I can't say whether his communications would have been coherent. I have yet to come across another like him.

It seems possible that two people who know each other in physical reality could train themselves to journey together into nonphysical reality. So far I've made only one attempt to get a friend to join me in the out-of-body state. That's how I encountered my first Sleeper.

I had awakened that morning about 5:30 A.M. After getting something to eat, I went back to bed. I found myself out of body and decided to visit Alan, a good friend of mine. The mere thought of him was enough to transport me instantly to his bedroom, several miles away. I was a little disoriented at first because the color of the carpet in his room is rose, whereas it seemed to me that the dominant color on this visit was dark green. Hardly had I arrived when the idea of lifting Alan out of body struck me so forcefully that I couldn't tell if it had originated within me or had come from somewhere else, like a command. I approached Alan's bed, wriggled my arms under his physical body, and pulled him upward. I heard a slurping sound, such as firm gelatin makes when being poured out of a mold.

After Alan's astral form was completely out of his body, he stood groggily in the center of the room and began to move away from the bed. His motions were so slow and effortful that he seemed to be wading through water. I mentally projected a suggestion for him to turn around and look at his physical body, asleep on the bed—knowing that the great test of whether one is ready for out-of-body adventures is how he responds to such a sight. Alan turned in slow motion. The moment he caught sight of his body, his astral form began to quiver and fade, losing its outlines. Spiky waves rippled through him in herringbone patterns, like a television screen gone haywire. I overhead his thoughts: "Oh my God, I must have died! I've got to get back!"

Still in slow motion, but faster than before, Alan returned to the bed. Amused, I helped him get back into his body. He woke up immediately. I began thinking of my own physical body and found myself instantly back in my bedroom, wide awake.

I called Alan later in the day and found out that he was using a dark green sleeping bag as a quilt during the winter months, a fact I hadn't known. Alan's large mattress lies on the floor, which must be why I mistook the dark green color I had seen for the carpet. Unfortunately, he didn't remember the visit. That's a Sleeper for you.

11

Instructors

If a nonphysical entity provides instruction, as did the disembodied voice that told me about the importance of balancing thinking, feeling, sensing, and intuiting in the out-of-body experience described in chapter 2, then I call it an *Instructor*. The function of Instructors is similar to that of Guides, except that travel or touring is usually not involved. Such instruction may take the form of pure information, or it may involve a lesson of some kind.

In the following adventure, which occurred while I was sleeping, an Instructor posed a challenging problem that I was supposed to solve, as if it were a puzzle.

"We have a task for you," the Instructor said. The voice had a distinctly feminine cast. "We'll be placing you in a specially formulated reality. This reality will have definite boundaries and restrictions. Your task is to use what you find there to escape. You won't be allowed to leave until you've succeeded."

Before I had a chance to ask questions, the presence behind the voice vanished. I found myself in a combination bedroom and study, sitting at a drawing table. Behind me was a four-poster bed of elaborately carved wood. Heavy drapes of a deep burgundy color hung from the bed frame. They were tied back with a golden cord. To my left, I noticed a narrow window, apparently wider on this side of the thick wall than on the outside. Sunlight streamed in the window, and I felt a soft breeze with a salt tang brush my face. I concluded that I was in a castle near the ocean. I didn't verify my conclusion by getting up to look out the window, however.

Instead, I looked down at the drawing table, where I found a complex perspective study of a cathedral drawn in ink on a piece of parchment. The sketch was in the style of the Renaissance. Could this be a past life, I wondered—one in which I'd been an artist or an architectural draftsman?

The window had no glass. The castle must have been in a warm climate—Italy, perhaps. Could this be the sixteenth century? I reached up to scratch my head in perplexity—and found a floppy satin cap, like one I'd seen in a Renaissance painting. I couldn't remember what country or period this style of cap belonged to. Just a few moments ago, I thought I'd felt the breeze stirring in my hair. Had the cap been there before?

All at once, I remembered my task. I was somehow supposed to escape from this room—but how? As instructed, I looked for clues. A quick scan showed me that there was no door. Perhaps it was concealed, like a trap door. After all, I seemed to be a prisoner of sorts.

I looked down at the drawing table again. The architectural rendering was gone! In its place I found a piece of typing paper, turned sideways. On it was a child's crayon drawing of a landscape: a bright blue sky with a smiling Sun and puffy white clouds, green grass, and a poorly-drawn brown cow grazing by a metal gate. Before I had a chance to ask myself what such a drawing was doing in the Renaissance, however, I found myself inside it—a real-life figure projected into a cartoon.

A wind of colors blew by. The Sun set and a crescent Moon lying on its side rose up. The Moon had a big nose and was wearing a night cap. A music box began to play "Beautiful

Dreamer," and the Moon started to sing along in the voice of Frank Sinatra. A chorus line of five-pointed stars whirled and jigged between verses, occasionally chiming in. The brown cow never moved, however. It remained frozen in mid-chew, grass dangling from its mouth, faintly pathetic.

I walked around the cow to the gate and tried to open it with a shove. Maybe this was the way out. The gate wouldn't budge.

The Sun and the Moon seemed to be attached to a revolving wheel that kept spinning faster and faster. Day alternated with night so rapidly that they blurred together, flickering like a strobe light. I stood watching, wide-eyed, unable to believe what I was seeing—as full of wonder as if I'd been witnessing an uncommon natural event, such as an aurora or a meteor shower.

And then, just as suddenly as I'd been whisked into the child's drawing, I was outside it again, seated at the drawing table. I closed my eyes and shook my head to clear out the fog of what must have been a hypnotic trance, somehow induced by the child's drawing. When I opened my eyes and looked down at the drawing table, the architectural rendering had reappeared.

I scanned the room once more. Perched on a marble stand, which I hadn't noticed before, a black-and-white cat was washing herself. I looked over at the bed. It was reassuringly solid. In a nearby corner was a telescope surrounded by potted plants, as in my living room in Boston. On the floor, where there had been bare flagstones before, there was now an Oriental rug with a mandala pattern. Someone must have brought it in when I was sleeping, I figured. The strange experience of the child's drawing must have been the result of falling asleep while I was working.

Wasn't there something I was supposed to be doing? I asked myself, settling back to work on the drawing. Oh yes, I was supposed to escape from this room. But since there was no door, and the window was too small to climb through, it seemed that only some kind of magic would suffice.

The study vanished and I found myself wandering through a desert. With a clarity of logic that startled me, I resolved to seek out the witches and warlocks who must have been responsible for this bizarre change of scenery. Perhaps they could tell me how to escape from the reality in which I'd been imprisoned. After all, wasn't the woman who brought me there one of them?

I walked and walked. The desert remained as featureless as it had been when I first arrived. I was lost. But that didn't stop me. I kept on walking anyway. Suddenly, my perspective shifted. I seemed to be seeing myself from far away, looking down on myself as I walked. The desert planet I was walking on was so small that it spun beneath my feet with every step: I was wholly responsible for its rotation!

When I realized not only that I was getting nowhere, but that there didn't seem to be anywhere to go, I panicked. I began to feel that I would be trapped in this barren reality— wherever and whatever it was—forever.

Without transition, I found myself back in the architect's study. In bafflement, I surveyed the scene once more, as if to steady myself with its comforting solidity and homeyness. There was the bed, the tiger cat on the marble stand. Hadn't she been black and white before? I decided there must be two of them. The other one was probably under the bed.

I stood up, catching a glimpse of myself in a mirror on the wall behind the drawing table. I had jet-black wavy hair down to my shoulders—quite unlike the short brown hair I was used to seeing in my bathroom mirror. My nose was long and looked as if it had been broken. Beneath it, an enormous moustache flourished. The satin cap no longer sat on my head. It had been replaced by a broad-brimmed hat with a feather, like one that the Three Musketeers might have worn. A long cape was draped dashingly over my shoulders, and a rapier dangled from my belt. I must not be in Italy after all, I surmised, but France, in the eighteenth century.

As if giving the lie to my assumption, the Renaissance drawing was still lying on the drawing table. The rug, however, had taken on a distinctly Victorian cast. I noticed, down the hallway that I hadn't seen before, that the light was on in the bathroom—an electric light. Someone had done the bathroom floor in chic black tile, which contrasted nicely with the white porcelain of the commode. A tall green plant from the tropics provided the perfect accent.

I picked up the cat and held it to my face, reveling in its velvety, purring warmth. I walked over to the window to look out, wondering why I hadn't noticed the kitchen counter and sink now so obviously beneath it. Before I got to the window, however, I became distracted by a round table covered with a lace tablecloth. I put the cat down on the floor and sat down at the table. Someone had neatly arranged some change on the tablecloth: quarters, dimes, nickels, pennies, all with the presidents' heads facing upward. I began idly to count the change to see how many bus fares I could get out of it. I seemed to have an inexhaustible supply of pennies. No matter how long I spent counting them, there always seemed to be more.

All at once, it dawned on me who I was: the Count of Monte Cristo, imprisoned within the Chateau d'If. And this money was the treasure I would use to avenge myself on my enemies!

A door concealed in the wall near the foot of the bed opened and a woman entered.

Aha! I thought. It's the jailer's daughter—she has fallen in love with me and comes now to help me escape from the Chateau, so that I won't have to sew myself up in a shroud, as planned.

It wasn't the jailer's daughter. It was the Instructor who had brought me here.

"You haven't done too well with your task," she sighed.

"What task?" Thoughts of sweet revenge had driven it from my mind.

"The task I assigned you: to escape from this reality," the Instructor replied. "All you've done is immerse yourself more deeply in it."

"But you said there would be clues, and I haven't perceived a single one," I whined, embarrassed at the Instructor's exasperated tone.

"Let me ask you something," the Instructor said. "Where on Earth are you able to walk through a crayon drawing while the Sun smiles at you and the Moon and stars are singing? And what business do you have doing architectural renderings of cathedrals in an archaic style you know nothing about, while your study contains bits and pieces of every historic period from the last five hundred years? When have you ever looked like Athos, Porthos, or D'Artagnan—or the Count of Monte Cristo, for that matter? We threw in everything but the kitchen sink to get you to realize this was a dream—and we finally had to put that in too!

"All you had to do was realize the utter impossibility of everything you were perceiving and tell yourself you must be dreaming. Then you could have gone through the gate in the child's drawing. It would have taken you directly into nonphysical reality."

"What about the desert?" I asked, abashed.

"You got very close to freeing yourself at that point. You erased the dream images you had surrounded yourself with and began to head through the area between the Dream Zone and the rest of nonphysical reality. You were intuitively seeking the Otherwhere Gate, which, as you may recall from a previous visit to this Boundary Zone, was set in a desert. You can't enter Otherwhere unless you've left your dream images behind. This is why the Boundary Zone is as devoid of sights and sounds as the Arabian desert.

"You even sensed that your 'captors,' a group of Instructors such as myself, could be found on the other side of the desert—which of course is true, since we reside in Otherwhere. The problem, however, was your assumption that magic would help you escape from the Dream Zone.

"Because thought instantly manifests itself as experience in nonphysical reality, the transformations of objects, people, and settings experienced in dreams may seem magical. But believing in such magic wasn't enough to free you from the Dream Zone. You had to recognize that you yourself were the source of that magic—because you were *in* the Dream Zone.

"We gave you a little help at that point by shifting your perspective, so that you'd see that you were getting nowhere. Although you were no longer trapped in the dream's original setting, you were not yet free of the Dream Zone. We were concerned that you might interpret the disappearance of the Renaissance setting as the solution to the problem we'd posed.

"When you realized you were trapped on that tiny desert world, you remembered the problem. In order to resume working on it, you recreated the original setting, thinking you would go over that setting again, searching carefully for clues. The first time you hadn't realized that the bed itself was a clue that you were dreaming, and that the problem we'd posed was one of *perspective:* you are the architect of your dreams, but you can't free yourself from them until you realize this fact.

"Because you'd made the assumption that you were reexperiencing a past life the first time you found yourself in the architect's study, on your later visits to that scene we began to add anachronisms. After you returned from your adventure within the child's drawing—an experience we hoped was sufficiently bizarre to jolt you into lucidity—you noticed the Victorian rug and the objects from your living room.

"These anachronisms turned out not to be jarring enough to trigger the awareness that you were dreaming, so the last time you returned to the room we added more—the eighteenth-century costume, the kitchen sink, the chic bathroom, and the change.

"For good measure we transformed the cat's markings—and even your own features. And still you were unable to acknowledge that you were dreaming. At the point when you decided that the dress, the change, the castle, the sea air, and the sense of being imprisoned meant that you were the Count of Monte Cristo, you were too deeply immersed in the illusion to consider questioning it. We had to bail you out.

"Throughout the entire experience you were like the cow in the child's drawing, unable to leave the Dream Zone, passively accepting whatever you saw, and chewing it over in your mind until the most glaring inconsistencies seemed to make perfect sense."

By the time the Instructor had finished speaking, I felt stupid and ashamed. My dreams are rarely as irrational as my experience within the child's drawing had been. Really, a moon singing "Beautiful Dreamer"? What more would it take to get me to recognize that I was dreaming?

"Feeling sorry for yourself won't do a bit of good," the Instructor said mildly. "Surprisingly few people would be able to pass that test, as simple as it seems in retrospect. The problem is that most humans are addicted to physical reality. You assume that if your physical senses provide you with information about something, it must be real. So if you dream of seeing, hearing, touching, tasting, or smelling something, you accept its reality without question. Only through developing other criteria for determining whether something is real or not will you be able to pass through the Dream Zone and into the rest of nonphysical reality at will."

12

Instructors, Round Two

Several months after my failed attempt to solve the problem posed by my Instructor in the previous chapter, I was given a second chance. Once again, the adventure took place while I slept. I found myself in a crowded cafe. It was Sunday morning (even though in reality it was Saturday). People had gotten up later than usual and were eating brunch. The smell of exotic coffees mixed with the steam rising from Belgian waffles.

I looked through the large windows at the front of the cafe. It seemed to be a beautiful spring day outside. Someone was reading *The New York Times* Sunday edition, while waitresses in French maid uniforms scurried across the black-and-white tiled floor. Three glass deli cases held croissants, salads, and rich desserts. Behind them on a counter rose an elegant, highly polished brass cappuccino machine.

I couldn't recall ever having been in such a cafe in Boston. Something about the rush and bustle of the place made me think of New York City. But the cashier was an older woman who works at Today's Bread and Water Cafe, a favorite haunt of mine in Jamaica Plain. The management of the real Today's Bread had recently done some renovations, adding wooden facades to the counters to improve the atmosphere. The new tile and the hiring of waitresses for the self-service cafe seemed like logical next steps. Never mind that I had been to the cafe only a few days before and there was no evidence of such improvements—or that in my dream I'd entered the cafe through a rear door that was usually locked.

I sat down at one of the tables, eyeing a Black Forest cake that sat on top of one of the dessert cases. Moments later a tall-ish young man with long, blond hair rushed up to me. He had a tanned face, high cheekbones, and a prominent, unshaven jaw.

"There you are," he said briskly. "We've been waiting. We have some work for you to do. Come with me."

I kept trying to figure out where I had seen this man before. Then it dawned on me that he resembled the actor David Carradine in his youth. Before I had a chance to ask him how he knew me, the man grabbed me by the arm and hustled me into an area of the restaurant that was not a part of the real Today's Bread. It was an oddly angled room that narrowed down to a heavily bolted iron door at the far end. Although the front of the cafe was all windows, there were no windows here. The walls were painted a soft peach color that rose up to a molding about eight feet off the floor. Between the molding and the ceiling, a distance of about two feet, the wall was painted white. At intervals along the wall stood tall floor lamps that resembled the pillars of an Egyptian temple. Diffuse light came from finely styled lotus blossoms of frosted glass on top of each pillar.

There was room for only a few tables in this part of the cafe. At one, an attractive older woman, with her long silver hair combed back and tied in a ponytail, sat facing the iron door. She was totally absorbed in a book. At another table, which was piled high with papers and a calculator, sat a second youngish man, with dark, tightly curled hair, a beard, and a very pale complexion. He seemed to be waiting for the return of the David Carradine look-alike. I guessed that the two of them owned or managed the cafe.

The blond man led me to a point about halfway between the entrance to this portion of the cafe and the iron door. He set up a stepladder that had been leaning against the wall and directed me to climb it. When I reached the top of the ladder, the molding was at chest height.

"The molding needs to be restored," the manager explained, as if I were a carpenter.

Sure enough, a section about three feet long was missing. The manager handed up three pieces of wood of different lengths, some nails, and a hammer. Then he returned to his seat.

The manager seemed confident that I would know what to do. But I wasn't at all sure of myself. I took the three pieces of molding and held them up to the wall, one at a time. By eye, I marked where each one ended and set the edge of the next piece at that point. In this way I discovered that I had exactly the right amount of molding to fit in the available space.

All three pieces of molding had rough, splintery edges, as if they had at one time been a single section that had somehow been torn away from the wall and broken apart from each other. My next task was to figure out the order in which they fit together, by carefully examining and matching up the delicate tines of wood left on the ends of each piece when they were snapped apart.

Once I solved this puzzle, I began working out a strategy for affixing the pieces of molding to the wall. I might not be able simply to nail them down, one after another. The last piece would have to be carefully pressed into place, so that its tines meshed with those of the molding still remaining on the wall. I wasn't sure I would be able to do it, since I had no saw, sandpaper, or carpenter's glue. Perhaps I could fit a piece of molding in place, support it with a couple of nails driven in beneath it, then add the other two pieces in the same way, nailing them all to the wall after I'd fit them together properly.

I began from the left. When I got to the last piece, it seemed to be two inches too long. I must have fit them together incorrectly, I thought. I removed the three pieces of molding from the shelf of nails I'd created and rearranged them. When I got to the last piece, I was annoyed to see that it was two inches too short. Feeling frustrated, I removed the pieces of molding and tried fitting them together again, this time beginning at the right. Once again, upon getting to the last piece, I discovered that it was too long. I tried another arrangement. As before, the last piece came up too short.

I glanced down at the managers, embarrassed at this display of incompetence. They peered at me quizzically. Afraid that they might think I was a flake, I turned my attention back to the molding with renewed vigor. I was surprised to find that the white paint had entirely peeled away from one section. Had it flaked off during my increasingly desperate attempts to fit the three pieces together?

By now I was sure that the managers would be unhappy with my work. Not only had I been unable to complete the job, but the molding would have to be repainted, once it had been restored. I hung my head, shrinking away from the withering gaze of the managers. My confidence level fell. I felt that I'd been exposed as a fraud. Why hadn't I just told the managers that I knew nothing about carpentry?

Suddenly, I heard a clunk as one of the pieces of molding fell to the floor. I looked up at the two remaining pieces in amazement as they diminished in size, their paint flaking off. In a few seconds they had both slipped through the widely spaced shelf of nails I'd hammered in to support them and had fallen to the floor.

I bolted down the ladder in a panic, as if the place were haunted, hoping to escape through the iron door. But it was locked. Feeling cornered, I turned around as the tall David Carradine look-alike approached me. He smiled gently.

"Calm down," he said soothingly. "This is only a dream."

The manager led me back to the stepladder. He picked up the three pieces of molding, which had reverted to their original size.

"Why don't you give it another try?" the manager said kindly. He patted me on the back, as if to say that he had every reason to believe that I would succeed.

I climbed up the ladder, wondering how to proceed. It occurred to me that if this were, in fact, a dream, and if the books I'd read on the subject were correct—that once one knew he was dreaming he could shape the dream reality in any way he wished—then I should be able to restore the molding simply by willing it to become whole.

I replaced the pieces of molding on the shelf of nails, without trying to fit them together. Then I climbed back down the ladder. I allowed my eyes to run along the undamaged portions of the molding on either side. Then I closed my eyes and imagined that the molding ran unbroken along the length of the wall. When I opened my eyes again, I raised my right hand, palm outward, and traced the path of the molding from one end of the room to the other. All the while I concentrated on my image of an unbroken molding.

I had the strange sensation of using unfamiliar mental muscles. A power seemed to emanate from my outstretched hand. As it passed over the three fragments of molding, they blurred and ran together. Seconds later, it was impossible to tell where the molding had been broken.

"I guess this really *is* a dream," I thought to myself.

I began turning toward the managers, sure that they would be pleased with my work. But suddenly I heard a loud click. Instinctively, I turned toward the iron door. It began opening slowly.

Startled by the movement of the door, the silver-haired woman, who had been quietly reading all this time, jumped up from her table.

"My goodness," she said, "I'll be late." She slammed her book closed and rushed out of the cafe.

I turned to look back at the iron door. It was now fully open. The Carradine look-alike walked over to me, beaming.

"Congratulations!" he said, shaking my right hand heartily with both of his. The other manager came up behind me and put his arm around my shoulders. I wondered why they were making such a big deal out of my having restored the molding. Together we proceeded through the iron door into a courtyard.

It was a fine spring day. The flagstones of the courtyard were wet, as if it had rained recently. Tables with closed umbrellas were surrounded by a terraced garden and a high stone wall. The garden was blooming profusely: whites flashing against purples, yellows and oranges contrasting with vibrant blues and reds—all surrounded by greens more lush than any I've seen on Earth. Some distance away, I noticed an open-grillwork gate in the wall.

"You've just succeeded in using the dream state as a means of gaining entrance into Otherwhere," the Carradine look-alike explained, sensing my confusion at his congratulations. "We're pleased, because you didn't fail this test, as you did the one in the castle tower."

"But I thought I had to figure out for *myself* that it was a dream," I said, perplexed. "How could I have passed the test when you just came right out and told me?"

"You believed me," the manager replied. "You could easily have ignored what I said, talked your way out of what it implied, or forgotten it completely the moment you went back to work on the molding. Instead, you accepted my statement as a working hypothesis, set up an experiment that would either prove or disprove it, and then performed that experiment. Because the results of your experiment were consistent with your understanding of the properties of the dream state, you concluded that you were dreaming. You may have had some prompting, but the realization that you were, in fact, dreaming was entirely your own."

"How come I wasn't prompted in the tower adventure?"

"Ah, but you were, although indirectly. When you entered the child's crayon drawing, as you may recall, the moon was singing 'Beautiful Dreamer.' Unfortunately, you didn't get the hint."

The two restaurant managers and I made our way to one of the tables in the courtyard and sat down. It began to dawn on me that they weren't restaurateurs at all, but Instructors.

"That's correct," the David Carradine look-alike responded, having read my thoughts.

"But why do you look like David Carradine?" I asked.

"You'll have to figure that out for yourself. After all, you're the one responsible for how you perceive us."

I thought long and hard about why I would perceive one of the Instructors as David Carradine. All I could remember about the actor was that he starred in a television show called *Kung Fu* in the early 1970s—something about a master of an ancient Chinese martial art wandering around the American West. I glanced at the Instructor and shrugged my shoulders.

"What do the words *kung fu* mean?" he prompted. Before I had a chance to argue that I knew no Chinese, he continued. "Didn't you come upon these words once, when you were flipping through a translation of the *I Ching*?"

"Why, yes. I remember seeing that *kung fu* meant *inner light*, and wondering what that had to do with a martial art."

"There you have it." The Instructor smiled. "You see me as David Carradine because I'm a master of a certain discipline that leads to illumination, or inner light. Do you know anything of Tibetan dream yoga?"

"Not much," I replied. "I've read a few books on lucid dreams that mention it."

"Well, the purpose of dream yoga was to use lucid dreams as a pathway to what the yogis called the *Clear Light*. The dream yogis realized that human beings are addicted to physical reality. Anything perceived with the five senses is unquestionably real for most people. And in dreams, anything you can see, hear, touch, smell, or taste is also unquestionably real—until you wake up.

"The yogis believed that both the physical world and the world of dreams were equally unreal, but that dreams could be used as a means of discovering the true nature of reality—the

Clear Light. Only lucid dreams could be used for this purpose. So the yogis developed a number of techniques for achieving lucidity in dreams. Part of their training involved going directly into the dream state from the waking state without actually falling asleep. Once there, they would consciously strip away all dream imagery until they could perceive the Clear Light.

"As you know, if someone makes no effort to translate adventures in nonphysical reality into images and words, he experiences only a sense of immersion in energy patterns. Light is a form of energy, and will often be the only image such people will use to represent to themselves what happened. Thus the Clear Light is a translation of immersion in Otherwhere. The *clearness* of this light means only that it's unattended by any imagery.

"As you know, many of the questions that have plagued humanity throughout the ages—such as why are you here, and what happens after you die—can be answered through visits to Otherwhere. Even if someone who had experienced the Clear Light of immersion in Otherwhere chose not to translate his adventures into physical terms, certain knowings not previously available to him would appear spontaneously in his mind. These knowings would be the result of his having been present within the Clear Light.

"Many techniques for gaining entrance into Otherwhere have been devised throughout the ages—all of them aiming for the illumination that comes from immersion in the Clear Light of Otherwhere."

"It would seem that English is full of words that link the concepts of wisdom and light, such as *illumination* and *enlightenment*," I remarked. "Are you saying that all one has to do to achieve enlightenment is find some way into Otherwhere?"

"That's exactly what I'm saying," the Instructor replied. "As a matter of fact, my colleague and I designed this morning's lesson to demonstrate how you and others may use lucid dreams to enter Otherwhere.

"The first step is to realize that your dreams are as essential to your spiritual well-being as bread and water are to your physical well-being. This is why we chose Today's Bread and Water Cafe as the setting of our lesson. Just as it would be a physical hardship to go a day entirely without bread and water, so is it a spiritual hardship to go a day without remembering your dreams. Why? Because dreams contain as much information about your inner world as *The New York Times* Sunday edition contains about your outer world—if only you can learn to read them.

"Many people think that the distinction between being awake and being asleep is as obvious as that between black and white—hence the black-and-white tile of the cafe floor. Actually, there are various gradations of wakefulness, even while you're asleep. My colleague and I distinguish the following levels of wakefulness in dreams:

"If you recall no dreams at all upon awakening, and don't remember even that you dreamed, then you were as dead to the inner world as you were to the outer. This is Level Zero.

"If you remember that you dreamed, but are unable to recall a single image or feeling, some small portion of yourself was awake within the dream state. This is Level One.

"If you recall disjointed fragments of dreams, or isolated images or feelings, then you were even more awake within the dream state. This is Level Two.

"If you seemed to be watching yourself in the dream, rather than participating in it, then you achieved Level Three.

"Full participation in the dream action means that you achieved Level Four.

"You've achieved Level Five when the dream plots are long and involved.

"Then comes Level Six, in which colors and sounds are especially vivid. Generally speaking, the more detail you recall in a dream, the more awake you were within it.

"The presence of textures, smells, and tastes, indicates the extraordinary degree of wakefulness of Level Seven.

"Then comes the ability to think rationally, using mental processes characteristic of the waking state to solve a problem. That's Level Eight.

"If you rationally apply the miraculous powers available in the dream state—the abilities to fly or to alter your environment at will, for example—then you've achieved Level Nine.

"In Level Ten your usual waking consciousness becomes fully present within the dream state—upon recognizing that you are, in fact, dreaming. At this point it becomes possible to enter Otherwhere.

"The technique of using lucid dreams to enter Otherwhere is simple, but it takes time to develop. First you must begin paying attention to your dreams. Years ago, there were periods when you remembered hardly any dreams at all. That was Level Zero. Eventually, you began to keep a dream journal—an excellent way of stimulating wakefulness in dreams. Upon retiring each night, you suggested to yourself that you would remember your dreams. It wasn't long before you began remembering that you'd dreamt and recalling fragments of dreams. You were already at Level Two.

"In order to increase the degree of wakefulness in dreams, all you needed to do was increase your degree of interest in them. Making a commitment to writing them down every day helped. You could then notice fluctuations in wakefulness from night to night. Had you then had access to the schema we just gave you, you could have made notes about which level of wakefulness each dream represented. Looking back on these notations after several weeks or months would have given you an idea of your progress.

"Learning to interpret your dreams also helped increase your interest in them. The more convinced you were that your dreams had value—that it was worthwhile to spend time writing them down and interpreting them—the more likely you were to experience higher levels of wakefulness within them.

"By this time your dreams were fluctuating between Levels Four, Five, and Six. Playing with your sleep schedule allowed you to increase your level of wakefulness in dreams even further. You experimented with waking up and writing down a dream immediately after it occurred, no matter how many hours remained until you needed to rise and begin your day. The longer you stayed awake after writing down the dream, the more likely you were to have a Level Six or higher dream during the next sleep cycle. You were sleeping more lightly, then, and so could bring more wakefulness to your dreams—while still getting the rest that you needed.

"You discovered that sleeping six hours or less, getting up, having something to eat, and keeping busy for a couple of hours, then returning to bed can produce Level Eight and Nine dreams—even though you didn't know at the time what to call them. Sleeping longer than eight hours at a time also produces this effect. And your twenty-minute naps, too, became opportunities to explore lucidity in dreams, since it was possible in that brief time to slip through the twilight state into the dream state without having actually fallen asleep.

"The ability to generate Level Ten dreams—to initiate and sustain lucidity—is a skill. Like all skills, it requires practice. In particular, you need to be on the lookout for anomalous elements in your dreams—anachronisms such as a chic yuppie bathroom in a Renaissance castle, for example. To recognize an anomalous element as such can lead to the conclusion that you're dreaming.

"Once you've made this realization, if you want to use the lucid dream as a means of entering Otherwhere, then try to change something within the dream. You won't be properly prepared for a journey into Otherwhere until you've reminded yourself that in nonphysical reality thought creates your experience almost instantly. At this point, all you need do is look for or create a door or gate. Pass through it and you'll be in Otherwhere.

"Now the fact that you could smell coffee and Belgian waffles in the beginning of the dream meant that you had achieved Level Seven.

"The stepladder in the other room indicated that you had several levels to go before achieving Level Ten. After you climbed the ladder and began to consider the problem of restoring the molding, you were thinking rationally. By this time you'd achieved Level Eight. Rational thought, however, wasn't enough to solve the problem. That's why you could never get the pieces of molding to fit together. You began to react emotionally to this apparent failure, believing that my colleague and I thought you were a flake. So the paint began to *flake* off of the pieces of molding. Thus you were reminded that thought manifests itself instantly as experience in nonphysical reality, of which the Dream Zone is a part.

"Because of your previous confidence and the subsequent proof of your inability to perform so simple a task, you felt *exposed* as a fraud. So the wood beneath the paint was exposed. You *shrank* from what you perceived as our critical gaze, and so the pieces of molding shrank in size. Your self-esteem began to *fall*, and so the pieces of molding fell to the floor.

"You tried to run away from the problem. You could have awakened at that point, recalling a nightmare about inadequacy. Instead, you chose to become more awake within the dream. Instinctively, you knew that the goal of the exercise was to go through the iron door into Otherwhere. But as long as you were unaware that you were dreaming, you were as if imprisoned within the Dream Zone. That's why the iron door was locked. The only way out would have been to return to physical reality. But my colleague and I were blocking that exit.

"At this point I reminded you that you were dreaming. This information allowed you to achieve Level Nine, in which the solution to the problem of restoring the molding became obvious: all you had to do was will the dream reality to change and the molding would restore itself. Once this task had been completed, you were able to conclude that you were, in fact, dreaming. Thus did you achieve Level Ten, and the door to Otherwhere opened wide to admit you."

"What about the act of restoring the molding—does that have some special meaning?" I asked.

"Certainly. When you were in high school, you often achieved Level Nine, in which you were able to transform the imagery of a dream as you pleased. Since then you've lost the awareness that made such transformations possible. The purpose of this morning's lesson was to *restore* your ability to *mold* the imagery of a dream.

"The awareness that you're responsible for all imagery encountered in the dream state is the pillar of Tibetan dream yoga and allows you to enter the Clear Light. That's why the lamps in this room look like pillars. They're topped with lotus flowers because the act of envisioning a many-petalled lotus is one of the dream-yoga techniques for achieving lucid dreams. We don't necessarily recommend such a technique. We simply wished to make a certain connection clear, using dream imagery.

"As you can see, my colleague and I intended every image in the dream to contribute in some way to the lesson we wanted you to learn. That's why there was a calculator on our table, and why you perceived us as managers—we were managing your perceptions in a carefully calculated fashion."

"What about the woman reading the book?"

"As you recall, she was facing the door into Otherwhere. There are many people in the world who have an interest in exploring psychic phenomena. They love to read about other people's adventures in altered states of consciousness. But if a door that would allow them to undertake such explorations on their own were to open, they would make up excuses not to go through. The most common one is that they don't have time."

"What does this have to do with me?"

"Well, you're providing them with reading material that not only recounts your adventures, but also explains how to gain entrance into Otherwhere. You may be excited about offering others the opportunity to have adventures of their own. But a time commitment is required in order to achieve such adventures. Not everyone who reads your book will be willing to pay attention to their dreams every day for several years until they've cleaned up their uncentering emotions and achieved the levels of wakefulness necessary to enter Otherwhere. Your book may show them the way, but you shouldn't gauge your success as a writer on how many people try the techniques you've outlined and succeed."

So there we sat, my two Instructors and I, chatting pleasantly in a cafe on the other side of time, surrounded by empty tables, garden terraces, colorful flowers that all meant something other than their physical appearances implied. I'll provide the rest of our conversation at a later point in this book.

13

Shades and Facilitators

Over the years, I've made several visits to the Afterdeath Zone, the place we go when we die. I prefer this term to the more common "Afterlife" because it has none of the strongly Christian connotations of the latter. I have nothing against Christianity, but I would rather invent my own translations of what I perceive in nonphysical reality than have them predetermined for me by someone else's translation tables.

The nonphysical species most likely to be encountered in the Afterdeath Zone is, of course, the souls of the dead. As deficient as English can be when it comes to describing nonphysical reality, it has no lack of words that refer to the dead: ghosts, spirits, spooks, specters, phantoms, wraiths, and so on. Most of these terms refer to apparitions of the dead in physical reality. To describe the dead when observed in their own environment, I prefer the term *Shades*. This word has none of the frightening associations attendant upon ghosts, specters, or phantoms, and none of the jocular skepticism of spooks. Its similarity to the word "shadow" aptly suggests the immateriality of the soul after it has departed from the body.

Just as shadows mimic the body's outlines, Shades often take on the semblance of their former selves—but not necessarily how they looked at the time of death. Frequently, they'll appear as they did in their prime. Some Shades may have no form at all, manifesting themselves instead as points, spheres, or ovoids of light.

In the *Divine Comedy*, Dante equates the lack of human form with advanced spiritual development. As he ascends from level to level in Purgatory, he notices that it becomes increasingly difficult for him to make out the faces of the souls he encounters, because the blaze of light surrounding them is so bright. The phenomenon becomes even more pronounced in Paradise, where the quasiphysical form a soul has taken may be totally washed-out by this light:

Just as the sun, when its rays have broken through
a screen of heavy vapors, will itself
conceal itself in too much light—just so,

in its excess of joy that sacred soul
hid itself from my sight in its own ray . . .

(Dante 1970, 67)

During the lab session at The Monroe Institute that I described in chapter 1, I encountered the Shades of existentialists in a kind of cave. The beings of light that I ran across later, and which I perceived as highly spiritual, seemed to exhibit characteristics similar to those Dante described in the lines cited above. Yet my experience at the lab occurred more than a year before I'd read those lines.

The following encounter with a Shade, that of my maternal grandfather, demonstrates that the form taken by such an entity can change with its mood. My grandfather died in the fall of 1989, at the age of ninety-two. He had been an important influence on me, introducing me to the books of the medium Edgar Cayce when I was very young. A deeply religious man, my grandfather was never sure whether Cayce's mediumistic work was sanctioned by the Bible, despite the fact that the nonphysical entities who spoke through Cayce had helped an enormous number of people through physical and psychological crises.

In 1980, I developed mediumistic abilities of my own. I began to channel a nonphysical entity named Charles, who helped people in the same way that Cayce had. I hesitated to tell my grandfather what I was doing, for fear that he would worry about my spiritual welfare—and his own for possibly having misled me. When my first book, *Menus for Impulsive Living*, came out in the spring of 1989, however, I sent him a copy for Father's Day. I included a letter, explaining that I'd written the book with the help of Charles.

I thanked my grandfather for having played an instrumental part in the development of my mediumistic abilities by introducing me to the work of Edgar Cayce. I also assured him that the information I was channeling had been beneficial for the hundreds of people who had consulted me. My grandfather lived two thousand miles away in Colorado, so I wasn't able to discuss these matters with him in person. A few months later, he was dead.

About two weeks after the funeral, I encountered my grandfather in the Afterdeath Zone. He appeared to be in his forties, very strong, tall, not stooped, hair gray rather than white, and there was more of it. At that age he had been an assistant high school principal—an impressive authority figure. He drew himself up to his full height and shook his finger at me.

"Go back to the Bible!" he said, imposingly.

"Grandaddy," I replied, "if you hadn't encouraged my interest in psychic phenomena, you wouldn't be talking with me right now!"

He dropped his hand, taken aback.

"Did you try to visit the family before the funeral?" I asked.

"Why yes—I came to dinner the night before and sat at the

foot of your parents' breakfast room table," he answered, still bemused.

Because the table had extra leaves in it, the foot had been pushed almost against the patio doors that led out of the breakfast room. There was no room for anyone physical to sit there, which must have been why Grandaddy chose that place.

"Did anyone notice that you were there?"

"Not at all. No matter how I tried to attract someone's attention, no one saw me."

"Didn't you think that was strange?"

"Of course I did. I'm not used to being ignored by my own family!"

"They weren't ignoring you," I explained. "It's just that most people are unable to see the spirit of someone who has died. They don't know how to look, just as most people don't know how to travel into the Afterdeath Zone to visit their loved ones. The only reason I can do it is that I've studied these things—thanks to you!

"The fact that I'm here should more than justify your having introduced me to the field of psychic phenomena," I continued. "But I would still like to put your mind to rest about my being a medium. The best way I know to do that is to let you see for yourself that what I've done has been for the greater good, through what's called a *mind merge*."

Though Grandaddy still seemed nonplussed, I could tell I had his full attention.

"A mind merge is a way of exchanging information in nonphysical reality," I explained. "When you're in a body, the boundary of the skin sets you off from all other things and becomes one of the ways in which you define yourself. But over here, in nonphysical reality, everything is energy. Boundaries between one thing and another are not so firm and clear.

"In nonphysical reality, one's individuality is a kind of local disturbance in the overall flow of energy, like a wave in the ocean. Just as you can watch a single wave travel toward the shore, so can you identify a particular entity in nonphysical reality by the quality of disturbance it creates. By disturbance, I don't mean turmoil or disruption, but a kind of vibration that broadcasts ripples, like those that emanate from the point where a raindrop falls into still water.

"Right now, you and I are like two raindrops that have fallen close together. The ripples we send out intersect and interact with each other, allowing us to communicate. We can change the rate at which we vibrate—or send out ripples—in an attempt to understand, or become more like each other, at least in terms of the broadcasting wavelength of our thoughts. This act will pull us closer together, until at last we merge. At that point we'll have access to whatever memories or thoughts we've agreed to share, and will experience them as if they'd been our own."

"How do we change our vibrational rates?" my grandfather asked.

"First, let's agree that the purpose of the mind merge will be for you to see and understand what it has meant for me to develop psychic abilities of my own."

"Agreed."

"Then you must think about the love you've always felt for me," I continued. "Add to that love an intense desire to understand me. Release any fear of losing your sense of identity through the mind merge. In fact, you might want to imagine that your identity is like a tense muscle you would like to relax. As your love increases and your identity relaxes, you'll find that the two of us are drawn closer and closer together, until at last we merge—but only for a moment. In a burst of energy and insight, the information we've agreed upon will be exchanged. Then our respective identities will reestablish themselves, like stretched rubber bands snapping back to their original shapes."

At this point, I noticed a certain stiffness about my grandfather's image—an expression of his rigidly religious belief system. I wondered whether he would be able to overcome this rigidity in order to effect the mind merge. As I worked on relaxing my own identity, Grandaddy struggled with his. He was having a hard time, but I could feel that his willingness to understand was strong.

We seemed to be standing several feet apart in a landscape from my childhood, a place whose familiarity to both of us made us feel safe with our experiment. The distance between us became highly charged with emotion. Like two magnets, we felt ourselves irresistibly drawn together. The sensation of merging was like an affectionate, familiar hug, only deeper and richer in ways impossible to describe. Despite the fact that we'd agreed upon sharing only the memories of my psychic development, I let slip everything I knew about the Afterdeath Zone, figuring that Grandaddy would find it useful.

The merge seemed to last only the briefest of instants. When it was over, Grandaddy looked much younger. Full of excitement, he seemed to be in his twenties, the time when he first began exploring his own interest in psychic phenomena.

"All of this goes against a lot of the things I was taught in church," he said. "It's hard for me to accept how old-fashioned my beliefs seem to be over here. I appreciate the insights you've given me about this place, but I hope you'll pardon me if I go see for myself whether it's really true."

And off he went, as excited as a kid turned loose at a carnival.

Aside from Shades, there's another species that one is likely to encounter in the Afterdeath Zone. I call these entities *Facilitators*. Their function is to help the Shades perform various tasks, from reviewing their former lives to preparing for new incarnations in physical reality.

The Afterdeath Zone consists of a variety of *stations* through which Shades must pass before they reincarnate. These stations are manned by Facilitators. For the most part, the Facilitators are Shades themselves, albeit ones well-advanced in spiritual development. They may choose to reincarnate occasionally, but most of their learning takes place in the Afterdeath Zone. When they do come back to Earth, they often take the role of spiritual teachers.

I strongly suspect that the first being I encountered in the Cave of the Existentialists experience was a Facilitator. It also seems likely to me that the figures of saints or of Christ often reported by near-death experiencers may actually have been Facilitators. Either the Facilitators assumed such guises in order to make the individual more comfortable about his near-death experience, or the high level of spiritual development achieved by these beings led the near-death experiencer to translate their presence in religious terms.

This is not to say, however, that Christian saints might not be among the company of Facilitators. In the afterdeath state, spiritual attainment doesn't seem to be the exclusive property of a particular religion. It would be hard to tell the difference between Christian, Moslem, or Hindu saints. This is why I prefer to identify Facilitators by their functions rather than by their identities in previous lives.

The Facilitators fulfill a variety of functions in the Afterdeath Zone, depending on the station to which they've been assigned. Thus they may be broken down into subgroups identified by the specific tasks they perform. One night my Guide arranged for me to watch a documentary that provided an overview of these tasks.

I was brought to an area of nonphysical reality that I perceived as a conference room large enough to seat a dozen people at several small round tables. All the spaces were filled, except the one reserved for me. I had the distinct impression that my companions weren't human. Their forms were vague, but somehow alien. Before I had a chance to become alarmed, however, the documentary began. At first I seemed merely to be watching it. Moments later I was actually inside it, personally witnessing the things it described, while a voice explained what I was seeing.

"After the physical body dies," said the narrator, clearly an Instructor, "the soul keeps trying to reenter it. The soul often feels frustrated and afraid because it doesn't understand why the body won't respond. Certain entities in nonphysical reality are responsible for exhuming such souls. Since these entities are nonphysical, the six feet of earth on top of a coffin doesn't exist for them. They gently squeeze the soul out of the dead body, as if the latter were a tube of toothpaste. Actually, what they're squeezing out is the individual's memories.

"Memory isn't localized in the brain but distributed throughout the body, in every cell. As long as any of this cellular memory remains, it acts as a kind of homing signal that draws the soul back to the body. When all of the individual's memories have been squeezed out of the body, the soul takes up residence in the Afterdeath Zone. This exhumation process isn't necessary when a body has been cremated.

"Once the soul has been completely released from the body, it often wanders—as a Shade—through nonphysical environments reminiscent of its life on Earth. Since thought creates experience in nonphysical reality, the Shade's own memories are responsible for generating such environments.

"Because the Shade recognizes the feel of nonphysical reality from prior experience in the Dream Zone, it sometimes assumes that it hasn't died but is merely sleeping. It will try to wake up. As it attempts to alter its state of consciousness in order to awaken, a nonphysical entity will prevent it from leaving the Afterdeath Zone."

The Gatekeeper who fulfilled this function was represented in the documentary by a three-headed dog, like Cerberus in Greek mythology. The dog barked, growled, and bared its fangs until errant Shades stopped trying to leave the Afterdeath Zone.

"The three heads of the dog symbolize past, present, and future," the narrator continued. "Time as such doesn't exist in nonphysical reality. For the Shade, past, present, and future seem to be happening at once. This can be quite confusing to the recently deceased, who are more used to the linear sequencing of events they experienced in physical reality. They may try to get back to physical reality by concentrating on the last things they remember—under the assumption that their lives will carry on from that point.

"Meanwhile, they'll attempt to exclude all other past memories and any visions of their 'future' experience in the Afterdeath Zone. The Gatekeeper reminds them that they're in nonphysical reality and that they must learn how to remain simultaneously aware of past, present, and future. Such reminders force recently deceased individuals to accept the idea that they can't return to physical reality because their bodies are dead. Shades find these reminders shocking and irritating, like the loud bark of a dog.

"In nonphysical reality, thought and motion are closely connected. Merely thinking of some destination is often enough to transport one there. When the Shade finally accepts the fact that the body is dead, it enters a state like depression, in which thought and motion slow down and eventually cease. It becomes self-absorbed, unresponsive to anything happening outside itself.

"As the Shade draws into itself, it gradually loses its human shape, which up until this point has appeared as an idealized version of its former body. The Shade's final form is completely inert: a compact ovoid, as tightly sealed as a clam. *Harvesters* periodically sweep through the areas in which the recently dead congregate, collect these ovoids, and transport them to another region of the Afterdeath Zone."

The next portion of the documentary focused on a large building with many levels, a kind of laboratory. Each level of the building contained row upon row of shelves that rose from floor to ceiling. The floor plan was similar to the stacks of a library. But instead of books, the shelves supported long lines of deep wooden drawers.

"Harvesters bring each ovoid here," the narrator said. "It is then assigned to a particular level based on its size. The size of the ovoid reflects the amount of experience the Shade assimilated in the course of a lifetime. The Shades are stored in these drawers, where they undergo a transformative process. The drawers seem to be made of wood in order to symbolize how the Shade, while alive, had naturally grown through various cycles. Just as the rings of trees indicate years of rain and drought by their thickness, so for a Shade some years are thick or rich with events and others thin or drab.

"The entities working in this area can locate any Shade through a cross-indexing system that uses personality traits in the same way a library uses call numbers in a card catalog."

Technicians on each level were busy with what looked like alchemical apparati—crucibles, flasks, tubes, and alembics. They were intent upon distilling phials of liquid light. The phials came in a variety of colors. Every hue of the spectrum seemed to be represented.

"The phials of liquid light represent awareness," the narrator continued. "Their myriad hues indicate the many ways in which human emotions can color one's awareness while alive. During this phase, the Shade must distill the emotional coloring from every event of its life in order to arrive at a pure awareness of what it learned from that event. This is the process that ancient alchemists referred to as transforming base metals, or raw experience, into gold, or pure awareness."

The Technicians carried clipboards that prescribed different types of liquid, their dosage, the frequency of their administration, and the locations of the recipients. When they weren't overseeing the distillery, the Technicians were opening the drawers, taking samples of the contents, pouring in a few drops of liquid awareness, and noting the results.

"The Technicians make observations on how the Shade's transformative process is progressing. They take samples of the Shade's awareness in order to see how much emotional coloring remains. The stronger the emotion, the more powerful the hue. The Technicians then distill this awareness to the next stage of purity before adding it back to the drawer, which challenges the Shade to purge itself of even more emotion.

"Eventually, the contents of a drawer will begin to emanate a brilliant radiance. At this point, the Shade has purged itself completely of every emotion that the events of its life contained. Everything that was to have been learned from these events has been understood. The Shade will now manifest itself as a clear light: it's nothing but pure awareness. One of the Technicians will release it from the drawer, and it will be sent to another region of the Afterdeath Zone."

The next phase of the Shade's growth took place in a university-like setting.

"Here the Shade may enroll in seminars about life on Earth," the narrator said. "It will study the climates and geophysical characteristics of particular regions, and major events of political, scientific, spiritual, and demographic significance that could have an impact on its life in the area it's thinking about incarnating in. Simulations and other teaching aids, such as the quasiparticipatory documentary that you're now experiencing, are used extensively in these seminars. There are also classes about the kinds of things that can be learned in physical reality, especially from the enormous variety of relationships that may develop there.

"One frequently attended course is called 'Choosing a Body.' Here the Shade learns how to match personality traits and physical characteristics and how to choose parents in order to enable the lessons of time, place, and relationships to occur. As the final exam for this class, each Shade takes on a pseudophysical form—an expression of all the choices it has made in the process of selecting a body. In a simulation of life on Earth, it progresses rapidly through each period of its prospective physical development to make sure that it has a full understanding of how the body it will adopt is likely to grow.

"Between classes, Shades gather with their friends, like students in a college cafeteria. They make bets and dares, bargains and contracts about encountering each other in physical reality. They speak of their next lifetime as if it were just another class for which they're about to register.

"When the Shade feels ready to sign up for a new life on Earth, it progresses to a region of the Afterdeath Zone in which it will find a rounded air-lock chamber. This chamber is the

Reentry Gate that connects nonphysical and physical reality and opens into the womb of every pregnant woman. The Shade is reminded of certain agreements it must honor about what it means to be present in physical reality, such as that no two objects may take up the same space, and that time will be perceived as a linear succession of moments instead of as a simultaneous Now. The Shade is then admitted to the chamber.

"Notice that there are no windows in the chamber. No one in nonphysical reality can see what happens when a Shade passes through the Reentry Gate. Shades might not be so eager to return to Earth if they knew what was in store for them. When passing through the Reentry Gate, the Shade finds that the awarenesses accumulated during its stay in the Afterdeath Zone get compressed so that they'll fit into the body of a newborn infant. Often the shock of this compression causes the Shade to forget much of what it has learned. A kind of trap door opens out from under it, and it finds itself sliding down a chute into physical reality. This chute is the birth canal."

14

Further Encounters with Shades and Facilitators

So far we've seen three types of Facilitators in action: the *Exhumers*, who squeeze the soul's memory out of the body; the *Harvesters*, who collect Shades ready for the emotional distillation process; and the *Alchemists*, who oversee that process.

Of course these are my own terms for describing the functions of the entities in question, just as the building with the endless rows of wooden drawers is a personal translation of something nonphysical. Other people might experience the same things quite differently. Dante, for example, wrote about the Mount of Purgatory, where souls purify themselves on seven levels, corresponding to the seven deadly sins.

It may seem as if there's a world of difference between sin and the emotional coloring of one's awareness. Yet the key factor here is the concept of *purification*. Dante and I have both encountered regions in the Afterdeath Zone in which a purification process occurs. It may be that the same things are being purified in both of our accounts, and that Dante and I have merely translated them differently because of our divergent belief systems.

Compared to Dante's *Paradiso*, being shut up in a wooden box may not seem like the most attractive vision of the Afterlife. This image also is a personal one. I believe that its dry functionality indicates that the documentary was made from the Facilitators' perspective. For the Facilitators, the most important thing is overseeing the emotional distillation process. The library-like organizational structure exists purely for their convenience, to help them keep track of the Shades in their charge. The Shades themselves have a different perspective on this distillation process, as demonstrated by the following encounter.

Once again I found myself in an underground cavern. It appeared to be man-made. Some parts of the rock were rough-hewn. Others had been carved into elaborate designs, apparently with religious significance. The place seemed to be very old.

I looked around, wondering where I was. Suddenly, it occurred to me that people who believe that the only way of gathering information is through the five physical senses may experience nonphysical reality as an endless blackness or void. The closest analogy, in physical terms, would be a cavern in which all light has been extinguished. Caves have often provided a natural metaphor for the Afterdeath Zone, as in the ancient Greek notion of Hades. It's possible to reshape a cave, or to create an artificial one—just so has humankind carved the void of the Afterdeath Zone into a variety of forms with religious significance.

An underground river ran through the cave. I dove into it and let the strong current carry me along. Another unexpected insight came immediately into my mind—not the result of instruction, but of being somehow receptive to the energetic ambiance of the environment in which I found myself. I realized that within the Afterdeath Zone there are several *energy streams*.

Once again the cave image provided a useful metaphor to describe them: underground rivers. One of these energy streams, I suddenly knew, carries people to and from physical reality. Another allows them to travel between regions of the Afterdeath Zone. The third is like a cold plunge: it startles people into realizing that their earthly personalities are not the be-all and end-all of who they are.

In Greek mythology, the first energy stream was called the River Styx. Souls had to cross it to enter Hades. In Roman mythology, the third energy stream was called the River Lethe. It brought forgetfulness of life on Earth. There were three other rivers in the Greek and Roman underworlds, but I wasn't familiar enough with the legends about them to identify the second energy stream—the one that I was traveling in.

After a while, I got out of the energy stream and began wandering through huge galleries that seemed to have been occupied long ago, but which now were abandoned. I saw no one and had no sense of what the galleries were used for. There was only the creepy feeling that they were ancient and that no one had been in them for a long time. They were like the long-disused wing of a huge mansion.

All at once, I realized that I was perceiving the structure that some long-dead religion had used to understand what goes on in the Afterdeath Zone. All of the people who once believed in this structure had moved on to other lifetimes. Their religion was now a matter of interest only to scholars.

Eventually, I came to another energy stream. The area around it resembled a spa or health resort. The main focus was the cold plunge: the River Lethe.

A Shade was seated by the side of the plunge. She seemed to have come from a wealthy and highly cultured background—an American society matron in her mid-seventies. She was unaware of my presence, yet I had no trouble reading her thoughts. She was about to go back into the memories of a particular time in her life. Apparently, the function of the spa region was to give Shades an opportunity to heal themselves by remembering difficult events and figuring out why they had occurred.

Somehow I accompanied the woman into her memories, which both of us experienced as if they were happening for the first time. I saw that the woman was in her early forties in this particular memory. She had been widowed for a couple of years. She was traveling in England with a younger woman. I wasn't sure if the younger woman was a friend or a relative. They were driving through the country together and had stopped at a farm where horses were kept. The horses had been especially groomed for fox hunting.

As the women got out of the car to look at the horses, a young man in his late twenties came out of the nearby stable. He approached the women and they began to talk. Evidently, he was responsible for taking care of the horses. The older woman found herself sexually attracted to the young man. She was very embarrassed by this and was afraid that her companion would notice. The attraction seemed completely harmless to me. It didn't lead to any shameful behavior. Yet the woman acted as if her fantasies about this man were sinful—and making them real would be unthinkable.

After the two women left, the older one did her best to pretend that the incident had never occurred. Much to her annoyance, her friend kept referring to the very nice man they'd just met. The older woman grew stone-faced and silent.

Coming out of the memory of this incident, I once again found myself by the side of the cold plunge. The woman dove in and was carried a short distance by the current. Somehow I knew that this was necessary so that she could enlarge her perspective on the events she had just recalled. She was so completely immersed in reexperiencing them that without the cold plunge she might have forgotten she was dead.

When the woman came out of the plunge, I sensed a new awareness dawning on her. She had been widowed three years before the trip to England. She was still mourning the death of her husband, and the friend had thought that an overseas trip might help her leave her grief behind. The older woman's higher self had been responsible for stimulating her attraction to the young man. The encounter was to have been a part of her healing process, a rediscovery of her sexuality after the long period of mourning. The woman's higher self had not intended for her to become involved with the young man, but only for her to recognize that her sexuality had not died with her husband.

This realization would have helped her open herself to the possibility of drawing a new mate into her life. Instead, it was sabotaged by her religious beliefs in the sinfulness of sexual thoughts—that imagining the deed was as bad as actually doing it. She also felt guilty and embarrassed that she'd violated her intention to remain chaste and pure in memory of her late husband.

She somehow hoped that, if he was indeed looking down on her from Heaven, he would be proud that she had erected a monument of chastity in his honor. The result of these beliefs was that she never remarried. Her later life wasn't miserable, but it was certainly not as happy or as fulfilled as it could have been.

The woman's emotional reactions to her husband's death had colored her perceptions. Through reliving the encounter with the young man in England, she was able to distill for herself an uncolored awareness of what that encounter meant—from the perspective of her higher self.

As I stood by the side of the energy stream contemplating the widow's life, a Facilitator approached. This entity was human in form, but seemed to be without gender. It was in charge of training people in how to use the cold plunge. The Facilitator had taken my long period of standing by the side of the energy stream as hesitancy to use it. After demonstrating what to do, the Facilitator stepped aside to let me try it. I did feel hesitant. If this was Lethe, the River of Forgetfulness, I wasn't about to plunge in. I hadn't died yet: I still needed my memories of who I was!

The Facilitator assured me that the only things that are forgotten after a plunge into Lethe are one's illusory perspectives on earthly life. Somewhat comforted, I decided to jump in after all. The cold water provided a kind of electric shock. When I came out, my awareness seemed to be crystal clear. That clarity remained with me long after I'd awakened.

I've mentioned that the Afterdeath Zone is divided into a number of stations. The spa I just described—a place where people can heal themselves of painful memories—is one of them. On another occasion, I visited what, for some people, may be the first station they'll pass through after death.

Just after going to bed, I found myself in a state of consciousness somewhere between waking and sleeping. I could clearly hear both the rain falling outside and the footsteps of the woman who lived in the apartment below mine. Yet I felt as if I were drifting through space.

After a gentle twist—like somersaulting through a precise but odd angle—I arrived at a threshold, which my mind interpreted as an opening in heavy gray walls. The walls seemed to be made of huge, ancient blocks of stone. As I crossed the threshold, I immediately felt an intense pressure bearing down on me, as if I were many fathoms below the surface of the sea. The sensation wasn't pleasant. I could barely move. My arms were pinned to my sides.

A man approached me. He looked to be in his thirties, had a very white and shining face, a moustache, dark eyes shaped like almonds, and a long scar on his right cheek. He would have been handsome, had it not been for his sternness.

"How did you die?" he said. His nonverbal communication had a no-nonsense air about it.

"I'm not dead, just sleeping," I replied, a bit taken aback.

"That's what they all say!" the man retorted.

He came closer, informing me that the truly dead only appear to maintain the gender characteristics of the body they've left behind. In actuality, their new forms come equipped with both sets of sexual organs. Those of the opposite sex appear almost invisibly—latent energy patterns that will develop more fully as the individual becomes conscious of the fact that the soul is neither male nor female, but androgynous.

I looked down at myself, surprised to discover that I was naked. Yet I wasn't embarrassed. I've noticed that when visiting nonphysical reality my form—with or without clothes—is merely a convenience. As I'd explained to my grandfather, it's the ripples I send out that determine my true identity. I could have instantly manifested any costume I wished merely by thinking about it. But somehow I knew that the entity with whom I was speaking would see through the disguise.

"Well, I'll be damned!" he said, pointing. "You've only got the ones you were born with!"

Because he was stationed at a threshold and seemed to have some interest in the state of anyone wishing to cross it, I identified the man as a Gatekeeper. I got the distinct impression that he knew all along I wasn't dead. Perhaps all he wanted to do was draw my attention to this process of sexing the soul. It must be startling indeed to an individual who refuses to acknowledge that he has died to be shown that a second set of sexual organs is now emerging from his astral body.

"That's right, young man," the Gatekeeper said, reading my thoughts. "While this shock may not be the decisive factor in getting someone to accept the fact that he's dead, sexing the soul will certainly begin to undermine his resistance. As for you, it served the purpose of providing some assurance that you didn't get here in the usual manner!"

The Gatekeeper allowed me to cross the threshold. I entered what felt like a vast enclosed space.

"Welcome to Immigration!" the Gatekeeper said. "Everything that happens here is designed to convince the recently dead of the fact that they've died. No one can move on to the other stations of the Afterdeath Zone without first having made this acknowledgment. The pressure you feel represents an intense focusing of energy on this single goal: it's necessary because so many people refuse to embrace death as a part of life."

I left the Gate and entered a very crowded space. There was barely room for me to move. Row upon row of people extended off into the distance. There must have been tens of thousands of immigrants to the Afterdeath Zone, standing quietly and waiting. Everything was a dull, brownish gray. There was just enough light to perceive form, but not enough to register color. Mists swirled about, making it difficult to see much detail.

In front of me was yet another society matron—this one in her late sixties and clearly of considerable wealth. She wore an expensive dressing gown, as if she had died in her sleep. On my right was a woman in her mid- to late twenties, in ski clothes and a ski mask. Had she died in a ski accident or on a ski trip? In between these two was a black man in his middle forties. His shoulders arched upward and he held his arms stiffly to his sides—a pose I associated with extreme shock and terror. The only part of him that moved were his eyes, wide with fear. He seemed to be holding his breath.

Just trying to make conversation, I turned to the society matron and asked her how she had died. Her whole body shuddered, so I knew she'd heard me. But she didn't reply. In fact, when I uttered the word "die," a tremor ran through the entire crowd, like the ripples caused by tossing a rock into calm water. In a prankish mood, I began to shout "Death! Death! Death!" at the top of my lungs—or maybe I was just thinking it very loudly, since there's no such thing as true speech in nonphysical reality. All around me people winced and recoiled, gritting their teeth and stiffening their backs, as if I were shouting an obscenity.

Meanwhile, more people were being brought in. None came voluntarily, and some almost had to be shoved across the threshold. The crowd rearranged to accommodate them. In this process of reshuffling, the terrified black man bumped into the woman in ski clothes. She turned on him, enraged.

"This is what I have to say to you, buster!" she screamed, then gave him the finger. She seemed to believe that this was simply a crowd of people somewhere on Earth waiting for something to happen—an outdoor rock concert, perhaps.

The black man looked even more terrified and confused at the woman's anger. To calm her down, I said, "That's a very attractive ski mask you have on."

The woman took it off and showed me its special features, pointing out the designer's logo inside. I noticed that she had long brown hair and brown eyes, a broad, pretty face with a few freckles on the cheeks. She looked at me with a roguish smile and said, "You're not so bad yourself!"

I ignored the remark, a little squeamish over being admired by a dead person, but also knowing that she found me attractive simply because she'd somehow sensed I was still alive. Now that she had removed her ski mask, she could see more of what was going on around her. She asked me about it. I tried to explain, based both on what I already knew about the Afterdeath Zone and on close observation of what was going on in Immigration.

The woman was particularly interested in the two entities who moved continuously through the crowd, addressing now this person, now that. The fact that they were always on the move made them conspicuous among the throngs who were immobilized by the pressure I'd felt when I crossed the threshold. One was the man I'd met at the Gate. The other seemed to be in his early fifties. He had black hair, a little thin, with some gray in it, a clean-shaven, squarish face. He was somewhat overweight. His most prominent feature, however, was the cigar stub perpetually hanging from his lips.

I explained that these two men were Facilitators, in charge of this particular station of the Afterdeath Zone. After I'd observed the nature of their work for a time, I dubbed the one with the cigar the *Minister* and the one with the moustache, whom I had earlier identified as a Gatekeeper, the *Philosopher*.

"The task of the Minister must be to bring people here after their funerals," I explained. "The recently dead are allowed to attend funeral-home visitations and their own memorial and burial services—anything to help them acknowledge that they've died. But there's always something about the funeral that they're not happy with—someone who doesn't show up; or something that doesn't take place according to their expectations, whether set down in their wills or imagined while alive.

"They refuse to believe that the funeral they've witnessed is really theirs—even though their own physical bodies are on display, and the genuine grief of their friends and relatives is clearly visible. The Minister determines the exact nature of the funeral the individual would have preferred and enacts it in a special area of the Afterdeath Zone. He uses the principle that thought creates experience in nonphysical reality to construct lifelike images of the church and people, accurate in every detail, even the number of candles lit on the altar.

"Whatever the person expects to see at his funeral will be experienced as real. The shock of participating in one's own funeral exactly as one has imagined it is often sufficient to convince a person that he's dead.

"This is where the Philosopher takes over. His job is to determine the nature of the individual's expectations of the Afterlife. From these, he will deduce a course of instruction that will gradually eliminate dogmatic beliefs that might obstruct the afterdeath learning processes.

"Once the Minister has gotten someone to acknowledge his death and the Philosopher has determined his expectations of the Afterlife, this person will be transferred to another part of the Afterdeath Zone, where he will have a chance to live out those expectations. Meanwhile, a gradual process of reeducation will wean him from these expectations, so that he can move on to yet other lessons."

The woman in the ski mask took in everything I related to her. She became curious about what would happen to her upon leaving Immigration, since she was an agnostic. I told her that I didn't know. But as I spoke, I noticed that she seemed to be less affected by the immobilizing pressure of Immigration. Her stiffness had vanished. She left me, moving freely through the crowd until she came to a wall of heavy gray stone with a threshold like the one I'd originally crossed. She climbed up two stone steps, crossed the threshold, and disappeared from view.

It seemed to me that the two steps symbolized the two things that had to be accomplished in order for the woman to leave Immigration: acknowledgment of her death and determination of her expectations of the Afterlife. Because she didn't believe in any particular religion, she had no expectations of the Afterlife. This meant that once she realized she was dead, she could move on to the next phase of afterdeath training without undergoing religious reeducation.

I felt proud of myself for having helped this woman along. I began to look around for another person I could help in the same way. Yet I found myself amused by the idea of people having to see their funerals reenacted before they would believe that they were dead. In fact, the Minister and the Philosopher seemed like such characters to me—the one with his cigar, the other with his scar—both so seriously and tirelessly performing their duties. It occurred to me that, with their perpetual poker faces, these two Facilitators would gamble anything to get people to confront the fact that they're dead.

"Who are those guys, anyway?" someone near me said. I was so pleased with my gambling analogy that I playfully projected an image of the Minister and the Philosopher playing poker together to the person who had questioned me. "They're old gambling buddies," I started to say. Instantly, the Philosopher was at my side.

"Look, you're becoming a nuisance here," the Philosopher said. "It's time for you to go home!"

The Philosopher grabbed me by the neck, as if to march me back to physical reality. At his touch, an electric shock ran through me, returning me instantly to my bedroom, fully awake.

For many people, one of the most pressing questions concerning life after death is why the dead don't return to assure us that they've survived. Some small token of proof would mean so much to those of us who struggle to believe that there's an Afterlife. The following visit to the Afterdeath Zone suggests an answer to this question.

I came into an area where a number of Shades were waiting anxiously. The mood was similar to that of a train station when the train is long overdue. After a while, a horse-drawn vehicle came by, a kind of open touring car driven by one of the Facilitators. The touring car reminded me of a story I'd once read by E. M. Forster, "The Celestial Omnibus," in which a child is transported to Heaven in a similar vehicle driven by Dante. The association helped me to understand that the touring car was a form of transportation between physical reality and the Afterdeath Zone.

The Facilitator stopped the car in front of me. Here was the same entity I'd encountered in Otherwhere's Grand Central Station, although he was then piloting a gondola. I greeted him with a bow of respect.

"Have you been transferred to another line of work?" I asked.

"No," the Facilitator replied. "My position still requires that I take the dead back into physical reality to visit their living relatives."

"What happened to your gondola?"

"Whether I appear as the driver of an omnibus, or as Charon, ferryman of the dead in Greek mythology, is entirely up to you. My function, however, remains the same in either case: I facilitate travel between physical reality and the Afterdeath Zone.

"There are two ways to travel between physical reality and the Afterdeath Zone," the Facilitator explained. "One is by using the River Styx, the energy stream that connects the two realities. It's possible for any living person to use this energy stream. But most people have forgotten it exists."

"Is this energy stream the same as the canal I saw under Grand Central?" I asked.

"That's correct. To come to the Afterdeath Zone, you could either take the Afterdeath Ferry or simply dive in.

"The other method of traveling between physical reality and the Afterdeath Zone may be used by both the living and the dead. It usually requires a Guide, such as myself. Although the few living persons who make use of this guidance may travel in either direction, the dead usually go only one way. A few of them are permitted to return briefly to Earth from time to time, but only under certain conditions.

"The first is when they absolutely refuse to believe that they're no longer focused in a physical body. Since they seem to have the same form that they did before dying, many Shades assume that they're only dreaming they've died. A journey back to Earth can help convince them that this is not the case. As they witness their own funerals or see their families grieving for them, as they fruitlessly try to get their loved ones to notice them, or as they come to realize that they're visible only to delirious alcoholics and drug addicts, they eventually resign themselves to the fact that they're dead. Then they're ready to begin the learning processes required of them in the Afterdeath Zone.

"The second condition is when there's a great need for comfort on the part of a loved one who's still alive. The loved one may not be able to see or communicate directly with the Shade, but may be surprised by a feeling that the Shade is somehow present. More intuitive individuals may see or even receive messages from the Shade. But since psychic abilities tend to go undeveloped in your society, such visits are often wasted: loved ones almost never notice them.

"The third condition involves a kind of incentive program. As you know, part of the learning in the Afterdeath Zone requires Shades to confront memories of even the most difficult circumstances of their lives, in order to understand what they learned from these events. Because many Shades resist going back into painful memories, they're rewarded for each time they do so with a kind of token. The token symbolizes the extent to which their self-awareness has grown as a result of processing their painful memories. After a certain number of tokens have been collected, Shades are permitted to return to Earth for a brief visit to check on the well-being of their loved ones."

I watched the Facilitator sort through the crowd of anxious Shades. As each one displayed his or her collection of tokens, the Facilitator nodded or shook his head. If he nodded, the Shade got into the vehicle. If he shook his head, the Shade stepped back, crestfallen. The Facilitator selected only a handful of Shades to accompany him back to Earth. But he allowed a few to get into the vehicle without checking their tokens—those who had been summoned by the great need of a loved one.

I wondered why the Facilitator allowed so few Shades to come along with him.

"I have to be very careful," he replied. "A lot of the learning acquired in the Afterdeath Zone can be undone by a single visit to Earth. It's easy for Shades to perceive when the choices of a loved one are inappropriate: their learning in the Afterdeath Zone has required them to identify their own inappropriate choices. Furthermore, the beliefs of a loved one may not admit the possibility of communication with Shades. The frustration of seeing what a loved one needs to do while being unable to convey a message about it can cause a Shade to believe that the universe is arbitrary and unfair. This belief can generate resistance to the Shade's further education in the Afterdeath Zone.

"If you wish, you may call this the *CO Line*—short for *Celestial Omnibus*. It's a way of getting to and from the Afterdeath Zone by bypassing the Dream Zone.

"What's the advantage of bypassing the Dream Zone?"

"The Dream Zone presents all sorts of distractions for the living. As you've discovered, even with the best of intentions to become lucid while dreaming and cross over the boundary into

Otherwhere, you rarely succeed. The advantage of bypassing the Dream Zone is a higher degree of lucidity from the outset of your adventure. This is not to say that you can't become fully lucid when you've taken the Earth-to-Otherwhere Line—even though it passes through the Dream Zone. It's just that a little more effort is required.

"As far as the dead are concerned, we try to keep them out of the Dream Zone—more for the benefit of their surviving relatives than their own. When people on Earth dream of a dead relative, in most cases they're perceiving an image created from their longing to be comforted, or because the deceased individual represents a certain aspect of their own characters.

"Yet sometimes people feel that they've truly been visited by a dead relative in a dream. *That* experience has a much greater vividness and sense of reality—as if the deceased individual had actually been there, supplying comfort or pertinent information.

"In such cases, the dead have *not* entered the Dream Zone—but the living have entered the Afterdeath Zone, carried along by the strength of their yearning. The idea of having journeyed into the Afterdeath Zone is too scary for most people, so they tell themselves the 'visit' came in a dream.

"We don't allow such visits to take place in the Dream Zone so that the living can learn to distinguish between the dream symbol of a deceased person and the actual presence of that person. This sort of distinction is basic to learning how to tell the difference between experiences in the Dream Zone and those in the Afterdeath Zone."

15

The Shadow Worlds

During my visit to Otherwhere's Grand Central Station, part of which I recounted towards the end of chapter 6, the Facilitator who ran the Afterdeath Ferry had told me about bus lines to the Shadow Worlds. Each bus line ran through a tunnel that was visible from the station's main platform. There were three such worlds: Alternate Was, Alternate Is, and Alternate Will Be.

I visited all three of the Shadow Worlds that same night. What I experienced in each is the subject of this and the next two chapters. I'll resume my account where I left off in chapter 6, in the midst of a conversation with the Facilitator who was manning the Afterdeath Ferry.

"The spirits of the dead—Shades, as you call them—use the Alternate Was worlds to experience what life would have been like had they made other choices at the major turning points of their existences on Earth." The Facilitator went on to say that because nothing in nonphysical reality takes up space as we know it, an infinite number of possible realities can exist there without encroaching upon one another.

"Every person alive creates Shadow Worlds without being aware of it," he told me. "Such Shadow Worlds have no past prior to the point when a certain kind of decision was made, but they provide complete run-throughs of all the alternative consequences of that decision.

"As a part of the educational process that every Shade must undergo between lifetimes, he or she will take a number of field trips into the Shadow Worlds. The purpose of these trips is to look at moments when a major decision was made that in some way diverged from the soul's master plan for one's growth.

"Both free will and predetermination operate in physical reality. The soul predetermines the *what* and *why* of an individual's experience—his or her life purpose, and a number of other important lessons. It's up to that individual to decide *how, where, when,* and *with whom* to realize these plans. Sometimes people choose to avoid fulfilling their life purpose or learning the lessons that the soul has outlined for them. That's when a Shadow World comes into being. Shades go there to live out the consequences of having chosen *not* to avoid realizing the soul's master plan for their growth.

"A feeling of satisfaction is generated by the soul whenever one lives according to its plans. Subsequent to one's diverging from the soul's plans, his experience is usually less than satisfying. Going into the Alternate Was worlds allows a person to experience the greater satisfaction of having made decisions more aligned with the soul's plans. This can act as an incentive to make decisions that are more aligned with one's learning and life purpose in future lifetimes."

"In contrast to the Alternate Was worlds, the Alternate Is and Alternate Will Be worlds are for the benefit of the living. The Alternate Is worlds allow people to see what the present would be like had they made a different decision at some important point in the past.

"The value of visiting an Alternate Is world is that one can always choose to create a lifetime of greater satisfaction, of greater alignment with the soul's plans. The only irrevocable decision is to kill oneself, by suicide, accident, or prolonged illness—each of which, from our perspective, is an expression of resistance to fulfilling the soul's plans. Dissatisfaction can grow in strength until it actually weakens the will to live.

"To see how much more satisfying one's life would be now, had a certain past decision been made differently, can lead a person to consider ways of restructuring his or her current life in order to realign it with the soul's plans.

"Alternate Will Be worlds help people see the consequences that would develop from an important decision that they're considering. The value of making a visit to an Alternate Will Be world is that people can find out for themselves which decisions would bring the satisfaction they desire and which would not, thus enabling them to make the most appropriate choices upon returning to Earth.

"People are free of the reincarnational cycle only when they're capable of living an entire lifetime without diverging from the soul's master plan for their growth," the Facilitator explained. "Because life on Earth is so full of distractions that can obscure the nature of one's lessons and life purpose—peer pressure, for example—it's more or less inevitable that deviations will occur.

"Visits to the Alternate Is and Alternate Will Be worlds can help a person get realigned with the soul's plans, after—or even before—a deviation has occurred. Deviations uncorrected at the time of death make it necessary for someone to confront a similar set of conditions in another life—in which, hopefully, he'll make a more appropriate decision.

"It's the purpose of the Alternate Was worlds to help people see where, when, how, and with whom their decisions caused them to deviate from the soul's plans, so that they'll be well aware of the circumstances under which they made inappropriate decisions and can avoid doing so in their next incarnations."

When the Facilitator had finished his explanation, I heard a clamor from the upper platform.

"Sounds like the bus to the Alternate Was worlds has

arrived," the Facilitator remarked. "Why don't you see if there's room for you. You'll learn a lot more from a field trip of your own into the Shadow Worlds than I can tell you."

I bounded up the stairs to the upper platform, anxious not to miss my chance to visit the Shadow Worlds. The people gathered there had picked up their bags and were queued up before a bright yellow school bus. I took my place at the rear of the line, wondering if there would be room for me. When I got to the door, I saw that the bus was jammed—but the driver waved me in anyway. Because I was the last one in, I stood in the stairwell looking out the front window.

The bus driver was a woman in her fifties. She had auburn-colored hair, obviously dyed, a permanent wave, and wore a floral-print dress of a style that had been in vogue some thirty years ago. Her glasses, with their upturned and pointed frames, also seemed out of date. Although a little dumpy, she seemed soft-spoken and kind as she announced that we were on the B & C line, bound for the Alternate Was worlds.

We moved toward the leftmost of the three Shadow World tunnels. The tunnel was pitch black, and for some reason the driver neglected to turn on her lights. I speculated that she either knew the way too well to need them or that she could see in the dark. Then I remembered that I was in Otherwhere, where the physical laws I was familiar with on Earth often don't apply. The tunnel seemed solid enough—but that didn't necessarily mean it was real in the usual sense of that word.

Suddenly, the bus emerged into a dazzling blaze of sunlight. We seemed to be driving down a narrow country road surrounded by fields of intensely green grass and bedecked with brilliantly hued wildflowers. The bus began to pick up speed. Up ahead, I could see where the pavement ended in a dirt road. A strange shimmering, like heat waves, floated up from that point.

I couldn't understand why the driver was speeding up instead of slowing down. It seemed to me that we were in danger of damaging the bus when we hit the dirt road. What if it was rough or deeply rutted? I closed my eyes so I wouldn't have to watch the accident occur. Even through my eyelids, I could sense the brilliance of the flash of light that came when we passed through the shimmering. When I opened my eyes, I was sitting in a Burger King in Mansfield, Ohio.

It was the winter of 1980, my senior year in college. I was on tour with the school wind ensemble, in which I played principal clarinet. We were traveling by bus and had stopped for lunch, while on our way to a concert. I was eating a fish sandwich.

One of my friends, a saxophone player named Michael, was sitting across from me. He was talking very animatedly about his plans to go to graduate school and study filmmaking. His goal was to become a college professor in the field. As Michael spoke, I noticed that the bus driver was sitting next to him. Michael ignored her, or perhaps she was visible only to me. She seemed to be waiting for something to happen, an encouraging smile on her kind face.

Michael went on to justify his major in English, a little defensively. Apparently, he wasn't sure whether this would be the best preparation for film school. But then he turned his trump card: all the writing he had to do because of his major was the perfect training for producing his own scripts. While Michael spoke, I nodded my head at appropriate points to let him know that I was listening.

Something was bothering me. I couldn't quite place it. Aside from the fact that the bus driver was certainly not a part of my memory of that day in Mansfield, something else didn't feel quite right. Then it dawned on me: Michael had transferred to another school in the fall of 1978. He couldn't have been on tour with the band in 1980. I became confused. The scene had seemed more real than a memory, as if both Michael and I really were eating together. Now it began to wobble and fade, as if it had been enclosed in a balloon that was leaking air.

Suddenly, I found myself sitting in the front seat of the bus, as if I'd never left it. The driver explained that the Shadow

World we had visited wasn't mine, but Michael's. She reminded me of what Michael had told me about his life when I ran into him by chance several years later. Shortly after transferring, he decided that he was gay and became very active in the gay social scene. He moved to a large city, settled in a predominantly gay neighborhood, joined a gay health club, and worked as a waiter in a gay restaurant. He eventually graduated with a degree in filmmaking and video, but hadn't gone on to film school. Since then he'd taken an occasional class in film or video production, but had never completed his master's degree. Five years after graduation, he was still working as a waiter.

"While it's true that Michael eventually would have had to come to terms with his sexuality," the driver said, "in many ways, his remaining at the small, midwestern college where you met would have been a better choice than transferring. The relative isolation of that school from any kind of gay community would have helped him focus more clearly on his career goal.

"Of course, he could have done equally well going to school in a larger metropolitan area. The problem, however, was that he chose the social acceptance of absorption into the gay community *over* fulfilling his life purpose as a filmmaker and teacher. You remember how bitter and cynical he was when you spoke with him. That's the result of his having cut himself off from fulfilling his life purpose and seeing no way back to it, given the choices he'd made since transferring. Acceptance is *still* more important to him than self-realization."

I hadn't been in contact with Michael for several years. His bitterness made him an unpleasant person to be around. Finding out why he'd become so cynical about life made me sad.

"Even though I've lost touch with Michael, I assume he's still alive," I said. "And if that's true, then couldn't he choose to realign himself with the soul's plans at any time?"

The bus driver nodded her head.

"So why couldn't I somehow let him know what you've told me? Wouldn't it help him get back on track?"

"He wouldn't listen," the driver replied. "Most people know, deep down inside, which of their decisions have deviated from the soul's plans. Many of them prefer feeling wistful and nostalgic about the way things could have been—had they lived differently—over doing anything to change their lives for the better. Bitterness is the inevitable result of such thinking.

"They would rather invent excuses why they can't—they're too old, it's too late, they're not good enough, they don't have the time or the money, they'll risk losing the approval of family and friends—rather than investigate the options available for change."

"It sounds as though you've written him off," I said, feeling upset by the Facilitator's apparent lack of sympathy for Michael. "That doesn't seem fair. I thought that it was the purpose of Facilitators and Guides to do everything they could to help people keep themselves on track—both while they're alive, and after they've died."

"That's certainly true. Every night for the last ten years, Michael has had dreams about the danger of choosing acceptance and approval over self-realization. But he refuses to remember them. Dreams have no meaning in his belief system. And that goes double for spiritual presences such as ourselves. Furthermore, you have to *want* help before you can recognize it. Michael doesn't want help, so he'll be unable to recognize it, even if you were to repeat our conversation to him word for word.

"You've got to understand that the great irony that governs his life—and the lives of so many people in the world—is that the source of his bitterness is the frequency with which he tells himself that he's happy the way he is. There's nothing you or we could do to convince someone who's always telling himself he's happy that there's an even greater happiness to be gleaned from fulfilling his life purpose. What he has isn't happiness; it's comfort. And comfort, in the sense of avoiding change, is the greatest enemy of self-realization—and therefore of true happiness."

With that, the bus driver turned the ignition key. The bus's engine roared into life.

"Ready to go back to the station?"

I nodded, looking out the window. The Burger King in Mansfield had long since disappeared. We seemed to be moving through a thick, gray fog.

"What happened to everyone else?" I asked, suddenly remembering the formerly packed bus.

"They're still out in the Shadow Worlds, I imagine," the bus driver replied. "One of us will come by to pick them up when they're through. Some will stay longer than others because they've got more work to do. You can always tell who's booked an extended stay in the Shadow Worlds by how much baggage they've got with them at the station. I run the B & C Line—short for *Bitterness and Cynicism*. What people carry with them on this line is the emotional baggage that comes with choosing comfort over growth: all the dissatisfaction and unhappiness of having become something other than what their souls had planned for them to be."

I was deeply disturbed by my experience in the Alternate Was world. I'd been told that this set of Shadow Worlds was used primarily by the dead. Was Michael still alive? I hadn't seen him for several years. What if he'd contracted AIDS and died in the meantime? We had no mutual friends, so there was no way of tracking him down. And what would I say to him if I did?

A little more than a year after I had this adventure, I was walking through Boston's South End on my way to a dance concert. As I passed an alley, I was startled when someone walking down the alley called my name. It was Michael. How much he'd changed since we met almost fifteen years ago. He was wearing a bandana over close-cropped hair, a large, pirate-style earring, a body-builder's tank top, and very tight workout shorts. He told me that he'd finally finished his master's degree. In fact, he'd just moved to New York to look for work.

He was only back in town for a couple of days to tie up loose ends.

I was glad to hear about the degree. And I was really surprised when Michael said that in some respects he wished that he hadn't transferred. It seemed that he *had* gotten himself back on track. Then he told me about his final project. It was a short film about being gay, struggling for family acceptance, testing positive for the AIDS virus, how the years have changed his attitude towards it all. "You know," he said, "the kinds of things my friends and I are dealing with."

16

The Alternate *Is* Worlds

The bus driver pulled into Otherwhere's Grand Central Station. I'd been so absorbed in our conversation that I hadn't seen how we got back. Another school bus was parked ahead of us. Lots of people were milling around on the platform, but only a few had gotten onto that bus. The others seemed to be waiting for the one that I was on.

"Better get off before you're trampled," the bus driver said wryly, eying the crowd. "It looks like they're holding the Alternate Is bus for you."

I thanked the driver for her kindness in answering all my questions, bounded out the door, and hurried toward the other bus, afraid I might miss it. Sure enough, just as I arrived at the door, the bus pulled away, heading for the tunnels. I began to jog alongside the moving bus, shouting and waving to get the driver's attention. To my great annoyance, no one on the bus spoke up on my behalf, even though I was in plain view. The passengers all seemed totally self-absorbed, unaware not only of me, but also of one another.

The bus wasn't moving very quickly. I lunged for one of the open windows and tried to pull myself through, wondering if I would fit. I managed to get my arms through the window, but the rest of me dangled precariously outside of it. To my great relief, the driver finally stopped.

"So *there* you are," the driver said in a sour voice. "We've been waiting for quite a while. Why don't you come through the front door like everyone else?"

I was surprised at the driver's nasty tone. Most of the Guides I'd met had been mild, gentle, and helpful. This one was a harridan.

I disentangled myself from the bus window and trotted up to the door. As I boarded the bus, I noticed that the driver was obese, her arms and head tiny in comparison to the ballooning bulk of her body. If she were to grow any larger, it seemed, her head and arms would utterly vanish, swallowed up by her huge torso. She wore a smock decorated with bars of clashing colors that were surrounded and separated from one another by black borders. The black dye apparently had not been colorfast. It had bled all over the other colors, as if someone had randomly sprayed the dress with black paint. The woman's longish hair was tightly, painfully pulled back in a bun, and there was a large wart on her right cheek.

"This is the F & A Line," the driver announced in a stentorian voice. *"Frustration and Anger*, bound for the Alternate Is worlds."

I took up my former position in the stairwell of the bus, even though there were plenty of empty seats. I wanted to experience the transition into the Shadow Worlds as fully as possible—this time with my eyes open.

Surreptitiously, I examined the driver of the F & A Line. I found both her nastiness and her bulk intimidating. But it occurred to me that the way I was seeing her probably had nothing to do with how she really looked. Unfortunately, I couldn't think of a discreet way to ask why she was so ill-tempered and fat. And I certainly didn't want to risk offending her!

As the bus resumed moving toward the central tunnel of the three that led to the Shadow Worlds, the enormous body of the driver began to shudder and heave grotesquely, like a volcano about to explode. I didn't want to witness the eruption of spleen that was about to occur and began to move toward the back of the bus.

"Don't go away!" the driver stuttered in a surprisingly sweet and giggly tone of voice.

I stopped, unsure of what to do next. Then it occurred to me that the paroxysms rocking the driver's body weren't the result of uncontrollable rage, but of laughter.

"You forget," she continued, struggling to gain control of herself, "that all communication in Otherwhere is telepathic. I've been aware of your thoughts all along!"

I felt flustered and embarrassed to know that what I was thinking had been so transparent.

"Don't feel bad," the driver said, much calmer now. "You're quite correct in assuming that what you perceive has little to do with who I am. But of course it has everything to do with my function. Just as bitterness and cynicism are the common denominators of those who travel into the Alternate Was worlds, so frustration and anger are the common denominators of those who travel into the Alternate Is worlds."

"Why, then, was the driver of the B & C bus so sweet and kind, while you seem somewhat put out?" I asked. "If what you're saying is true, I would have expected her to be as bitter and cynical as her passengers."

"The B & C driver deals mainly with Shades," the fat woman replied. "She's the heart and soul of their nostalgia and wistfulness for the life that could have been. That's why her hair, dress, and glasses seemed so old-fashioned to you. Because her passengers, for the most part, are already dead, they need to be treated with compassion and understanding, not more of the bitterness and cynicism they're trying to purge themselves of.

"I, on the other hand, deal solely with the living. I have to be an example of what frustration and repressed anger can do to people, so they'll be encouraged to change their ways when they return to Earth. That's why you see me as so overweight. Many people overeat out of frustration. Not only that, the virus that causes warts can only attack people whose body chemistry has changed under the impact of repressed anger. The size of the wart indicates the pitch of their anger.

"My dress represents what frustration and anger can do to people's perception of the world: it puts them in a black mood that dulls and distorts their outlook on everything. And my nastiness is an attempt to pull my passengers out of themselves. Frustrated and angry people are always brooding about how life has shortchanged them. Showing myself as worse off than they are in looks and temperament gives them some perspective: perhaps things aren't as bad as they think.

"This prepares them for their journey into the Alternate Is worlds, where they'll have a chance to see what life would look like now, had they not shortchanged themselves at some point in the past by making an inappropriate decision."

By now we'd passed through the dark tunnel and out into the sunlit field of grass and wildflowers I'd seen before. The scene was so beautiful that I became distracted from my conversation with the driver.

"Remember that nothing you see here is really as it seems," she reminded me gently. "What you're perceiving now is actually an energy field dedicated to growth—represented by the grass—and self-realization—symbolized by blooming wildflowers, which make the best of wherever they're sown. This energy field surrounds and permeates the Shadow Worlds, which exist solely for the purpose of aiding growth and self-realization.

"The paved road we're on now represents the hard facts of the life you're currently living. The dirt road up ahead represents the unfinished quality of the Shadow Worlds, whose histories go back only as far as the moment you diverged from the soul's master plan, whether that decision was made a day, a month, or a decade ago. The shimmering we're about to enter marks the boundary between what is and what might have been."

As the bus gained speed, approaching the end of the pavement, I was determined to keep my eyes open. But the flash as we entered the shimmering was so bright that it didn't matter. Eyes closed or open, I could see nothing of how the transition took place.

When my vision cleared, I found myself on a narrow city street. It was twilight. And a nearby street lamp had just come on. My friend Alan was leaning against the lamp post, his white Saab parked a short distance away. I looked up and down the street. We seemed to be in Fort Point Channel, a district of old warehouses along one side of Boston Harbor. Some of these warehouses had been converted into artists' lofts. The building behind Alan was made of old red brick.

I stood in the middle of the street, which seemed otherwise abandoned. It was so narrow that it could have been an alley. In fact, Alan's car was parked with the passenger-side wheels up on the curb to make room for other cars to get past. At the end of the block I saw the nose of the school bus, discreetly tucked away in a side alley so that no one would notice it but me.

I took a good look at Alan. He seemed different somehow— still tall, still fit, his brown hair streaked with gray. His face was ruddy and cheerful. An irrepressible enthusiasm glittered in his blue-gray eyes. He was calmer, more relaxed, and self-assured. He was wearing blue jeans, an expensive Italian leather jacket, and a white scarf draped elegantly around his throat—a more fashionable look than I've ever seen on him.

Alan arched an eyebrow at me as a taxicab pulled into the alley. A beautiful woman in her late thirties, about Alan's age, stepped out of the cab and paid the driver, after he'd unloaded her luggage from the trunk. As the cab drove off, the woman rushed over to Alan, her high heels clattering on the cobblestones of the alley. She also was fashionably dressed, the glitter of gold and gemstones on her fingers and wrists, a slinky lavender skirt that fell below the knees, with a long slit up one side, and a rose-colored cashmere sweater over a high-throated white blouse.

The woman embraced Alan and gave him a warm kiss on the cheek. Alan gestured for me to join them.

"Kurt, I'd like you to meet Catherine White, the opera diva," he said. "Catherine, this is my best friend, Kurt."

Together we walked a short way up the alley to a door in the red brick building. Alan asked how Catherine's flight from New York had been, then wondered whether she minded if I sat in on the recording session the two of them had planned for that evening. Alan explained that I'd come along not only to hear her sing in person, but also to watch Alan in action. I was curious to see whether the claims he made about the superior quality of the equipment in his custom-designed recording studio were true. The best way to do that, he said, was to hear the musician he was recording live, and then listen to the tapes. Since he and Catherine were old friends, he didn't think she would mind.

All of this was news to me. When I had last seen Alan, at dinner the night before I found myself visiting Otherwhere's Grand Central Station, he was telling me that the new high-end audio business he'd started a few months earlier was finally getting off the ground. As the Shadow-World Alan took out a huge key ring to open the door of his studio, Catherine smiled, saying that she would be honored by my presence at the recording session. I began to feel confused. Hadn't Alan told me that Catherine White had given up her budding career as a mezzo-soprano and moved to the Northwest, where she'd joined a highly restrictive and paranoid cult that had grown up around a charismatic trance medium?

Once again, the scene began to deflate like a balloon. I found myself back on the F & A bus—alone, but for the driver.

Although I was brimming with questions, I wanted to think through all the incongruities of the scene I'd just witnessed before asking about them. First, there was the presence of the mezzo-soprano. Alan had lost track of her years ago. Recently, however, he'd run into some people who had once belonged to the same cult that Catherine did. It was from them that he found out where she was and what she was up to, which certainly had little to do with opera.

Alan himself seemed different. Ordinarily, he pays little attention to what he wears, dressing casually in sweatpants and T-shirt, or in a plain business suit when he's selling stereo systems. Although he has often spoken to me about the problems inherent in modern music-reproduction equipment and recording processes, hinting that he has certain innovative ideas that might change some industry standards, he continues to sell the highest quality audiophile speakers, amplifiers, and compact-disc players by appointment. He doesn't own an expensive Italian leather jacket like the one I'd seen, nor have I ever seen him wear a scarf with such élan. At the time he drove a white Saab, just as did his Shadow-World double. I seemed to be the self that I usually am when visiting with Alan. I concluded that the Shadow World wasn't mine, but his.

"That's right," the bus driver interjected, once again having read my thoughts with ease. "About twelve years ago, your friend brought together the best recording equipment available and taped Catherine singing Schubert *Lieder* with a well-known Boston pianist. Alan's idea was to have the tape pressed into a disk and market it, not only as a showcase for the superb talent of both musicians—but also for his innovations in sound engineering. Once the tapes were made, however, he let them lie around—gathering dust, rather than carrying out his plan.

"Had he distributed the recording, favorable reviews would have encouraged Catherine to compete in the Metropolitan Opera auditions in New York—where she would be singing now. Alan would have generated sufficient interest in his sound-engineering ideas that investors would have helped him set up a recording studio. He would have been ideally placed for the compact-disc revolution that would occur shortly thereafter and would now have his own successful, though modestly-sized record company, as well as a famous sound-studio design, which he would have been called upon to recreate all over the world.

"Thus he could have combined his talents as a business-man, audio consultant, and sound engineer to create a truly satisfying career in the service of art, instead of that of commerce, which he now finds boring."

"Would it do any good for me to tell Alan about my visit to this Shadow World?" I asked.

"Perhaps. He's still alive, which means that he can always choose to realign himself with the soul's master plan for his growth. It seems doubtful that those old tapes of Catherine's singing would be of much use to him now. Recording technology has changed too much since then for his old ideas to have an impact. The important thing for you to emphasize when you speak with him is that his passionate denouncements of the recording industry's current approaches and his continual hinting that he knows better are indications that his life purpose lies more in the area of sound engineering than in audio retail. It's up to him to find some way of acting upon this knowledge in the present.

"While it's true that some people can obsess about activities and careers that have nothing to do with their life purpose, this is not the case here. The Alternate Is worlds come into being only when you've diverged from your life purpose—in order to show you the way back. You couldn't have seen Alan as a record company president and recording engineer if such roles had not been in some way an expression of his life purpose."

I looked out the window of the bus and saw that once again we were moving slowly through a gray fog.

"Before we get back to the station," I said, "I have just one more question. Alan seems pretty well-adjusted and happy as he is. I just don't see the frustration and anger that you told me goes along with failing to fulfill one's life purpose. Any comment?"

"Of course," the bus driver replied. "The bitter and cynical people on the B & C Line convince themselves that they should be happy with what they've got, even though their bitterness derives from how little what they've got truly satisfies them. The people on the F & A Line have the same problem, but to a lesser degree. Their beliefs haven't yet made it impossible for them to realign themselves with their life purpose. They keep telling themselves that someday they'll get around to doing what they know they need to do.

"This gives them hope, which is all but extinguished by the time they get to the bitterness-and-cynicism stage. The longer the F & A riders go without acting on this hope, the more likely they are to convince themselves they'll never be able to do so.

"It's never too late to fulfill your life purpose—unless you believe it is. And if you believe it's too late, you're already riding the B & C Line. As for Alan, the reason he rarely listens to music anymore is that his frustration at what he believes to be the inferior sound quality of today's recordings makes them utterly unenjoyable to him. This frustration comes out in the vehemence with which he criticizes them.

"Frustration is a milder form of anger, just as bitterness is a milder form of cynicism. Frustration, anger, bitterness, and cynicism represent points on a continuum of diminishing hope. Alan still believes in the validity of his ideas, so his hope is relatively strong. He hasn't yet found a way of implementing them, so he feels frustrated. If he were to believe that the world somehow prevents him from fulfilling his life purpose, he would lose hope. Anger would be the result, followed by bitterness and cynicism. As this belief grew in strength, his hope would diminish and eventually disappear."

The bus rolled to a stop. We were back in the station. Once again, I'd failed to notice the route we'd taken to get back.

"How quickly you forget," the bus driver gently chided me. "The station, the bus, the tunnels, the paved and unpaved roads, how I look—all these things are merely images, representations of invisible energy patterns. You see the method of entering the Shadow Worlds as a school bus because learning is the main purpose of such visits. The fog we seemed to be traveling through on our way back to the station was a manifestation of your confusion at the discrepancies between the Shadow Worlds you visited and the memories you carry with you. After our talk, you were no longer confused. The fog cleared and you found yourself back in the station.

"The station represents the human entry point into Otherwhere. Everyone who travels into Otherwhere does so to learn. When the learning is complete, one finds oneself back here, ready to depart on another set of lessons or to return home to Earth."

"Is it time for me to go home now—is that why you're telling me this?" I asked, a little disappointed.

"Not at all," the bus driver replied. "How could your tour of the Shadow Worlds be complete without a visit to the Alternate Will Be worlds?"[1]

---

[1] I told Alan about my visit to the Alternate Is world. Shortly thereafter, at a trade show, he encountered an engineer who designs speakers and recording equipment. Alan explained his ideas to the engineer, who is considered to be one of the best in the field. The engineer felt that Alan's ideas were as worthy of investigation as Alan believed them to be, and has taken time from his busy schedule to begin designing prototypes for the kind of recording system Alan has in mind.

17

The Alternate *Will Be* Worlds

When I left the F & A Line, I expected to find another school bus parked in front of the tunnel to the Alternate Will Be worlds. I was surprised to see instead a tall, thin, blond man with hair to his shoulders, bushy sideburns, and a moustache, leaning against a Harley-Davidson motorcycle. He was dressed like a Hell's Angel, in black leather chaps decorated with shiny pointed studs. Beneath his leather vest was a Grateful Dead T-shirt. Instead of a helmet, he wore a black leather cap whose visor hid his eyes from me. The sprawling Harley sported two sidecars. Three large black dogs waited in the sidecar on the left. The other one was empty.

I left the Alternate Is bus reluctantly, not at all sure whether I should approach this formidable character. The dogs, however, seemed glad to see me. They came bounding up to me, practically knocking me over with their affection—prancing, nuzzling, and licking my hands as if I were an old friend.

"Howdy, pardner," the Hell's Angel said as I approached. He spoke with a broad accent that reminded me of people I'd met out West—warm and amiable, easygoing. I felt even more at ease about him when he looked up and I saw his eyes. They were calmly, serenely blue, without a trace of the hard edge I'd expected.

"This is the R & S Line," he said. "Stands for *Regret and Self-pity*. We're on our way to the Alternate Will Be worlds. Hop in." He gestured toward the right-hand sidecar.

As I settled in, the motorcyclist snapped his fingers. The dogs obediently jumped back into the sidecar on the left. Swinging his long legs over the saddle of the Harley, he gunned the engine. We sped toward the rightmost of the three Shadow World tunnels with a roar.

Once again, we entered total darkness. When we emerged this time, we were on an interstate, not a country road. The four-lane highway reminded me of I-94, passing through the arid hills of eastern Montana. We seemed to be going west.

We hadn't been on the highway long when the cyclist took an unmarked exit. The ramp curved down a short way and turned into a dirt road through grasslands. Instead of the brilliant green of the fields that preceded my entry into the Alternate Was and Alternate Is worlds, however, this grass was faded and dry, if not dead.

The Hell's Angel accelerated as we approached the shimmering that marked the end of the exit ramp. After passing through it with a flash, I found myself in an unfamiliar landscape that reminded me of Kansas or Nebraska: no hills, just acres and acres of rolling fields of wheat. It was very hot and dry, like a day in August. The wheat seemed to be suffering from a drought. A warm breeze rustled through the stalks with a hiss.

Some distance away was a Victorian farmhouse, plain and gray, its yard piled high with junked automobiles and farm equipment, all rusted out. A few miles away, the grain elevators of a small town loomed against the horizon.

Nothing moved at the farmhouse. No cars drove down the road. The town, hardly more than a railway junction, looked deserted. Apparently, this was a place totally devoted to the work of planting and harvesting. It seemed as if there was nothing else to do for miles.

I turned around to see what was behind me and was surprised to find a small campground called "Timberlost." It was empty, dry, and dusty. The name seemed appropriate, since there were no trees in sight. Behind the campground, utterly incongruous, rose the high flat facade and wooden shutters of a Federal-style mansion, such as I would expect to find in a New England town, not all by itself on a wide expanse of prairie.

I turned back to the Hell's Angel in puzzlement, but he'd already anticipated my question.

"You've been planning a camping trip in Idaho this summer, right?"

I scowled and nodded my head, failing to see the connection. This barren wasteland bore little resemblance to the forested mountains and clear streams of the parts of Idaho I'd visited in years past.

"And even though you've got several months to finalize your plans, you've begun to wonder whether you can afford the plane fare, right?"

Once again, I nodded.

"The landscape in which you now find yourself isn't a real place," the Hell's Angel continued. "It's a symbolic portrayal of how you'd feel if you decided not to go to Idaho."

I surveyed the desolate landscape, not comprehending the Hell's Angel's words.

"You would feel a sense of loss at not being able to camp out in Clearwater National Forest, right? That's the meaning of the Timberlost Campground. And staying in New England, represented by the Federal mansion, would seem as dry and dull as the landscape before you. Sure, there's plenty to do in Boston—much more than in the little town over yonder. But your regret at not being able to get away into the wilderness of the northern Rockies would undercut your desire to find fun things to do in Boston. Just as the wheat fields here are suffering from drought, so your willingness to grow would begin to wither, your motivation to fulfill your life purpose dry up and turn to dust.

"You see, fulfilling your life purpose isn't the only thing that's important. You've also got to do things that increase your enjoyment of life. Without balancing work with the enjoyment of your presence in the world, you'll come to resent your life purpose. The world will come to seem as dreary as this landscape."

As the Hell's Angel spoke, he let one of the dogs roam free but kept the other two on leashes. Although they struggled to free themselves, he kept them pinned to his side. Thinking that he was treating the dogs unfairly, I was about to protest. The Hell's Angel interrupted me.

"It shouldn't surprise you that these aren't dogs," he said, straining with the effort of keeping them in check. "In nonphysical reality, past, present, and future all coexist simultaneously. On Earth, however, you have only the present. While you can recall the past and anticipate the future, you're largely unable to experience the future or the past as if it were the present.

"In the Shadow Worlds, though, you can easily experience the past or future as if it were the present. The dog that now runs free represents your own sense of the future, roaming over the Alternate Will Be world of what it would feel like not to go to Idaho. Thus you're experiencing the future as the present.

"Meanwhile, I'm keeping your sense of the past and the present tightly leashed, so that you don't become confused about what's what. Earth's insane asylums are full of people who've forgotten the difference between past, present, and future—often through blundering into the Shadow Worlds without the proper guidance."

The possibility of going insane while visiting the Shadow Worlds made me nervous. If they existed for the benefit of humankind, even though they were rarely used, why should they be so dangerous? The Hell's Angel picked up where my thoughts left off.

"As long as you're with a Guide, you'll have no problem in visiting the Shadow Worlds—you won't go insane. That's why I'm with you now, and why the bus drivers stayed with you on your field trips to the Alternate Was and Alternate Is worlds. The ones who are in danger of becoming lost in the Shadow Worlds are those who use drugs or alcohol to get here, or who've experienced some emotional or physical trauma so severe that they withdraw from physical reality into a fantasy world.

"From our perspective, such fantasy worlds are real—and are often, but not always, an Alternate Was or Is world. There are beings who try to rehabilitate such lost souls, but that's not my line of work, so I can't tell you any more about it."

Apparently finished investigating the Alternate Will Be world we were visiting, the one dog that roamed free returned and jumped into the Harley's left sidecar. My Guide turned the other two dogs loose and they followed suit. I took one last look at the desolate landscape. Regret at having missed the opportunity to go camping in Idaho washed over me like a wave whose strong undertow threatened to pull me into an ocean of self-pity. I began to feel frustrated that I had been unable to make the money I needed for the plane fare to Spokane, which was to have been my starting point. Then a wave of anger broke over me—resentment that the soul had assigned me a life purpose, as writer and counselor, which might not allow me to afford the kind of getaway that I so much needed to counterbalance it. Totally absorbed in feeling sorry for myself, I hadn't noticed that my Guide was watching me intently.

"It doesn't take much for regret to become self-pity," he said, startling me out of my reverie. "Many people create private hells for themselves out of such regrets. That's why you see me as a Hell's Angel. My function is to rescue such people from their private hells before they've even entered them—by showing them how they would feel if they were to decide against doing something they really need to do. That's the purpose of the Alternate Will Be worlds."

"So why are you wearing that Grateful Dead shirt?" I asked. "Is it because you're glad you're no longer alive and are therefore free of such regrets?"

"While it's true that I no longer feel regret about anything I've experienced during previous lifetimes on Earth, I wouldn't say that I'm grateful to be among the dead. That would imply that life over here, in Otherwhere, has a greater value than life on Earth. From our perspective, that isn't true. There are things that can be learned only here and not there. But there are also things that can be learned only on Earth. Learning is all that matters, and no lesson is more or less valuable than any other.

"To explain why you perceive me as wearing a Grateful Dead T-shirt, I have to make reference to your projected trip to Idaho. Not going would be only a minor regret, right? It might sap your motivation to fulfill your life purpose for a while, but not your will to live. Some people regret the decisions they've made so deeply that they truly believe they'd be better off—more grateful—if they were dead.

"The Alternate Will Be worlds can show them what life would be like if they weren't so hell-bent on feeling sorry for themselves. Regret isn't in itself a bad thing. It simply indicates that you've made an inappropriate choice, as far as the soul's master plan for your growth is concerned. Regret can actually be useful in recognizing and acting upon opportunities to make a more appropriate choice if a similar situation comes up in the future.

"Self-pity, however, is the great enemy of growth. When regret turns into self-pity, as you experienced a moment ago, frustration and anger soon develop. As you might have guessed by now, regret and self-pity are on the same continuum of diminishing hope that leads through frustration and anger to bitterness and cynicism."

My Guide gestured toward his Harley, as if to say it was time for us to move along. I tried to take a step, but found myself rooted to the ground. My Guide smiled at me and said, "Still paralyzed by self-pity, eh?"

It was true. Despite my Guide's words about the damaging effect that self-pity can have on the motivation to fulfill one's life purpose, and even the will to live, I hadn't been able to let go of feeling sorry for myself. How was I going to get to Idaho if I couldn't afford the plane ticket?

"That's the question, isn't it?" my Guide said, gently breaking into my thoughts. "Your other Guides may have told you that once you've absorbed everything there is to learn from a visit to one of the Shadow Worlds, you return to Grand Central more or less instantly. They probably didn't tell you that you actually have to *complete* that learning before you'll be able to leave."

"So what do I have to do?" I asked, still unable to move.

"Well, if the only remaining question is how to get to Idaho," my Guide replied, "then all you have to do is answer it. Usually, the answer to any question you might have about a decision you're about to make will be contained within the Alternate Will Be world that you've visited."

I thought back to the things I'd seen since we arrived in the desolate landscape of my regret at not having gone to Idaho: the dried-up wheat, the faded farmhouse, the tiny town with its oversized grain elevators, the empty campground, and the incongruous Federal-style mansion. No answers suggested themselves. I remained rooted to the ground.

"How did we get here?" the Hell's Angel prompted me.

"By motorcycle," I replied.

"And what kind of road did we come in on?"

"An interstate."

"Right—an appropriate symbol for the shifting states of consciousness necessary for travel in the Shadow Worlds. And what kind of landscape did you see?"

"It reminded me of I-94 in eastern Montana."

"And isn't Montana on the way to Idaho?"

I nodded.

"Then you have your answer. If you can't afford to fly to Idaho, then drive."

As my Guide uttered the word "drive," the desolate landscape began to deflate with an audible hiss. I watched until it had collapsed into a shrinking puddle the color of dry wheat. When it was completely gone, I looked back to where the Hell's Angel had been standing. But there was no sign of him, his Harley, or the three black dogs.

Suddenly, I realized that if the landscape was gone, I had nothing to stand on. In a panic, I looked all around me. There was nothing but unfathomable darkness, through which I seemed to be drifting slowly. I relaxed when I realized I wasn't falling, and gave in to a gentle, yet persistent pull, trusting I would find the guidance I needed, no matter where that pull might take me.

I seemed to be rising. The darkness gave way to a dull, orange glow that continued to brighten until I recognized what it was: sunlight filtered through my closed eyelids. I opened my eyes and stretched. I was back in my bedroom—no Shadow World, but the blue sky and birdsong of a new day beginning.

I was able to make my trip to Idaho after all, and I didn't have to drive. Money for the plane ticket became available through my work. The trip was everything I'd hoped it would be, a wonderfully relaxing adventure in the wilderness.

18

Overseers

During my many visits to the Afterdeath Zone, I've encountered not only Guides, Shades, and Facilitators, but also beings that seem to be somehow superior to these. Robert Monroe came across similarly superior beings during his own explorations of nonphysical reality. He called them INSPECS—short for *intelligent species*—"which presumes," as he put it, that "humans are not quite so" (Monroe 1985, 93). Monroe believed that INSPECS were directly involved in the evolution of human consciousness. My encounters with such beings have confirmed this idea.

Yet for me to adopt Monroe's term would be inconsistent. Since the words used in this field guide have been derived from the function of the entities described, such a label would imply that it was the function of the INSPECS to be more intelligent than we are—hardly a useful function. I prefer to call such beings *Overseers*, because they seem to oversee the spiritual evolution of humanity.

I've had a total of six lab sessions at The Monroe Institute, including the one in which I encountered the Cave of the Existentialists. Of the two beings of light that I questioned during that visit to the Afterdeath Zone, I believe the first to have been a Facilitator, and the second, who was much larger and brighter, an Overseer.

On another occasion in the lab, I experienced an altered state in which an Overseer temporarily merged with my consciousness and began to speak through me. Once again, the monitor was Rita Warren. (It may seem odd that the Overseer should use the vocabulary I've been describing throughout this book with such familiarity. Keep in mind that I'd been developing this vocabulary for several years before this visit to the lab. In the process of translating experiences in nonphysical reality I use images that already exist in my consciousness. Just so, a being such as the Overseer, in choosing to speak through me, will use the vocabulary that also exists there.)

"Overseers are available to selected individuals for the specific work of a single lifetime," the Overseer said. "Such beings were formerly human, but are now completely focused in nonphysical reality, without requirement of further incarnations.

"Many of the great religious teachers of the world are present among our company. Some occult disciplines have referred to us as 'ascended masters.' We don't particularly like that term, because it seems to confer special status on individuals working with us.

"Our function is to oversee the evolution of human consciousness. We ourselves move on to other kinds of development at the point when our positions are replaced by others who have achieved freedom from the incarnational cycle. During birth, much of what you've learned in the Afterdeath Zone about who you truly are is forgotten. An individual is finished with the incarnational cycle only after overcoming this forgetfulness and maintaining an awareness of his own and humanity's purpose through most, if not all, of a lifetime.

"We make ourselves available to individuals who have a talent or potential for furthering our work in some fashion, either because of developmental levels attained through having experienced many lifetimes in physical reality or because of what could be called accident of birth. Some family and cultural situations are more conducive than others to maintaining the awarenesses gleaned in the Afterdeath Zone."

At another point in his conversation with Rita, the Overseer asserted that there is a Council of Overseers, with various stations or assignments. He went on to say that attempts over the centuries "to assign names and specialties to archangels and angelic hierarchies represent an awareness of this Council." He assured Rita, "that the Council is not a hierarchy in the political sense."

"Is it a hierarchy in terms of the development of the individual soul?" Rita asked.

"There are stations within the Afterdeath Zone that are occupied by advanced human consciousnesses between lifetimes. It is part of the human development for individuals both to experience life on Earth from as many perspectives as possible, and to pass through the various stations of guidance within the Afterdeath Zone, as Facilitators. The Council of Overseers is entirely free of the incarnational cycle. In terms of acquired wisdom, we are beyond the facilitating level. Our greater understanding of the human evolutionary process determines the greater extent of our influence.

"Within the Council itself, there is no hierarchical order, only the balancing of one function against another. Because all functions are equal in their importance to the well-being of humanity, we have no single leader. All of us are at the level of development in which the needs of any lower level are the only important factors to respond to. Among us, there is no politics."

"Have all of the Facilitators been in human form at one time or another?"

"Yes. These are individuals who have experienced many lifetimes in human form, and who are taking a break, as it were, from the incarnational cycle. The Hindu term *Bodhisattva* has been invented to describe such individuals, although somewhat incorrectly. The concept implies that such individuals are free of the incarnational cycle, which is not necessarily true.

"Facilitators are more likely to carry the awarenesses gleaned from retraining in the Afterdeath Zone with them into a particular lifetime. Positions in cultures and families that will help them maintain the integrity of such awarenesses will be provided for them. Such individuals will often be deeply spiritual, perhaps teachers of some sort."

"Does the concept of responsibility apply to your role in the lives of such individuals, or in their roles in humanity at large?"

"Our work with an individual is mutually agreed upon. Observation of the individual's early years is critical. We must gauge the extent to which any work done on our behalf might be distorted by culturally prevailing beliefs, or family background and training. Periodically, attempts will be made to guide the individual toward the work of others who have contracts with us. Such exposure can help him overcome blockages based on culturally and parentally derived belief systems. Contracts are then arranged during sleep training periods."

The Overseer spoke through me several times during my sessions in The Monroe Institute lab. On another occasion, it mentioned several individuals with whom contracts for furthering the work of the Council had been made.

"There are many maps of nonphysical reality—the Afterdeath Zone, in particular—scattered throughout the history of your art and literature. These can provide useful translation tables for orientation within nonphysical reality. Why should every individual who explores nonphysical reality start from scratch? The Council has commissioned certain people to produce such maps. Hieronymous Bosch, painter of *The Garden of Earthly Delights*, was commissioned in this way. So were Dante, and your own Robert Monroe.

"It is not rare, this commissioning. But varying levels of what could be called signal-to-noise ratio come through in the maps, depending on the intrusion of public symbol systems and personal distortions caused by fear of the unknown."

Bosch's triptych, *The Garden of Earthly Delights* was painted in the early 1500s. The left panel shows Adam, Eve, and Jesus in Heaven, surrounded by animals—including a few bizarre creatures, such as fish with wings and three-headed birds. The right panel depicts a scene from Hell, in which people are being tortured in grotesque ways by demons. The larger central panel is the Garden of Earthly Delights, where hundreds of naked figures debauch themselves with food and sex.

Earlier in the lab session, I had made a visit to the Afterdeath Zone. The imagery of the painting had helped me translate what I was perceiving: it was as if I had stepped into a living version of *The Garden of Earthly Delights*. The Overseer implied that Bosch had created the work so that people like me would have a better time understanding certain regions of the Afterdeath Zone.

The area I'd visited was one where Shades would go to purge themselves of obsessions about what they believed would make them happy. If the individual had been overpious, obsessed with the idea of getting into Heaven, he might end up in the region depicted in the left panel. Because thought creates experience in nonphysical reality, Heaven would look like his beliefs about it. The bizarre creatures in the painting served the function of encouraging him to question the validity of what he was perceiving, in much the same way that the anomalies in my Count of Monte Cristo experience were intended to get me to realize that I was dreaming.

If the individual had been obsessed with negative emotions such as fear, anger, jealousy, or hatred, he would end up in the hellish region depicted in the right panel. There he would be tortured by his own thoughts, much as the individuals in the Cave of the Existentialists had been.

If the individual had been obsessed with food or sex, he would end up in the central panel, in which he could indulge himself in imagining sensual pleasures until he grew weary of them, let go of the obsession, and moved on to other stations of the Afterdeath Zone.

On one of his own visits to nonphysical reality, Monroe came across what looked to him like an enormous pile of wriggling fishing worms. With a shock, he realized that the worms were actually deceased human beings—thousands of them—obsessively engaged in an orgy (Monroe 1985, 88–90). It seems likely that Monroe had happened upon the same region of the Afterdeath Zone described in *The Garden of Earthly Delights* but had translated it with a different set of images.

The first time I visited the Council of Overseers, I was traveling with a friend in the Rocky Mountains. We'd pulled into a rest area to take a nap. On impulse, I decided to use one of The Monroe Institute's Hemi-Sync tapes to help me relax. I put on the headphones of a portable cassette player and lowered the back of my seat.

A few minutes later, I seemed to be seeing the surface of a swimming pool projected on the screen of my closed eyelids. Light played over the water in the pool, reflected and refracted in an ever-changing pattern of complex wave forms. In the center of my vision was an extraluminous clarity, like the peak of a brighter wave. Upon closer inspection, this clarity seemed more like a gap in the rippling background than a wave. Hardly had I noticed the gap when I found myself falling into it.

Suddenly, I was in a large chamber. Between fifteen and twenty beings sat at long tables arranged in a square—the Council of Overseers. Their figures were dim, but they seemed to be dressed in business suits—perhaps a symbol of their efficiency, or that they "meant business." On the walls of the room were maps of the Earth. At first glance, they appeared to be flat. Closer examination showed that they were actually three-dimensional and alive with movement.

One of the Overseers directed his attention toward me. His communication seemed both insistent and patient: "There's something you have to do, something you need to remember."

Before the Overseer could tell me what it was, I was startled by footsteps crunching in the gravel of the rest-area parking lot and woke up.

A couple months later, I made a visit to the Afterdeath Zone while asleep. Again, the Zone appeared to me as a cave with a strong archaeological feel, like one that had been inhabited by different cultures over long periods of time. Each culture had left behind the remains of its beliefs concerning the Afterlife. I wandered aimlessly through several regions which ancient civilizations had called Heaven—the happy hunting ground of an unnamed Indian tribe, teeming with buffalo; an Egyptian temple with carved columns resembling papyrus plants. I drifted from level to level of Afterlife imagery, coming eventually to an area that seemed to be at the center of the Afterdeath Zone, like a grand cavern in the middle of a mountain.

There I found four radiant beings, three male and one female. The males were dressed in business suits, as in the previously related encounter. They sat at a stone table shuffling papers, like some kind of cross-examining committee. The female wore a skirt, blouse, and suit coat. Leaning against the table, she had the no-nonsense air of a lawyer.

"We are the Overseers in charge of the Afterdeath Zone," she said. "Nothing happens here but by our decree. In ancient Greek myths, we were represented as the judges of Hades: Minos, Rhadamanthus, and Aeacus—although these are not our real names. But our role is not to judge the souls of the dead. It's up to them to judge for themselves which of their actions on Earth furthered and which hindered their growth. We determine the principles upon which the Afterdeath Zone must run.

"So we're like the fair-minded, but firm law-givers that Minos and the others were while alive. As you can see, there are four of us, not three. None of us have any particular attachment to the forms you now see. We're beyond the level at which gender roles make a difference in the way we perceive ourselves. However, I've chosen this female form to emphasize a point: the Council of Overseers is not a patriarchy. The soul is without gender. Here, we are each our whole selves, androgynous."

The Overseer brought forward a document that seemed to be drawn up on parchment, in a fine calligraphic hand.

"This is your contract with us," she said. "It exists as energy, not in the quasiphysical form you're now perceiving. We've commissioned you to do some mapping of nonphysical reality."

"How long has this contract been in effect?" I asked, surprised.

"Your grandfather encouraged you to read the writings of Edgar Cayce at a young age. Thus your belief system was more conducive to working with us than that of most of your peers. We made our first attempt to reach you when you were fourteen years old, just as your interest in mysticism began to wane in favor of music. At that time you had a series of out-of-body experiences. They frightened you, because you did not know what they were. You set up mental blocks that prevented us from reaching you again in that fashion. During your junior year in college, we arranged for you to meet the trumpet player who introduced you to Robert Monroe's first book. From our perspective, there was no better way to prepare you for mapping nonphysical reality than through exposure to the work of someone who'd been similarly commissioned."

My friendship with the trumpet player had lasted only as long as it took for me to read the book and return it. This was a great disappointment to me. I'd always hoped to find a friend with whom I could share my interest in mysticism. That interest had virtually died out for lack of anyone to talk to but my grandfather, who lived many miles away. I was beginning to feel used, manipulated by the Overseers for some obscure purpose. The Overseer's explanation made me wonder how much of my life was my own.

The Overseer broke into my thoughts. "If anyone was *used*, as you put it, it was the trumpet player. He performed a valuable function for us, and one no more difficult than loaning a book. You both tried for weeks to establish a friendship, but discovered that you had virtually nothing in common. That wasn't our fault. As for the question of how much of your life is your own, we would have to reply: *all* of it. Most of your adventures have taken place while you were sleeping, something you would do regardless of our contract with you. Except for the time required to write down your experiences, they've hardly interfered with your waking life."

I had to admit that this was true. The adventures occurred at the rate of one or two a month, sometimes with much longer periods between. They rarely upset the schedule of my daily life. On the other hand, I would sometimes feel depressed for weeks afterwards. I was afraid that the changes taking place in me as a result of what I was learning were turning me into some kind of freak—and that I would end up spending the rest of my life alone and unloved, rejected by society, family, and friends. It was hard to accomplish anything when I felt this way. Clearly, the Overseers were responsible for my depression.

Once again, the Overseer interrupted my thoughts. "We can't be responsible for your emotional reactions to experiences in nonphysical reality. Such reactions are chosen by *you*. You could feel sorry for yourself and become a hermit, as if what you've learned has made you somehow contemptible. You could equally well feel blessed by divine revelation, go preaching to the multitudes, and have yourself martyred. Your life is what you make it."

"I don't remember agreeing to any kind of contract with you," I grumbled, refusing to give in to the Overseer's unassailable logic.

"Perhaps you've misunderstood what we mean by 'contract,'" the Overseer said mildly. "From our standpoint, the agreement to work with us is established by a certain kind of willingness. You weren't willing to have out-of-body experiences at age fourteen, so there was no contract.

"During your freshman year in college, you saw a film by Jean Cocteau based on the myth of Orpheus. The movie moved you deeply—the idea of the poet venturing into the realm of the unconscious to bring back works of art. What is the unconscious but nonphysical reality—the Dream Zone, and beyond it the Afterdeath Zone, which Cocteau portrayed so vividly?

"Your fascination indicated to us that you might have the right inclinations after all. A year and a half later, we made another attempt to reach you, through the trumpet player. You were willing to tell him your experiences. You were willing to read the book. You were willing to work on releasing the mental blocks to out-of-body experiences you erected in high school. We required none of this. These actions were chosen of your own volition. There still was no contract. You had demonstrated willingness—from our standpoint, the same thing as a talent for the kind of work we require of you now.

"Years later, you read Monroe's second book, *Far Journeys*. Excited by his adventures in nonphysical reality, you wrote in your journal that you wished you could have similar experiences. We began giving them to you—testing you, as we have many people throughout the ages. Unlike most people, however, you remembered your experiences—willingness. You wrote them down—willingness. You studied them for consistencies—willingness. You came to the Otherwhere Gate, failed to get through, and became more determined to do whatever was necessary to cross that boundary—again willingness.

"We also tested you by showing you what the evolution of human consciousness looks like from our perspective. You accepted what you saw. On a trial basis, we admitted you to Otherwhere. You began to systematize what you learned there for the benefit of others. From that point on, we had a contract. As you can see, your willingness to fulfill it has determined every article."

I was abashed. For years I'd resisted my adventures, fearful of how they would change me. I'd completely forgotten that I'd asked for them.

"At last you know what it was that you needed to remember: that you have a contract with us for mapping nonphysical reality, and that you agreed to do this work of your own volition."

Only once have I ever gotten any idea of who might be among the members of the Council of Overseers. For several years before the adventure I'm about to relate, I'd been devoting a lot of time to developing a career as a poet. I'd been published in several dozen literary magazines, won a number of awards, and my poetry manuscript had been a finalist several times in national competitions. But that year everything seemed to grind to a halt.

No magazines were accepting my verse for publication. I sent out a hundred poems and all were returned to me with rejection slips. I began to have doubts about my calling as a poet. Full of self-pity, I wondered whether I had anything of significance to say to a reader—whether people even read poetry anymore, as they once did, for news of the spiritual world and man's place in it.

One night I found myself again in the presence of the Council of Overseers. This time I had the sense of being surrounded by dozens of shadowy, but frighteningly powerful spiritual presences. A different spokesperson than the woman in the previous adventure addressed me. After greeting me in a friendly fashion, he responded to the questions about my calling that had so much been occupying me.

"The Council does not take poetry lightly," he said. It *can* be a way of guiding others, even if it seems not to have much of an effect in your country. There are indeed individuals whom we've chosen for such a purpose. The Irish poet Seamus Heaney is one of them. His extraordinary success is a result of having found his way to, or stumbled upon, a form of spirituality much needed in the world—a set of values. It doesn't violate the Christian perspective with which he was brought up, while finding ways to praise the richness of life that modern man can hear and respond to.

"In a time and a country so full of violence, that ability to praise the richness of life is much needed. Therefore, the Council has helped him reach the largest number of people possible—first in the English-speaking world, then beyond it, through the inevitable translations of his work that will come in the wake of his having recently been named a Nobel laureate.

"Poetry can also become a means of achieving enlightenment on one's own, in private. One of our own members certainly demonstrates that this is so." With these words, the spokesperson for the Council introduced me to one of the shadowy presences that surrounded me. She rose, but did not approach me. I was shocked to recognize her as Emily Dickinson, the nineteenth-century American poet. I've spent years avoiding her work, which for some reason I've never been able to develop a taste for.

The Council spokesperson smiled, fully aware of the impact that this introduction was having on me. He continued: "The body of Emily Dickinson's poetry was produced as a kind of final examination, before she would be allowed to enter our ranks. In it she demonstrated her awareness of every aspect of the human condition and found a legitimate spiritual perspective on it. She isolated herself so as not to be distracted from her purpose by the larger outside world, and to demonstrate that enlightenment could be achieved within the context of a minutely observed and deeply experienced localization of life.

"Grand spiritual pilgrimages weren't needed. She preferred not to publish her work so as not to be deflected from the process of its production by fame or the social aspects of a literary life. She did, however, generate enough interest in this work on the part of a few outsiders that it would be looked into after her death and then ever more widely distributed. She never married because the gender-role restrictions for women during the time in which she lived would have prevented her from achieving enlightenment. The fact that she was a woman, though, would demonstrate to posterity that enlightenment is not an exclusively male prerogative."

The implication of the Council spokesperson's message was clear. It shouldn't matter to me whether my poetry would be published or not. I could nevertheless use it as a private means of developing myself spiritually. I would of course continue to seek publication. But after my visit to the Council, I no longer concerned myself with trying to figure out what the editors of literary magazines were looking for. That put me beyond the temptation to write what I thought might get published, or to suppress the impulse to write what might be a crucial poem for my spiritual development on the basis of my doubts about its publishability.

19

The Evolution of Human Consciousness

The lawyer-like female Overseer in the last chapter had mentioned a final test, in which I'd been shown how the evolution of human consciousness looks from the perspective of the Overseers. I remembered the event well. It occurred only a few weeks after my first unsuccessful attempt to go through the Otherwhere Gate.

I'd just gone to bed when a voice in my head announced, "The adventure begins this evening." I drifted off to sleep, thinking that I'd manufactured the voice. A couple of hours later, I awoke. The adventure had indeed begun. It took me most of the next day to write down everything that had happened to me during those few hours. Here is what I wrote:

As if in an unusually vivid dream, I become a single blade of grass—deeply green, and about seven inches tall. A strong wind blows me this way and that, and I feel exhilarated. There's something ecstatic about being caught up in the motions of an invisible force.

All at once, I become aware that I'm surrounded by millions upon millions of other grass blades, all of about the same height and shade. The wind blows over us and we swirl about, responsive to its every movement. My joy in being a grass blade expands a hundredfold as I undulate with my fellows in huge wind-shaped patterns.

I make a startling realization: I can simultaneously maintain an awareness of myself as a single grass blade and as a multitude of grass blades. Yet my unique beingness has a precise location within the vast tapestry of grass that surrounds me. That location doesn't change, regardless of whether I focus on the singular or the collective me.

The perception of myself as a grass blade fades, and I find myself in the presence of a radiant being—one of the Overseers.

"Very good," the Overseer says. "You learn quickly."

I'm puzzled by this response, unsure of what I've learned. The Overseer senses my confusion and responds gently.

"We've designed a set of images and sensations in order to illustrate certain aspects of the human condition," he says. "Our intention is to show you how the evolution of human consciousness looks from our perspective.

"Your immersion in the beingness of a grass blade has allowed you to sense, in symbolic terms, the common denominator of all human experience: time, in the guise of change. Time is as invisible as the wind, and yet its effects—change—can be perceived throughout the course of any event, like wind-shaped patterns eddying through a field of grass. It may seem as if most people avoid change, yet there are those who find it as exhilarating as the rambunctious, mechanized rides of your amusement parks.

"Perception of change occurs in three stages: how it affects oneself; how it affects those immediately surrounding one; and how it affects regions, nations, and the world at large. Such perceptions can help someone discover his unique position—or function—within the larger whole of humanity."

Without warning, the Overseer vanishes, and I find myself once again within the consciousness of a grass blade. The Sun comes out from behind a cloud, and I feel a sudden thrill. Its warmth fills me with happiness and satisfaction, and a passionate yearning for more. If I stretch myself a tiny bit taller, I can *have* more. Before, when there was only wind, I had no idea how wonderful light could be. I was just tossed about, this way and that. Now I'm growing! I take in sunlight and transform it so that I become larger and can take in more sunlight. My joy increases constantly, yet it's always on the edge of what I can bear. As I get used to a certain level of ecstasy, I extend myself to contain more. A perpetual orgasm!

I'm so self-absorbed that I hardly notice anything around me. Suddenly, my perception expands and I realize that I'm in a field of countless other grass blades. At first I rejoice, thinking that all of them must feel the same ecstatic urge toward growth that I do. But then I notice that something's wrong. Not every grass blade strives as I do. It's true that some are growing more quickly than I am, but others are growing more slowly. There are even a few brown spots, where the grass is dying.

I return my attention to my own upward surge, a little less joyously. Again I feel that I'm part of a much larger whole, within which I hold a unique place. I can shift the focus of my awareness between the singular me and the collective me, as before. Yet there are parts of the collective me that resist growth, choosing to die instead. There's nothing I can do about it but use the sobering thought of their eventual death to inspire me with an even stronger urge to grow.

"You're doing well," the Overseer says. As he speaks, the field of grass winks out of existence. "Change is not the only factor that influences the human condition. There's also the powerful motivation to grow. Just as the Sun feeds a grass blade with the light that's essential to its growth, so does the soul feed the body with life force. A grass blade converts that light into its own substance. You do the same thing with life force, converting it into love. There are a million ways to do so—all you have to do is enjoy yourself. The more love you create, the happier you are.

"Just as the blade of grass yearns to draw in more sunlight, so do you yearn to increase the amount of life force flowing through you. The only way to do that is to expand your capacity to love. People who experience life as change alone allow themselves to be passively buffeted along by it. They tend not to grow in their capacity to love. It takes an ecstatic embrace of all that life has to offer to induce true growth.

"The differing speeds of growth you noticed among your fellow grass blades were the result of different degrees of embracing life. Those who embrace life fully grow more quickly, those who resist it grow more slowly. Less life force is available to the latter. They may be prone to debilitating diseases. Blocking the conversion of life force into love is a sure way to kill oneself."

The Overseer finishes speaking. Without warning, he transforms me into a grass blade yet again. Someone has transplanted me. I now grow from a very rich soil, almost black. I feel myself exultantly drawing the nutrients from this soil and adding them to my bulk. In addition to extending myself upward, my color is deepening, my girth broadening, and my fiber strengthening.

I sense the presence of other grass blades around me. We ripple in a light breeze, stretch toward the sun, and broaden, deepen, and strengthen in a similar rhythm, rejoicing all the while in our togetherness. Celebrating this glorious companionship, I extend my awareness as far as I can. To my amazement, I discover boundaries—and so close! Gone is the sense of millions upon millions of other grass blades. Now I feel the presence of only a few thousand.

Gradually, I begin to register something beyond the boundaries: more grass blades. But their vibrations are gritty, less resonant; their growth patterns more erratic; their physical expressions thinner, weaker, lighter in color. Aha! Their soil isn't as dark. Fewer nutrients are available to them.

Extending my awareness even further, I discover that I reside in one plot among many. My plot is small. It's at the center of the field. The other plots grow in size the farther they are from the center. Their soil becomes lighter in color, and the grass correspondingly weaker.

I say to myself, "Why should I enjoy these wonderful nutrients when others suffer for lack of them? I must try to help the grass blades in plots where the soil is not as rich as mine!" But I can't move—I'm firmly rooted in the ground! Then I realize that to grow joyously with my fellows would be more productive than vainly striving to help others. We can support each other with our willingness to grow. Perhaps the plots farther away will sense the joy and satisfaction we take in our growth and strive to be like us.

From time to time, new grass blades are transplanted to our plot. Each addition makes us stronger, more sure of ourselves and our growth. The sense of well-being that we broadcast to the other plots increases in power. Some of the grass blades in these plots begin to lean toward us, yearning to join in. Perhaps they too will be transplanted.

The scene fades. "You're doing exceptionally well," the Overseer says. "So far you've had no resistance either to our teaching aids, or to the information conveyed. We may be able to take you through the entire cycle.

"The third stage in the evolution of human consciousness involves discovering the extent to which your beliefs influence the rhythm of your growth. Your beliefs shape your breadth of character, strength of will, moral fiber, and depth of experiential processing—all of which are essential in converting life force into love. Beliefs provide you with the rich soil from which you draw your experience—nutrients—in order to promote growth.

"The intention to maximize one's growth may require him to transplant himself from one belief system to another. He may need to leave behind the cultural, regional, familial, and historic soils from which he arose for others that will be more supportive of who he is. The majority of people in your culture, for example, believe that success is the only satisfaction. If their definition of success is making a lot of money, they'll strive to do so, regardless of whether their work promotes growth. You, on the other hand, believe that satisfaction is the only success. You choose work that satisfies you. Satisfaction is one of the by-products of growth—the aftertaste, as it were, of converting large amounts of life force into love.

"Those who believe that satisfaction is the only success are at the center of the human population. They recognize that any special aptitudes, talents, or passionate interests they may have are worthy of development. In developing themselves, they not only grow, but may also produce something of value for others. Life has a purpose for such people: self-actualization, with the goal of rendering service to humanity.

"Many people don't believe in themselves or their abilities, or even that life has a purpose. Their belief systems do not nourish them in the way that yours nourishes you, thus limiting their growth. Yet it's inappropriate for you to proselytize for your lifestyle. People whose beliefs are farther removed from yours might not understand your views. You must commit yourself instead to your own process of self-actualization. Others may sense your happiness and satisfaction. They may wish to feel the same way about life. If they ask about how you came to this happiness, by all means tell them—they're ready to be transplanted."

The Overseer finishes speaking, and I brace myself for another abrupt transformation. This time I'm surprised to discover that I'm no longer a grass blade, but a gloriously unfurling flower in the midst of a large garden. I feel such satisfaction at the beauty of my brightly hued petals, knowing that I've produced them from within myself. How wonderful it is to let the world see what I've done! And how supremely self-confident I am that my beauty will be appreciated!

A bee buzzes up to me and lands on one of my petals. I feel ticklish as it walks over me, pushing this way and that, gathering nectar and pollen from my insides. I feel ravaged and ecstatic at once. I'm being raped, plundered. But I can do nothing to prevent the bee from having its way with me.

Part of me flies away on the bee's legs. It rubs off onto another flower who, like me, has been pillaged. A mysterious process of regeneration begins. That's why I feel so satisfied! The bee has left part of another flower within me as well. Already I sense my impending decay. The mysterious process is causing me to close and shrivel and envelop myself. Other latent versions of me that will blossom in distant futures begin to form, like scabs covering the wounds of my ravishment. Soon they will harden into their own tiny universes of as-yet unrealized potential: seeds.

My perspective shifts abruptly. Now I have buzzing wings, which vibrate my whole body. I can hover and dart and curlicue around. Between my back legs hangs a funny bulbous bottom with a secret danger contained inside: my sting. I go from flower to flower, landing on petals, and then crawling into the best position to gather the sweet nectar at their centers—a kind of lovemaking that fills me with an orgiastic high, as if nectar were some kind of mind-altering substance. Somehow the vibrational frequency of my buzzing interacts with chemical processes inside me to metabolize this high, converting the nectar to honey. In between flowers, my body feels heavier and heavier until I wonder if I can keep on flying.

Suddenly, I can no longer bear the idea of visiting more flowers. The rush of joy that their nectar usually sets off in my brain no longer seems pleasurable. I have no other thought than to fly back to the hive. The heavier I feel, the more nectar has been converted to honey, and the more urgently I need to get back to the hive. I can't continue living if I don't empty myself!

Back in the hive, I store my honey in one of the hexagonal units of beeswax. The honey throughout our hive has the same flavor because my relatives and I have all descended from the same queen. This honey is our food—but more than that. It thinks for us, it guides us. Although we use it to fuel our bodies, we do so only to make more. It is our god, our life force. Some will be used by us, and some will be taken away—for who knows what purpose.

Once again, my perspective shifts. Now I'm a green grape on a vine. I feel myself slowly filling with sweet juice pumped into me from a source I can't perceive. It just keeps coming, and I keep trying to find room—gradually, oh so gradually, pushing at my boundaries as I expand like a balloon. I turn the focus of my attention toward where the juice enters me. I discover a kind of pipeline with a slow but steady flow. The pipeline also fills other balloons that hang alongside mine, all joined to a single stalk. Higher up the pipeline, still other stalks branch into clusters of balloons, all filling slowly with juice, all gently and imperceptibly expanding.

Again my perspective shifts. Now I'm a raspberry. I'm constructed of dozens of tiny sacs, all emanating from the same interface. The sacs push against each other as they fill with sweet juice. But my consciousness is more focused on the interface—the center of a former flower which is like the brain behind myriad tiny eyes, all clustered together. Each eye captures a slightly different facet of the world, like the composite eye of a bee.

A sudden jolt brings me back into the presence of the Overseer.

"If you were to entitle the previous stages of development as follows—*Time as Change, Growth through Love,* and *Nourishment from Beliefs*—then the current episode could be called *Creativity: The Instinct to Bear Fruit.*

"Exercising creative abilities is the primary manner of converting life force into love. The first type of creativity is physical. Its fruit is the body.

"The body is beautiful, just as a flower is beautiful, simply because it exists. What you *call* a beautiful body is culturally determined. The body's true beauty is in its simple, spontaneous pleasure in being, confident that it has a right to exist, unpretentiously aware of the sensual delight it affords to itself and to other people.

"The creativity exercised on behalf of the body involves maintaining it, through healthy diet and athletic activity, and developing its potential as a vehicle for self-expression and sensual delight. Thus do you convert life force into the love of being present in the body.

"The second type of creativity is expressive. Its fruit is the personality. In your daily interactions with people, part of you rubs off on them, and part of them on you—just as the bee picks up pollen from a flower, and at the same time leaves behind some that had been gathered previously. If you see characteristics in someone else's personality that appeal to you, you may seek to develop them in yourself, shaping your own personality as if it were a piece of sculpture. The creativity exercised on behalf of the personality involves not only shaping your own personality but also learning to love both yourself and others. Learning to express such love is in fact one of the primary ways of shaping the personality. Thus do you convert life force into the love of being human.

"The third type of creativity is reproductive. Its fruit is a future generation. The phrase *making love* indicates that the sexual act is an important way of converting life force into love. Lovemaking involves both the physical and expressive aspects of creativity, since it can contribute to the love of being present in the body, and the love of self and other. When it's used for the purpose of procreation, the conversion of life force into love produces a child. Reproductive creativity doesn't stop after bringing a child to birth, however. Rearing a child and shaping its personality is just as creative an act as the mysterious process of regeneration that formed it in the womb.

"The fourth type of creativity is transformational. Its fruit is wisdom. Just as a bee gathers nectar, so do you gather experience. The bee transforms this nectar into honey, and you transform your experience into learning or wisdom.

"Learning to perform a task requires a certain amount of creativity: you may have to adjust your perceptions of the task or your expectations of yourself in order to master it. Such adjustments involve the transformational aspect of creativity. Learning isn't the only way of transforming experience, however. Creative application of the many self-help techniques currently available to your world can help you convert even the most painful experiences into wisdom. Gathering and processing experience allows you to convert life force into love, not only through enjoying what you do, but also through releasing yourself from emotions that block such enjoyment. The wisdom acquired in this fashion can be passed on to others, nurturing them in the same way that the honey gathered by the bee nurtures the other bees in the hive.

"Experience can make you high. But at the end of a day rich with experience, you feel heavy, drowsy, like the bee full of honey. Sleep allows you to process your experience, through dreams. Just as the bee can't survive without emptying itself of honey, so are you unable to survive without sleep.

"As you learned earlier, not everyone desires to grow. The same thing is true of acquiring wisdom. There are those, however, who learn not just from their own experiences but also from the experiences of others. They tap the hive of human wisdom, as it were, nourishing themselves with learning so that they'll be able to transform their own experiences more creatively. Their wisdom thinks for them and guides them. It's their god, just as honey is the god of the bees.

"The fifth type of creativity is artistic. Its fruit is a work of art.

"When you compose a piece of music, you fill it with your love of the melodies, harmonies, and formal principles you've chosen to work with. As you develop these musical materials, the piece expands in range and scope, just as a grape expands as it fills with juice. While composing, you'll be transforming experience into wisdom in other areas of your life. Such transformations will have an effect on what you write. In a sense, you'll be encoding these transformations into the piece. When it's performed, the audience will participate in your process of transforming experience into wisdom, and will learn from it. They'll also be refreshed by the love you've stored in the piece, just as they would be refreshed by biting into a grape.

"The same is true of all works of art: both love and the artist's process of transforming experience into wisdom will be contained within them. Even violent works can teach a viewer or listener ways of coping with or rebelling against the presence of violence in the world.

"Works by the same artist will have a similar flavor, despite differences in what they express—like grapes that have grown from a single stem. Similarly, the works of artists alive during a certain time period may also bear stylistic resemblances to one another, a result of their having to confront similar challenges in converting experience into wisdom. In our analogy, these were represented by clusters of grapes descending from different stems.

"We come now to the raspberry, which sums up very nicely the reasons for creativity. Every creative act, whether physical, expressive, reproductive, transformational, or artistic, allows you to convert life force into love. This love fills the product of that act like the juice fills a raspberry. Just as a single raspberry is made up of a number of tiny sacs of juice joined to a common interface, so your life is made up of a number of projects inspired by any of the five types of creativity you've chosen to explore. These projects are like the composite eye of the bee: each one allows you to experience a different facet of the world, or of what it means to be human."

Before I have a chance to absorb all that the Overseer has said, he vanishes. Now I'm the gardener—not, however, an actual person. I have no human form. I'm an invisible, mobile energy plexus, a gathering into folds of a thin, omnipresent energy field, making it thicker, more locally intense—as if a sheet of paper could simultaneously maintain its flat thinness and also be crumpled into a ball. The paper is like the field from which I, the ball, arise. Within this field, I'm the only moving part. I can't move beyond it. Nor have I created the field from myself. Wherever I am is the center of the field. I move by crinkling the energy field into paper-ballness in one direction, while leaving behind me a trail of wrinkles that gradually subside back into the field's original smoothness and uniformity.

As if superimposed upon this perception of myself is another more ordinary one: an image of a gardener working in his garden. I'm aware that both the gardener and the garden are metaphors for something else. The human portion of me needs these metaphors in order to make sense of the reality in which I find myself. As the gardener, I plant seeds, ordering patterns of flowers by shape, color, texture, and number of petals, and deciding what goes where and when. I establish beehives, erect trellises for grapevines. I gather bunches of grapes and eat them for sustenance. I remove portions of honeycomb and take them somewhere far away from the garden, where they'll be used for unknown purposes. The garden has been in existence for so long that there are many varieties of seeds available—and many possible arrangements of them, which I take ceaseless delight in executing.

The flowers, beehives, and grape trellises fade away as the Overseer resumes his explanation.

"The fifth stage in the evolution of human consciousness is learning to see things from the perspective of your own soul, the nonphysical portion of you that establishes the lessons you need to learn and guides you through them. The garden is your life, and the soul is its caretaker. For the soul, your life is a work of art: a place to try out every possible association of human characteristics and expressions. The seeds are latent potentials: talents to be activated once you've been born into physical reality. Your task is to develop these potentials, to bring the seeds to flower.

"Although the soul sets up the patterns of events, or lessons, that will help you grow, it doesn't control your life. These patterns of events are like grape trellises—supportive structures you can wind yourself around in any way you see fit.

"It's the soul that assigns the task of transforming life force into love and storing it in your creative acts. The soul is nurtured by this love. Like a beekeeper, the soul gathers the love you've produced to nourish itself. It also passes some of this love on to other beings, just as a beekeeper might sell a portion of his harvest of honey.

"Your sensations at the beginning of this episode were an attempt on our part to show you how the soul perceives itself in its own environs—a vortex of energy moving through an energy field that completely surrounds it."

I want to ask what sort of being the soul might provide with a portion of its harvest of love. But before I have a chance to do so, I find myself floating out in space. I have a human form, one that's mythological in stature, titanesque. At the periphery of my vision, I can see the Earth: blue water, green land, brown deserts, white clouds. Pouring from every portion of its surface, in tiny trickles and spectacular gushes, is a flow of golden-white light. These streams unite into a river that meanders in my direction. It passes me and continues along to an unknown destination.

I dip my hand in the river and pull up a honeycomb, a bunch of grapes, and a carton of raspberries. I sample a cell of honey, a grape, a single raspberry. Then I return the rest to the river, where their forms dissolve back into golden-white light. I seem to be checking the quality of love contained in these products of human consciousness.

The river of light disappears from view, and my tutor resumes his explanation.

"Beyond the soul is the oversoul, or mass consciousness of humanity. While you have an individual identity, a unique function within this gigantic whole, you can also see life on Earth as if from the perspective of that whole. The oversoul monitors the refinement of the love distilled from life force through experience and creativity. This distillation is in turn gathered by more advanced consciousnesses than yours, in much the same way that you might gather honey from a beehive.

"They, in turn, transform and refine it as you have, just as the life force that you've converted into love was itself a cruder form of love, passed onto you by a level of consciousness less spiritually advanced than yours. And so it goes, up to the highest level of spiritual development, that of the Creator."

By now I've gotten used to the Overseer's sudden comings and goings. It doesn't surprise me at all when he vanishes yet again. However, I'm unprepared for the absolute nothingness that greets me after he's gone. There are no images this time to help me make sense of my experience. I can't see, hear, feel, or move. Before I have a chance to panic, the Overseer flips back into view.

"We are most pleased that you've been able to proceed through the entire sequence of lessons on the nature of human consciousness evolution. For the sake of completeness, we wanted to let you know that there's another stage of development beyond the ones you've witnessed so far. You could call it *graduation*. It will take you to that higher level of consciousness that your present self nourishes with the love you produce here. No direct experience of this stage can come until you've completed your Earth-focused cycle of learning.

"Even we Overseers are unaware of the learnings that will occur after graduation. One thing is certain: taking place entirely in nonphysical reality, they would be more or less impossible to translate into terms your current consciousness could understand."

20

The Grand Tour

On the night I had the experiences recorded in the previous chapter, a voice had told me that "the adventure" would begin that evening. It was my first foray into Otherwhere. Many of my subsequent adventures have appeared in earlier chapters. All of them, it turns out, were leading to the events that occurred on the night of September 6, 1991.

Although I'd been exploring Otherwhere for five years by that time, and had taken copious notes on my adventures, I was nearly overwhelmed by the magnitude of this one. A typical adventure might take three to eight hours to record, because of the challenge of turning nonphysical experiences into words. The present one, however, took me three months of almost daily work to write down. This and the following chapters recount that single adventure.

It began innocuously enough. In the midst of a dream, I climbed onto a bicycle and began riding through a nondescript gray-green landscape for what seemed like a long time. Eventually, I came to a well made of field stone. I leaned the bike against the well and peered over the edge. When my eyes had become accustomed to the darkness inside the well, I saw that it contained a spiral staircase. I climbed over the wall of the well to find out where the stairs might lead. Down and down I went into the darkness, which was not pitch-black, but half-lit, like dusk. I could see each great slab of stone clearly as I stepped down to it, spiraling around the stairway's central column again and again. Then the steps stopped. I passed through a stone arch and into a cavern.

The cavern was huge, large enough to contain a bustling metropolis. Tall skyscrapers stretched toward the ceiling of the cavern, but none of them quite reached it. Each building was of a different height, giving the impression that one could climb nearly to the ceiling simply by jumping from rooftop to rooftop.

As I approached the city, I came upon a small knot of people who seemed to be sightseeing. They were consulting maps, guidebooks, and pointing this way and that. Everyone wore sunglasses, mufflers, oversized sweaters, baggy pants, slouch hats. Bulges appeared in the strangest places beneath the tourists' ill-fitting clothes, as if a circus sideshow were traveling incognito, trying vainly to disguise its freakishness.

An attractive young woman with brown curly hair and a fresh, smiling face began clapping her hands together, trying to get the group's attention. Wearing a national park ranger's outfit, she was the only one of the group whose face and figure were clearly visible. In contrast to her shapeliness, the amorphus forms of the others looked very strange indeed.

"Welcome to the Human Afterdeath Zone," the young woman said, loud enough that I could hear. I hurried over to join the group, along with several stragglers who seemed to be having trouble walking, as if this were an unfamiliar means of locomotion. "I'll be your guide on today's tour. Those of you who feel it necessary to use names may call me Karin," she continued. "Please feel free to ask questions at any time."

The group moved toward the high Gothic arch of a stone gate, apparently left as a monument to former times, since the wall which once held it was no longer in evidence.

"Why are we underground?" one of the tourists growled, craning his muffled neck to scan the cavern ceiling.

Karin stopped and faced the group. "Good question," she said. "The Earth has a long history of peoples who believed that the Afterdeath Zone was a kind of underworld. An anthropologist might assume that such a belief originated in the practice of burying the dead beneath the ground. There were other groups, of course, who believed that the dead went to a place in the sky. These peoples cremated their dead to help them on their journey. To confuse matters even more, some religions taught that the dead who were buried underground went to Heaven or that the cremated dead went to an underworld. In a way, both traditions were right, but far too literal.

"Where the human dead go has nothing to do with burial, cremation, or any other means of disposing of the physical body. When the body dies, the soul retires to nonphysical reality. Since Earth's atmosphere is invisible, the sky became, for some peoples, a symbol of the nonphysicality of the dead's abode. Other peoples maintained a tradition of interaction with the dead and had to have some means of reaching them. Placing an underworld inside the Earth symbolized the presence of nonphysical reality within themselves. It was below the level of waking consciousness, just as the underworld was below the surface of the Earth. Because humans are addicted to physical reality, they can perceive nonphysical reality only in physical terms. Thus, if the underworld is below the ground, then it must be in a cave. A cave is one of the few direct experiences of being underground available to most humans."

The tourist grunted, apparently satisfied. Karin turned to face the gate.

"This style of architecture was commonly used for the portals of Christian houses of worship during a time when many of the beliefs characteristic of this religion were codified. In one way or another, these beliefs have had an impact on large segments of the Earth's population for many hundreds of years. The city on the other side of this gate is for the exclusive use of anyone brought into contact with this belief system, or any of its numerous variations. You may call it the City of Christendom, if you wish.

"Moslems, Jews, Hindus, Taoists, and Buddhists each have their own locales within the Human Afterdeath Zone—large cities like this one, because of the multitudes who adhere to each of these faiths. Religions with fewer followers also have locales of their own, but these would be perceived as towns or villages."

"Where are these other cities?" I asked. "The cavern seems to be totally occupied by this one."

Karin turned to look at me and arched her right eyebrow, as if surprised to see a normal-looking person among the motley crew of tourists. But she answered my question in the same matter-of-fact tone with which she'd addressed the first.

"Each religion has its own subzone within the larger reality of the Human Afterdeath Zone. You would probably perceive these subzones as contiguous, like countries on a map. Yet any nonphysical being would perceive these subzones as interpenetrating one another, in much the same way that television broadcasts interpenetrate one another. You see the City of Christendom because your perceptual equipment is presently attuned to the frequency band on which this subzone resides. You could attune your perceptual equipment to another frequency band, if you wished. You would then perceive a different holy city, just like changing a channel on TV."

One of the tourists looked down his nose at me as if he couldn't believe that I'd asked such an elementary question, or that our Guide had actually deigned to answer it. Before he had a chance to make a cutting remark, Karin cut him off.

"We have the unusual distinction," she said, "of having with us today a living, breathing member of the human race, unlike most of the individuals you'll encounter on our tour." A chuckle ran through the crowd. All eyes turned on me. "As is true of most humans, his understanding of the mechanics of nonphysical reality is relatively limited," she continued. "I hope you'll be patient with him if he asks questions whose answers seem self-evident to you."

Once again she'd spoken in a matter-of-fact tone, without a hint of patronization. Looking me in the eye, she said, "Welcome aboard."

We proceeded through the gate and found ourselves on a broad avenue. As we approached the center of the city, the skyscrapers, arranged in concentric rings, became smaller and smaller, until they were replaced by three-story, then two-story, then single-story buildings. A circular park of bright green grass separated these rings from a group of much older structures made of ivy-covered stone, rather than the chrome and glass of the skyscrapers. With a few exceptions, these structures seemed to be about the same age as the Gothic gate. Another greensward separated this ring from a central plaza, which contained a spectacular fountain.

At first I thought that the sculpted figures around which the fountain's waters played were mythological in nature— sylphs, dryads, a gigantic figure of Neptune wielding a trident. But when I got closer, I discovered that Neptune was really Moses. I recognized him by the tablet of commandments at his feet. The trident was actually the staff with which Moses had brought water from the rock when the Israelites were wandering in the desert. Moses' staff was cleverly directed toward the base of the fountain, so it seemed as if he'd just called forth the jet of water that rose from that point.

Our group walked clockwise around the fountain, admiring the finely wrought sculptures on each of its four sides. To the right of Moses was a tiered waterfall made to look like Jacob's Ladder. God was at its top, a three-dimensional version of William Blake's engraving *The Ancient of Days*—a long-haired, white-bearded, muscular old man. Water was gushing from his outstretched hands, like a blessing showering down on the orders of angels, whom I'd mistaken for dryads and sylphs. In front of the waterfall was Jacob himself, struggling with an imposingly winged angel.

On the side opposite Moses was a statue of Christ, carved from the central column of the fountain in such a way that he seemed to be walking over the pool of water at his feet. His arms were raised in a gesture of blessing. A jet of water poured from his mouth. At the edge of the pool beneath his feet sat several disciples with baskets of loaves and fishes, staring up at him with rapt attention.

On the side opposite Jacob's Ladder was a naked Adam, standing next to Eve as she reached for an apple. Eve was being encouraged to eat the apple by an enormous python curled around the Tree of Knowledge—the latter carved in frieze from the base of the fountain. Water poured from the mouth of the serpent and flowed in a deep channel around the feet of Adam and Eve. Perhaps this channel was intended to represent the Tigris or the Euphrates, the traditional boundaries of the Garden of Eden.

After we'd made our circuit of the fountain, our Guide addressed us. "Every holy city has such a fountain at its center, representing the flow of truth through the religion it was meant to serve. Here we have several scenes from the Holy Book of the Christians, each of which illustrates a fundamental truth in the Christian belief system. The commandments of Moses, for example, are one of the bases of Christian ethics, from which have sprung many of the laws of Christendom. That's why you see Moses striking a rock and bringing forth a stream of water, or truth.

"The scene of Adam and Eve in the Garden of Eden has always been a symbol of certain fundamental truths about the human condition. Here in nonphysical reality, an individual's needs are satisfied more or less instantly upon his recognition of their existence. This is the paradisal state with which all of you, with one exception, of course,"—Karin winked at me—"are quite familiar, or even perhaps take for granted.

"The soul is by nature nonphysical. When it incarnates in physical reality, it must have a suitable vehicle. Hands with opposable thumbs were highly desirable tools for the evolution of human consciousness. Thus, a primate species was chosen as the most advantageous vehicle for the human soul, which began to incarnate through this species' wombs.

"The goal was for humanity to experience a separation from the Creator, and from nonphysical reality, in order to discover its true identity or function, and then to evolve back to oneness with the Creator again. From the perspective of the Creator, this was merely a set of lessons to be learned. To humankind, unfortunately, it felt like a fall from *grace*, the state of connection with everything else that prevails in nonphysical reality.

"It was very painful for human consciousness to be present within a material body. In the early stages of the primate body's evolution towards its present human state, the soul remained only tenuously connected to that body. It had very little control of the body's doings. During this period, certain primate instincts became magnified and distorted by a kind of self-awareness that had never existed in it before, a product of the soul's presence in the body.

"Over many generations, before the soul was strong enough to govern them, or even realize that something might need to be done about them, magnified and distorted versions of the primate instincts for survival, sex, and social standing became genetically encoded. They formed the basis of a hybrid consciousness that was neither primate nor soul: the ego.

"As a hybrid consciousness, the ego can choose to align itself with the primate instincts or with the soul. It is this choice that's illustrated in the scene before you. The serpent represents the primate instincts tempting Adam and Eve, who represent humanity in its early stages of evolution. The serpent is trying to get them to follow *its* advice, rather than that of the soul. Yet the serpent didn't tempt Adam and Eve into performing an action that exiled them from paradise, or nonphysical reality. The serpent appeared afterwards, *because* of that apparent exile.

"What's the difference between good and evil? Good is defined by the soul as those actions which increase the presence of the soul in the body and which therefore further the evolution of humanity. Evil is defined as those actions that diminish or violate the soul's presence in the body, prompted by the magnified and distorted primate instincts. This distinction is perhaps the first and most important spiritual lesson for any human being to learn.

"Many scenes such as the one you see here, occurring between Adam and Eve, have been projected to receptive human beings over the centuries. These transmissions emanate from nonphysical reality, where there's no time or space, and must be translated into physical terms that include time and space. Such transmissions aren't always translated exactly as the Overseers intended them to be.

"The presence of the serpent in the Garden of Eden has caused more than one religious scholar to wonder why God would have allowed such an ignominious creature to mar the perfection of paradise. The answer isn't that God in His perfection planned all along that humankind would fall from grace— and planted the serpent in the Garden out of some unfathomable perversity—but that the individual who received the vision got the order of events mixed up. God never forbade the knowledge of good and evil to humankind. But humankind had come to believe that its painful separation from God and its presence within physical bodies was a form of punishment. There had to be some horrible transgression for which humanity was being punished. And since the only action in this scene was Eve eating the apple, that had to be the sin.

"Actually, it's the solution. Without knowing the difference between good and evil, as I've just defined these terms, no human being can evolve back to oneness with the Creator.

"In our fountain, water—that is, truth—pours from the mouth of the serpent because the voice of temptation is often one of the surest ways to discover the will of the soul. Every human being must learn to do exactly the opposite of what that voice says."

"But what about the part where Adam and Eve make clothes for themselves because they're ashamed of their nakedness?" I asked.

"The magnified and distorted primate instincts cause people to perceive one another as sexual objects, rather than as souls housed in bodies. This, and not nakedness, was what Adam and Eve were ashamed of. The idea of clothing was a possible solution to this problem—so that people wouldn't be continually distracted from their dealings with one another by sexuality. The fact that such distraction occurs even between fully clothed human beings can give you some idea of just how strong the magnified and distorted primate instincts are. Clothing isn't necessary in nonphysical reality, of course."

During Karin's discussion of Adam and Eve, I'd noticed that the other tourists were gawking at me. Several of them seemed to be struggling to find an appropriate reaction to her words. I saw rank disbelief, concealed laughter, pity, even awe. It was clear that none of them truly understood the human condition—it was too far removed from their experience of being. I'd begun to feel like a laboratory specimen under scrutiny and found myself tempted to lash out against the scrutinizers.

"If clothing isn't necessary for beings more highly evolved than we humans, then why is everyone in this group so overdressed?" I asked, petulantly.

At this, everyone but our Guide burst into laughter—not at all the reaction I'd hoped for. Karin waited until order had been restored and replied calmly.

"You may perceive that your fellow tourists are heavily clothed, but where they come from there's no need for clothes. What you see are their attempts to tone down and shield the alienness of their thought patterns so that their presence won't disturb the inhabitants of Christendom."

Abashed at having once again demonstrated my ignorance of the main principle that seems to govern Otherwhere—that everything I perceive there is energy, which I must translate into physical images in order to understand it—I slunk to the back of the group of tourists, hanging my head. They seemed to sense my embarrassment, but didn't respond to it. As a matter of fact, I got the distinct impression that they were puzzled at my reaction to Karin's words.

What was wrong, after all, with asking a question and receiving a straightforward answer? Information was information, as far as they were concerned. It seemed as if they didn't even know what embarrassment was. Meanwhile, our Guide went on to explain the remaining two sides of the fountain.

"Jacob, the individual illustrated here, was taken on a tour of Otherwhere and remembered what he saw more clearly than most. He represented the different levels of spiritual evolution that he perceived in Otherwhere as a ladder ascending to God. The basic lesson here was that humans, like all other beings in both physical and nonphysical realities, have in some way been separated from the Creator, and have been assigned the task of evolving back to oneness with Him.

"Humanity is not alone, therefore, in having experienced an apparent fall from grace. But humanity is one of the few forms of consciousness that feel sorry for itself over this fall, resisting instead of embracing the task of spiritual evolution.

"Jacob, like all human beings, had trouble deciding where his allegiance lay, with the primate instincts or with the soul. That struggle is symbolized by his wrestling with the angel, an image of his own soul.

"Christ, on the other hand, is one who was able largely to conquer the magnified and distorted primate instincts. Because he so strongly identified with the soul, he was able to perform a number of actions considered miraculous by his followers. Here you see him walking on water, a physically impossible act. Actually, at the time of this so-called miracle, he was out of body—yet able to impress his presence on the consciousness of his disciples, so that it seemed to them that he was floating over the waves. All of Christ's miraculous visitations to his disciples, including his so-called resurrection, were in reality out-of-body experiences. Combined with this incident is imagery from the Sermon on the Mount; which, from the perspective of the Overseers, has a much higher truth content than many of the other remembrances of Christ's words and deeds recorded in the Bible."

"Who built this magnificent fountain?" I asked as we completed our second circuit of it. I'd overcome my earlier feelings of embarrassment, but felt a little peevish at the giggles that greeted my question. Without missing a beat, Karin replied, "You did."

I was shocked into speechlessness. The sculpture was worthy of Michelangelo. Had I been an artist of that stature in a previous incarnation? Did I come here after my death and create this fountain, using what I had learned during that life? I became annoyed when I realized that the group of tourists were privy to my thoughts. Several of them could no longer contain themselves. Their laughter came in great guffaws.

Karin kindly came to my rescue. "Remember that the fountain symbolizes the flow of truth through Christendom. Truth is not physical, it's an energy. It flows through any number of scenes from the Bible. The Bible supplies images for these truths in the form of stories, some of which record actual events, others of which are purely symbolic.

"Here in the Afterdeath Zone, you're able to sense Christian truths as energies. These energies remind you of the stories associated with them, and you then represent these stories to yourself as sculptures. If they bear a resemblance to the works of Michelangelo, that's because you've seen pictures of his sculptures in books. Your memories become the raw material from which you've constructed this fountain. What the fountain represents is not your creation, but every aspect of its appearance is.

"Now, if you turn your attention to the circle of buildings surrounding the central plaza," Karin addressed the group, "you'll see that most of them seem quite old. It took many centuries for the official-line beliefs of Christianity to be codified. Some of the best minds of the Church's early days were occupied with interpreting the words of Christ, as they were passed along to his disciples. Unfortunately, the disciples only wrote down what they understood. So the teaching of Jesus is sadly incomplete, leaving a lot of room for interpretation.

"Branches of the new religion developed from disputes over the exact meaning of Christ's words and from debates over philosophical issues which, from the Overseers' perspective, were utterly meaningless. Volumes of cleverly worded arguments about such things as whether Christ was all divine, all human, or some seemingly impossible combination of the two were written. Arcane symbolism sprang up, often involving a triangle with God at one point, Christ at another, and a never very clearly defined concept called the *Holy Ghost* at the third. The Holy Ghost is really nothing more than a representation of one's own soul, or of the life force that animates the body.

"Terms such as *grace, sin, forgiveness, redemption* were coined and left intentionally vague. A priesthood sprang up as the official interpreters of Christ's message. Before long, the magnified and distorted primate instincts—in the form of spiritual survival fears, sexual guilt, and mind control—had infiltrated the new religion. Fear was invoked by telling people that they might lose their souls if they didn't manage their sexuality properly. Impossibly stringent limitations were established for sexual behavior, so that people were in constant fear of losing their souls. The beliefs of the Church were touted as the only way of guaranteeing salvation of the soul.

"Thus did the Church become an administrative structure primarily concerned with controlling large numbers of people through fear, and only indirectly with the promulgation of Christ's views.

"The buildings you see in front of you are a kind of university. The oldest ones have been around since the early days of the Church, when its official doctrines were established. Their purpose is to help people unlearn Church dogma so that they may arrive at an understanding of the fundamental truths that lie beneath it.

"Time and again the Overseers have sent individuals to Earth to reform the doctrines of the Church. A few succeeded, many failed. For the last five hundred years, the Christian religion has divided and subdivided like a one-celled animal, constantly spawning new versions of itself, which came to live alongside the old. Usually the rites of celebration changed, but not the corrupted structure developed in order to control the masses by using the fear of losing one's soul through sexual misconduct.

"Some of these offshoots have arrived at interpretations of gospel as creative—and as erroneous or irrelevant—as those of the great Church fathers of the Middle Ages. The circle of more modern one-story buildings that surround the ancient university contain classrooms in which these comparatively recent misconceptions are corrected.

"Beyond the one-story buildings you can see the skyscrapers rising, each concentric ring a little higher than the last, until the final circle brushes the cavern ceiling. Strange to say, only the uppermost level of each of these skyscrapers is inhabited. It may seem as if a lot of space is being wasted here, since the lower levels of the highest buildings are unoccupied.

"But remember," Karin said, directing this portion of her monologue to me, "there's no such thing as space in nonphysical reality. What you see here is an image that people on Earth can understand. The more far-reaching their view, and the more complete their perspective on the fundamental truths behind Christianity is, the higher the level of skyscraper to which they'll be assigned—once they've completed any necessary retraining in the university.

"The city is divided into segments originating from the central plaza, one for each country in which the Christian faith is practiced. The history and customs, even the language of that country, will modify its perception of the truth at the center of Christianity. Thus each country has its own set of viewpoints on Christianity. Every building in that country's sector will therefore have the same view of the central plaza.

"Around the outskirts of the city you'll find suburbs or villages in which atheists, agnostics, existentialists, and other dropouts from the Christian faith have a chance to explore the reasons for their often justified disaffection with organized religion. There are even ghettoes, as it were, for formerly Christian converts to other religions, such as Hinduism, Buddhism, or Taoism. The religion one is brought up with leaves a permanent mark on the way he perceives things, no matter how far afield he may go in later life.

"Eventually, such dropouts must arrive at an understanding of the fundamental truths behind Christianity. At that point, they'll move from their suburbs and ghettoes into the center of Christendom and prepare for their next lifetime, even if that lifetime will take place in another religious climate."

"Will we be going into any of the skyscrapers?" one of the tourists asked.

"No," Karin replied. "You'll have to satisfy yourselves with my description. The topmost level of each skyscraper actually represents an experience of what the Christians call Heaven. Heaven is a boundless energy plane in which each individual has the renewing and recharging experience of presence within the heart of God: not, of course, the Creator and Sustainer of universes itself—that would be overwhelming—but rather the powerful energy that is at the source of all humanity: its mission. That mission, of course, represents humanity's place *within* the great Creator and Sustainer of Universes.

"Using an analogy from Earth itself, the mission of humanity reflects the power that emanates from the Creator in the same way that the Moon reflects the light of the Sun. Someone who has accepted the Christian faith and who understands the truth behind Christianity will probably have done more to further the mission of humanity than someone within that faith who has little or no understanding of its truth. Thus, the individual with the greater understanding will find himself in one of the higher skyscrapers, where he'll experience himself as being closer to God."

Our Guide's words triggered my memory of the lab session at The Monroe Institute, in which, after visiting the cave of the existentialists, I had passed through an area that I was told was

Heaven. In the center of that Heaven was what seemed like a Sun that appeared to beat like a heart, sending light and love in all directions. The plane I was on extended into an apparently limitless distance. Other planes rose above that level like steps or tiers. The Sun/heart was on the highest of these tiers. I wondered whether this Heaven was the same as the one Karin had just described.

"Absolutely," she replied, reading my thoughts.

"I'm having trouble placing the expansive reality I remember into the upper level of one of those skyscrapers," I said, perplexed.

"Something you should always keep in mind about the Afterdeath Zone," Karin replied with a hint of amusement, "is that there are as many ways of perceiving it as there are classes of entities who make the attempt. I'm not just referring to how thought creates experience here. The function of any entity who visits the Afterdeath Zone shapes its perception. Its function acts as a filter that accepts certain energies and ignores others as irrelevant. Thus, a Shade sees things differently from a Facilitator. Only the Overseers can take in the whole picture. But everyone who works in the Afterdeath Zone—including yours truly—is aspiring toward election to the Council of Overseers.

"Such election is not a political matter but simply an expression of whether one is able to comprehend the whole of what happens here. Shades comprehend the least. After Shades come *Personal Trainers*, individuals who help people who are still alive by teaching them while they sleep. Then come the Facilitators who man the various stations of the Afterdeath Zone. There are three subclasses of Facilitators—*Personal Attendants*, who guide a particular Shade through the stations of the Afterdeath Zone; the *Technicians,* who are in charge of the operations that go on at any of these levels, including teaching the classes at the university; and the *Administrators*, who oversee the running of the stations.

"The Administrators have their own ranks, depending on how much of the Afterdeath Zone they're in charge of. So there are Administrators who oversee the instruction in the university, and other higher-ranking Administrators who oversee all activities that go on within the City of Christendom. Above those Administrators there is only the Council of Overseers itself, which has individual functions but no separate ranks."

"Where do you fit into this scheme?" I asked.

"Guides are Technicians in the process of training to become an Administrator. You could say that they represent the top level of the Technician subclass.

"Now, to get back to your original question. The images behind the City of Christendom are not merely of your own invention. Every Christian who comes here will see some variation of the city, the fountain, the university, and the surrounding buildings. Your friend Dante, for example, saw a mystic rose, in which Shades were arranged in tiers of 'blessedness' not unlike the levels of a Roman stadium. You perceive the same level-effect but are using a more modern image, that of skyscrapers. A Facilitator, however, would see only planes of energy, such as in your Sun/heart experience. To a Shade, Heaven would look like whatever it was believed to be, depending on that individual's personal interpretation of Christianity and understanding of its truths.

"On a tour such as this one, your function is to see things from more than one perspective, that of the Shade and that of the Facilitator. Thus, your confusion about how to fit the expansive reality of the Heaven you visited into one of the skyscrapers is understandable. You were trying to interpret one perspective in terms of another. From the perspective of the Shades, the notion of a stadium or of ever-higher levels of skyscrapers is necessary to help them understand that there are more comprehensive viewpoints above the one they were able to achieve in their last lifetime—and that in their next lifetime as a Christian, they should each strive to advance themselves beyond it."

"Sounds like yuppies who believe that it's more prestigious to live in an apartment or condominium on a higher floor, on account of the view," I commented.

"You've got it. Only most yuppies will probably end up on the lower floors here, unless they take the time to develop a more spiritual outlook on life."

21

The Civil Servant

"Now," Karin said, addressing the group as a whole, "if there are no further questions about the design of the City of Christendom, then we need to move on to the next phase of our tour."

No one spoke up, so she began to lead the group to a long, glass building opposite Jacob's Ladder.

"This is the Veterans Administration Hospital," she said, as we went through revolving doors into an expansive lobby. "Everyone who comes here is a veteran of the battle between good and evil— or between the soul and the primate instincts. The upper stories of the VA, as we call it, are very much like a hospital. Recently deceased individuals go there to rest. Before they're permitted to enter the VA, however, they must pass through a stage of purification, in which they'll release themselves of any illusions that may have distorted their perspective on life. This process occurs in the levels beneath the VA, which we'll visit first."

Our guide led us to the center of the lobby, where we were confronted by several banks of elevators.

"The human dead come in four types. The first type consists of those whose lives were dedicated to self-actualization, and who largely succeeded. The second consists of those who were aware of the need to self-actualize and did as much as they could, given the limitations of a too-conventional belief system. The third type consists of those who made attempts to satisfy the need for self-actualization, but encountered obstructions they were unable to overcome. And finally, the fourth consists of those who were unaware of the need to self-actualize and made no attempt to do so. The Overseers define self-actualization as the discovery and fulfillment of one's life purpose—which, as you know, is both one's function within the universe and also one's identity.

"It may come as a surprise to you that human beings are almost endemically unaware of who they are. The soul, of course, knows. But it's often blocked from transmitting that knowledge to the ego by the primate instincts. These instincts are capable of developing themselves into personality constructs that entirely supplant the soul. Thus, the magnified and distorted social instinct can manifest itself as a lust for power, turning a person whose life purpose involves leadership into a dictator. Likewise, the sexual instinct can cause someone to become a Don Juan or nymphomaniac—people who feel they have no identity other than that which their sexuality confers on them. And the survival instinct can produce people who are addicted to dangerous or self-destructive situations, or who are so fearful and anxious that they're unable to make decisions or to take action of any sort.

"These personality constructs may come in any possible combination or relative strength of the magnified and distorted social, sexual, and survival instincts. The Overseers refer to such constructs as *false personality*. All false personality must be eradicated before a soul can progress from Immigration, where it enters the Afterdeath Zone, to the VA. The process of purification I mentioned earlier allows people to heal any psychological wounds that they may have sustained in the battle between the soul and the primate instincts.

"The purpose of the VA's lower levels is to purge the soul of false personality, or illusion, of all the beliefs and attitudes that rationalized one's acting on behalf of the primate instincts instead of the soul.

"Now, if you'll all just step inside the elevator, we'll head to the lowest of the several levels beneath the VA and work our way up."

The group crowded into the elevator. As the door closed, Karin pressed a button and we began to move. Our descent seemed to take a long time. It was more like that of a freight than an express elevator. We came to a stop, but before the doors had opened, the elevator shook violently, as if in an earthquake. The quake was followed by several aftershocks. After they'd subsided—and Karin, clearly distressed, had regained her composure—the door of the elevator opened.

We found ourselves in another cavern. Except for the bank of elevators built into the rock, there were no buildings of any kind on this level, only a long, deep chasm that ran the length of the cavern, about twenty feet from where we stood.

An attendant of some sort, perhaps what Karin had called a Technician, was lifting what appeared to be a small ingot of pure gold from a platform erected on the edge of the chasm. He wore coveralls of a thick and heavy fireproof material and a helmet such as a welder would use to protect his face. His hands were encased in huge padded mittens, as if the ingot were very hot. He moved slowly and carefully back to the bank of elevators, still carrying the ingot. One of the three elevator doors opened to admit him.

We had come out of the doors on the right. The Technician had entered the doors on the left. Moments later, the middle pair of doors opened and two people emerged. One was dressed in the same coveralls, helmet, and gloves as the first Technician had been. He was accompanied by a man dressed in street clothes—navy blue slacks, the outlines of an undershirt visible beneath his plain white outer shirt. The man was tall and very overweight. He appeared to be in his middle fifties, with thinning dark hair and a white, pasty face. He moved as if in shock, unaware of his surroundings. The Technician maneuvered him toward the platform.

I was so intent on observing the scene as it silently unfolded that I was startled by our Guide's voice.

"As I mentioned earlier, there are people who never become aware of their life purpose, or even that they're required to discover and fulfill it. Such individuals rarely live beyond middle age. In a sense, it's a waste of life force for the soul to keep them going. The soul, of course, gives them every opportunity to become aware of who they are. It withdraws their life force only if it seems unlikely that any real growth will occur during this lifetime. Luckily, such people are relatively rare.

"The individual before you has just been brought from Immigration. Attuning your awareness to his energy field, you'll perceive that he was born on the East Coast of North America to Catholic parents. During adolescence, the individual became aware of a strong physical attraction to men. This awareness coincided with his indoctrination into the Catholic belief system, which condemns homosexuality. He always wanted to be a good person, but as he realized that nothing could be done about his attraction to men—he would not grow out of it, and no attempt to cure himself would work—he more or less resigned himself to a life of celibacy.

"Repression of his sexuality caused it to overpower his desire to be good in the eyes of the Church. Because he believed homosexuality to be base and immoral, he couldn't help but attract to himself the most degrading experiences. He would feel ashamed of himself, resolve to do better, and fail yet again. By the time he was in college, he was absolutely sure that when he died he would go directly to Hell.

"To atone for the sinfulness he perceived in himself, he chose a career in the human services field. Yet to help others in a counseling capacity was not his life purpose. What he really wanted to be was an actor. He was aware that the theater was a hotbed of homosexuality, and thought he was saving his soul by avoiding it. Actually, the theater would have been his refuge. Eventually, he would have written moving plays about his struggle to accept his homosexuality while at the same time laying the foundation for a morally upright and spiritually fulfilling life. These plays, of course, would have served as an inspiration for other gay men who had been born Catholic.

"Upon graduation from college, he began to work for a government agency. He feared he might lose his job if anyone suspected his homosexuality, so he developed a character as ordinary and unobtrusive as possible—note the plainness of his dress. He became afraid with each passing year that his friends, coworkers, and family might suspect he was gay simply because he hadn't yet married.

"His solution to this problem, however, wasn't to get married for the sake of appearances, but to develop a 'Mr. Nice Guy' persona. He would find ways to make himself essential to the lives of everyone he knew, at no matter what cost to himself. He was perpetually loaning money, doing favors, giving gifts, running errands—often responding to people's needs before anything was said. His weight problem was caused by sexual frustration and his resentment of all the people who took advantage of him. Yet he never dropped his false smile or raised his voice in anger.

"As he grew older, he developed a drinking problem. He ended up spending a lot of time in gay piano bars, the show tunes stirring in him a longing that he couldn't quite place— perhaps for a lover, he thought—although it was really a nostalgia for the life he could have led, but still dared not think about.

"He died of a heart attack, his constitution weakened by alcohol and obesity. Until his dying day, he hoped that he could buy his way into Heaven and the hearts of friends and family with the apparently selfless serving of others. While that could perhaps be someone's life purpose, it wasn't his. From the soul's perspective, his personality was irremediably warped by the primate survival instinct, which manifested itself not in terms of his physical but rather his emotional and spiritual survival. None of the lessons the soul intended for him were learned."

Hardly had Karin ceased speaking when the Technician stepped back from the platform, leaving the poor, unhappy man standing alone on the edge of the chasm. Was he going to jump? Should I try to save him? Can the soul commit suicide? The man stood there, apparently unaware of his surroundings.

I took a tentative step in his direction, but stumbled as the cavern began to rock back and forth, gently at first, but with ever-increasing intensity. A roar emanating from the chasm grew unbearably loud. Stopping my ears did nothing to block it—the sound reverberated through my entire being like an explosion. It seemed as if something were stirring deep within the chasm and had launched itself toward where we stood like a geyser. Any moment it would erupt into view—and suddenly it did.

The great reptilian head swung on its long green neck, towering over its victim, who still seemed dazed, unaware of its presence. Its nostrils flared as if relishing the scent of human prey. Its cold, unblinking eyes regarded the man impassively—first one, and then the other, cocking its head like a bird. A ruff of rainbow-colored scales around its neck flared out as the head reared back to strike.

The dragon opened its mouth, revealing a long, forked tongue darting over row upon row of gleaming teeth. It seemed to be licking its lips in anticipation of its meal. But the dragon didn't strike. Instead, it breathed a column of flame over the man on the platform—white-hot flame with the incandescence of magnesium, so bright that I had to cover my eyes with my forearms and turn away. Then came the aftershocks—the cavern trembled as the dragon slipped back into the chasm.

I uncovered my eyes, shaking as if from a rush of adrenaline. Standing on the platform where the man had been was an ingot of gold the length and width of my index finger. As before, the Technician came to retrieve it, entered the elevator on the left, and was gone.

A pall had fallen over our group. Even the unflappable aliens seemed subdued by what they'd just witnessed. In a low, quiet voice, Karin continued her explanation.

"That man's entire personality structure was based on the magnified and distorted primate instincts. Nothing that he did allowed him to discover and fulfill his life purpose. From the soul's perspective, it's as if he never existed. Here, that false personality structure is destroyed or purged. What's left—the gold ingot—is the core of identity the soul plants in every human being, that individual's essence.

"In a self-actualized person this core is continually expanded until it has all but driven out the primate instincts. The ratio of essence to false personality in such a person would be exactly the opposite of what you saw here: The gold ingot would be the size and shape of the individual standing on the platform, and the dross of false personality would be no bigger than one's finger. As it happens, self-actualizing people don't undergo this sort of purification process after death, as you'll see. For them, life itself was the process whereby they turned the base metal of false personality into the gold of essence."

"Is this what would happen to a criminal?" I asked, thinking of recent newspaper articles on mass murderers.

"It depends on the type of crime," Karin replied. "The soul sees the laws that govern the citizens of your world differently than you do. Someone may be thrown in jail for subversive activities, yet it may be a part of his life purpose to point out social injustice. Or an individual may lie or steal to fulfill his life purpose, if he sees no other way to do so. From the soul's perspective, the fact that the individual knows what his life purpose is means that he'll end up on one of the higher levels. He'll still undergo rehabilitation, though. He must come to understand that there may have been other ways to achieve his goals.

"All too often, however, crime becomes its own incentive. The individual intending to use it for his own or another's good often ends up subverting his essence in the process. Murderers may have done little or nothing to develop their essences. But they're subject to a different fate after death. Not Hell, as you imagine it, but a rehabilitation process that enables them to see how they compromised the growth of those they killed.

This process allows them to plan lifetimes in which they'll further their former victims' growth in some way as compensation. The areas of the Afterdeath Zone in which this rehabilitation occurs won't be covered by our tour."

"What happens to the essence once it has been removed from this area?" a fellow tourist asked.

"It's taken by a Technician directly to Emigration, where it will be deposited in an infant body as the core of a new human life, just moments before birth.

"If there's anything besides the essence left after the purging process, however, the individual had enough sense of his life purpose to feel a vague guilt about not having fulfilled it. Even though he may not have understood the concept of life purpose, he may have felt that there was something he should have been doing, if only he knew what it was. In such a case, the essence is alloyed with a small amount of learning. This guilt is one of the consequences of not having fulfilled one's life purpose. It could be said that the lifetime was dedicated to learning about this and other such consequences.

"The individual will then be taken to the VA instead of Emigration. There he'll have the opportunity to review all the moments when people and events conspired to show him his life purpose. He'll learn to connect the consequences of not having fulfilled his life purpose with their cause. Perhaps he'll be able to recognize more easily in his next lifetime the moments when his life purpose has been revealed to him.

"People are always attracted to events and individuals who will show them who they are. But they have to be ready and willing to see. Someone who feels the guilt I just mentioned is *almost* willing to see. But the man whose false personality was just destroyed here could see nothing. He was far too caught up in inventing ways to receive the approval of others. Luckily, it's relatively rare for someone to be that oblivious to his life purpose. Few people end up on this level.

"By the way, the threat of damnation that's such a powerful part of most organized Christianity refers directly to the event you just witnessed. But as you can see, damnation doesn't involve the loss of one's soul, which is immortal, but merely the stripping away of a personality that has blocked the growth of the soul."

"Where did the dragon come from?" I wondered aloud. Once again, the group turned to look at me, their expressions full of an amused tolerance that infuriated me.

"So you saw a dragon?" Karin said carefully. "Tell us about it."

I described the dragon in great detail. To my consternation, everyone on the tour applauded when I was finished.

"Well done," Karin said. "Everyone else experienced an energy, which arose from the depths of another energy, in order to consume a third energy, and leave behind a residual energy, which a fourth energy then removed. We all thank you for this lively representation, in physical terms, of what we just witnessed. You can be sure that none of us will forget it now!"

I wasn't sure whether Karin truly meant what she said or was gently teasing me. But several of the tourists were shaking their heads in wonder. Others were communicating in barely intelligible whispers, commenting on what they'd apparently experienced as a performance. But the adjectives they used— *amazing, palpable, exciting, realistic*—made me wonder what kind of performance it was.

Karin sensed my confusion and answered my question before I asked it. "Remember that in nonphysical reality, thought manifests itself instantly as experience," she said. "Not only did you describe the dragon, your thoughts caused everyone to experience what occurred on the platform in the same quasiphysical terms that you did, as if it were happening all over again.

"As for the dragon, you drew the imagery from the Adam-and-Eve myth. You could say that this is your version of the serpent in the Garden of Eden. Remember that the serpent represents the magnified and distorted primate instincts. If an individual's personality is consumed in life by these instincts, then that process is consummated here, beneath the flaming breath of your dragon.

"Many people in your society are desperately afraid that death represents an absolute extinguishing of the personality. They have good reason to be afraid. Your society does so little to help people discover and fulfill their life purpose and so much to promote false personality that no small number of Americans may end up having to face the dragon."

22

The Masseuse

We moved toward the elevator on the right. As we waited for it to arrive, I had the feeling that more than a few of my companions were observing me surreptitiously from behind their dark glasses. Previously, they'd ignored me, as if I were the tagalong kid brother, a nuisance barely to be tolerated. Yet when the elevator arrived, they politely stood aside, allowing me to board behind our Guide, as if I'd somehow gained their respect.

It was a short ride. When the doors opened, we entered yet another cavern. It was impossible to gauge its size. Within a few feet of the elevator doors, a thick, multicolored fog arose, blocking our vision. Karin cautioned us to stand back from the fog, as if it were somehow dangerous. On a platform at the edge of the fog stood a stack of what looked like flour sacks or sand bags. A Technician loaded them onto a cart, which he then pushed past us to the elevator on the left. Before he reached the door, the middle elevator opened. A small, dark-skinned woman of indeterminate age was led to the platform by someone who may have been her Personal Attendant. Technician and Attendant greeted each other silently as they passed. The Technician boarded his elevator with the cart and disappeared behind the closing doors.

Karin addressed us. "Once again, I ask that you turn your attention to the energy field of this woman. As you can see, she's black, born as an ethnic minority on the North American continent. During her lifetime, the possibilities of advancement for people of color, especially women, were relatively limited. Yet her father had distinguished himself as a medical doctor and, although his earnings were not as great as those of a white doctor, he managed to provide a comfortable upbringing for his children. Much of his early work had been for the army during the Second World War, and a sense of military discipline prevailed in the household. The woman before you resented this and did everything she could to distance herself from it, including drawing her father's disfavor upon herself by not going to college.

"Not having a degree made it even more difficult for her to find satisfying, well-paying work. Because of her upbringing, she felt it beneath her dignity to work for wages that were impossible to live on. Yet she had no trouble justifying prostitution as a means of supplementing her income, mostly because it went against the staunch Baptist faith of her father. She soon discovered that most of her clients felt lonely, unloved, and unlovable. She tried to provide them with more than mere sexual release—an open heart, a listening ear, a hint of genuine love.

"Eventually, she got married to a construction worker— once again to spite her father, who by now had practically disowned her. She had three children. Her husband was a drinker and womanizer. After six years of trying to persuade herself that she could change him, she decided that she deserved better. Her husband couldn't be depended on to provide child support, so after her divorce she was faced with the frightening prospect of having to raise her children on little or no money. Prostitution, she felt, was no longer a viable option, since she wanted to create a morally respectable atmosphere within which to bring up her children. She hit upon the idea of massage as a possible livelihood.

"Carefully balancing her welfare check against money made by selling marijuana to her friends, she managed to get herself certified as a massage therapist—essential, she believed, to distinguish herself from the prostitutes who advertised themselves as masseuses. As her children became older and entered public school, her practice thrived. Once again, she realized that what she was offering was an opportunity for her clients to feel loved.

"She began to draw and paint in her spare time. Unfortunately, exploration of her creativity was tied to marijuana use. She eventually came to believe that without pot it would be impossible to produce work of any lasting interest or value. But she had also discovered three aspects of her life purpose—as healer, mother, and artist—and had begun to fulfill them."

A movement within the swirls of fog beyond the platform caught my attention, distracting me for a moment from Karin's monologue. Something was inching itself toward the black woman who stood before us. As it approached, I began to realize that what I thought was swirling fog was actually layer upon layer of spider web, hanging thick as gauze from the ceiling of the cavern and trembling beneath what seemed at first to be a slight breeze, but which I eventually understood to be the movements of an enormous spider.

Apparently unaware of the spider's approach, Karin continued her summary of the woman's life.

"She was a proud woman—this much she inherited from her father, along with his nasty temper. She became interested in holistic health and attached herself to a holistic clinic as resident masseuse. The negative attitude of the medical establishment toward holistic health irritated her, and became a focus for the anger she had felt toward her father when growing up.

"Gradually, her career became subverted by her desire to find some respect in the eyes of the medical establishment—i.e., her father. The clinic by this time had begun to specialize in alternative treatments for people infected with the AIDS virus, with some small success in extending their lives. She took every opportunity to boast of this success, sometimes exaggerating it in such a way that she raised false hopes in the clinic's patients. Word got around to the patients' doctors, who eventually called in the American Medical Association.

"The AMA found a way to shut the clinic down. No one ended up in jail, but our masseuse was left feeling a powerful self-righteous anger at how men in general, and doctors in particular, had made it impossible for her to do the healing work she was born to do. She began to take her anger out on her children, restricting their freedom in order to regain the sense of control over her life that she felt men and the medical establishment had taken away. She punished her children unduly harshly whenever they tested her. In short, she became every bit as militaristic as her father had been—and couldn't bear seeing this in herself.

"Her marijuana use increased and her massage business began to fall off. She was too depressed to do her art work. A series of relationships with controlling and abusive men—her father over and over—had left deep emotional scars. One of them introduced her to crack, which she embraced as the only source of joy in her life. Back on welfare, she was unable to maintain her drug habit and take care of her children. Her parents tried to get her into a drug rehabilitation program. When this didn't work, they arranged for a state agency to remove the children from her care and place them in foster homes.

"Love of her children could perhaps have jolted her out of her drug-induced haze and encouraged her to straighten out her life. Instead, it became one more reason to hate her father, the medical establishment, the government, and a world in which men had all the power. Within weeks of the departure of her children, while under the influence of drugs, she fell down the stairs to her second-floor apartment, suffered a severe concussion, and died several days later in the hospital, without gaining consciousness. She was forty-three years old."

As our Guide spoke, the spider inched onto the platform. It towered above the woman standing there, who seemed not to see it. The spider crawled around and around her, spinning a cocoon-like web. Gradually, the woman's features disappeared. When all that could be seen of her was the dim outline of a female body beneath the web, the spider gently pushed her over on her side and dragged her deeper into the cavern.

Climbing through the tangle of its web, the spider attached a new line to the ceiling of the cavern and dangled the freshly wrapped woman there. Then it anchored the cocoon to the floor with three thick cables of webbing, each of which glowed a different color: green, red, and royal blue. I could see countless other cocoons dangling in the same way, their cables also colored, but more dimly—barely visible behind the foglike veils of webbing that permeated the cave.

"What differentiates this level from the previous one," Karin continued, "is that the individuals who are brought here had an awareness of their life purpose while alive, and may even have made attempts to fulfill it. Yet the magnified and distorted primate instincts were strong enough to prevent self-actualization from taking place. Just as on the previous level, the resulting distortions of personality must be purged."

I noticed that one of the tourists seemed to be looking at me intently. He had edged his way through the group to stand slightly behind me so that I had to look over my shoulder to see him. Shifting from one heavily booted foot to another, he seemed undecided about whether or not to say something to me. Finally, it came out, his thoughts timidly brushing mine with the sweetness of a gentle breeze.

"Could you do it again?" he asked, bashful as a child. "You know, the dragon." The outline of the creature I had seen on the previous level seemed to flit for a moment through the veils of webbing, like a film projected on a scrim. I looked at our guide, who nodded assent.

"Well, it's not exactly a dragon that I see here," I began, hoping not to disappoint him. I described the spider with its eight jewel-like eyes and jointed legs, its bulbous black body as big as mine, a yellow hourglass shape on the underside. I pointed out the layers of webbing, surprised at how closely everyone listened to me, since the spider's actions as it wrapped the black woman like a mummy and hung her from the ceiling were relatively undramatic.

"What's the spider doing now?" someone asked. I scanned the cavern until I found it.

"Apparently, it's making its rounds. I see it moving from one cocoon to another, testing the lines that hold them up. Now it has come to a cocoon in which the cables have lost their color. As it tugs at the cables, they break. It then gnaws through the line that attaches the cocoon to the ceiling. The cocoon drops with a soft thud. The spider climbs down to the cave floor and attaches a new line to the cocoon, dragging it over here and leaving it near the elevators. This one must have been a child, it's so small—about half the size of a grown man."

When I was finished, I felt as if I were surrounded by wide-eyed children, awe-struck by the wonders of storytelling. Karin thanked me for my graphic portrayal of the purging process and proceeded to explain it.

"The layers of webbing which you just saw represent the illusions spun by the magnified and distorted primate instincts as rationales for not fulfilling one's life purpose. An important part of the purging process is for recently dead individuals to be immersed in these illusions until they recognize them for what they are. This is why you saw the spider spin a cocoon around the woman we've been considering.

"The three colored cables represent the primate instincts: green for survival, red for sexuality, and royal blue for the social instinct. Gradually, these cables will drain away all aspects of the false personality based on them. The brightness of the cable indicates how much work needs to be done. As you can see, there are individuals in all stages of processing spread throughout the cavern—from this new arrival," she pointed to where the black woman's cocoon hung, "to those who've finished," she indicated the place where the spider had deposited the child's cocoon. "Eventually, a Technician will come by and pick up the cocoons of those who are finished, as you saw earlier."

As Karin spoke, I suddenly remembered the pile of what I had thought were flour sacks. They were all so small. Could all of them have been children?

Karin answered my question as if I'd asked it aloud.

"The size of the cocoons bears no relation to the size of the individual's physical body at time of death. Rather, it indicates the extent to which that individual had achieved self-actualization in the course of his or her lifetime. In this way, you can perceive the relation of essential characteristics to false personality.

"Individuals achieve this level only if *some* of their essential qualities have been developed. The whole personality is not extinguished, as in the previous level. But whatever has been distorted by survival, sexual, or social issues will most certainly be destroyed."

"What happens to the cocoons once they've been removed from this level?" I asked.

"They'll be taken upstairs to the VA. There the individuals inside them will undergo the process of purging each moment of their lives of any powerful negative emotions which may have affected them."

23

Mrs. Sackler

Once again we filed into the elevator on the right. When the doors opened, we found ourselves inside what seemed like a vast factory whose walls and ceiling were identical with those of the cave. The factory seemed to be divided into three sections. To our left were row upon row of industrial-sized washing machines. Dozens of Technicians were tossing large duffle bags full of laundry into the machines. Others were removing similar loads and carting them to some other section of the factory. A huge group of men of all ages and physical types sat with a few women in a nearby waiting area. Were they the owners of the clothes that were being laundered?

To our left was a series of bays like those in the repair shop of an automobile dealership. Here the Technicians busied themselves with examining the undercarriage, wheels, and engines of hundreds of different makes of cars. The center of the factory was filled with banks of high-tech machinery whose function I couldn't fathom. The Technicians who manned this machinery were preoccupied with pressing buttons and examining multicolored screens.

Before Karin could begin her explanation of what went on at this level, the central elevator opened and two figures emerged. One was a female Attendant. I couldn't tell whether she was young or old—not because she had one of those faces that can be guessed ten years on either side of its owner's actual age, but because she seemed quite literally to have two faces—two bodies, in fact, one superimposed on the other.

The younger of the two faces seemed to be that of a beautiful, but somewhat melancholy, woman in her late twenties, with long brown hair and large, sad, brown eyes. Her features were pale but finely sculpted. Her jaw had a tomboyish set. She was dressed in jeans, a red-and-black plaid shirt, and leather riding boots.

The older face was round and puffy—quite unlike the other, which was long and gaunt. Gray hair in tight curls surrounded this face. The eyes were blue rather than brown and held a kindly, somewhat mirthful expression. They were surrounded by the soft creases that years of smiles and laughter leave behind. And indeed the older face was smiling. This woman seemed to be about sixty years old. She was noticeably shorter than her younger counterpart, quite a bit heavier, and wore a flowery spring dress that reached to her knees, as well as pumps with low heels.

At first, I thought that perhaps I was seeing older and younger versions of the same person. After all, in Otherwhere, time is experienced very differently than it is on Earth. But it was unimaginable to me how the younger woman could have aged in exactly that way. Finally, it was the difference in the color of the eyes between the two faces that convinced me I was seeing two people who were somehow occupying the same space.

Behind the two-faced woman tottered a very much older lady. She walked quite slowly, with a cane in her right hand and her long-strapped pocketbook dangling from her left. She was a bit stooped, so the pocketbook nearly dragged on the ground. Her permed hair was tinted slightly blue. She wore a pillbox hat and her wrinkled face was caked with makeup, as if she'd tried to fill up its tiny rifts and valleys with enough powder to make her complexion completely smooth. On top of the powder she'd painted two bright red circles, so perfectly round that she might have been a marionette. Her thin lips were lavishly done up in a different red, but seemed a little off center. As she passed our group, she stopped to rest, looking directly at us through thick-lensed glasses.

"That's my daughter-in-law, Betsy Mae," she cackled in a southern accent, pointing to the two-faced woman with her cane. "She says we're going to get an adjustment. My goodness, it's been years since I've been to one of those bonecrackers. Can't say that I enjoy it, but I always feel better afterwards. And after that we're going to pick up my car at the shop. I haven't been able to drive for years—not since I broke my hip, you know. But I don't mind. Betsy Mae takes me everywhere now—not like those ungrateful daughters of mine!"

"Come along, Eunice," the two-faced woman said, taking her by the arm. "We don't want to keep the doctors waiting, now, do we?"

"I should say not," Eunice replied pleasantly. "I'm sure they have more important things to do than wait on the likes of me."

Eunice and Betsy Mae shuffled off in the direction of the high-tech machinery, leaving behind more than one quizzically arched eyebrow among the members of our group. We turned to face our Guide, brimming with questions. But she held her right index finger to her lips in the age-old gesture to remain silent and motioned us to follow.

We trailed Eunice and Betsy Mae, keeping enough distance between ourselves and them that we wouldn't be noticed. As they approached the nearest bank of machines, a Technician in a lab coat greeted them. He and Betsy Mae consulted one another for a moment while Eunice, oblivious to the fact that the conversation concerned her, asked loudly if the handsome young gentleman was married.

"Mrs. Sackler," the Technician replied patiently, "you realize that you're dead, don't you?"

"That's what they keep telling me," Eunice said agreeably. "It does take some getting used to, you know. I had the shock of my life when Henry came to get me at the hospital. He died twenty years ago of a heart attack, and my goodness did he look young! Almost like our wedding day. But what I don't understand is why Betsy Mae came along. Last I saw of her she was as healthy as they come. Could lose a few pounds, you know— but then she's always been fond of sweets. I just wonder what my son Jake is going to do without her, not to mention my poor grandchildren.

"But Mrs. Sackler, this isn't Betsy Mae. This is your Personal Attendant, Eva."

"Well she looks like Betsy Mae to me," Eunice said, squinting at her companion, "at least most of the time."

"Eunice," said Eva, "I can assure you that Betsy Mae is alive and well, and doing a respectable job of looking after your grandchildren, who are very nearly adults themselves by now. You've merely assumed that I'm Betsy Mae because of the similar functions we fulfill in your life. Just as she was such a help in getting you from one place to another during your last years, so am I helping you find your way around the Afterdeath Zone."

Eunice pondered her Attendant's words. "I suppose you're right," she said hesitantly. "I keep seeing that attractive young woman peek through. You weren't putting on a masquerade just to humor me, now, were you?"

"Not at all, Eunice. We're here to help you strip away any illusions that may have been a part of your life on Earth. Why would we want to replace them with others?"

"You see, Mrs. Sackler," the Technician broke in, "what you think about here in the Afterdeath Zone has an immediately perceivable impact on what you experience. If you think you're seeing Betsy Mae, that's your reality until you think something else."

The old woman peered intently at her companion, struggling hard to understand. She set her jaw in what seemed like a supreme effort of will. Gradually, the kindly face of middle-aged Betsy Mae dissolved and was replaced by that of melancholy Eva.

"Well done," said Eva. "You see, it was when I told you we had an appointment to keep that you began to see me as Betsy Mae."

"Bless her heart," Eunice said. "Her memory for that sort of thing always was better than mine. Well now, what about this adjustment you've been telling me about?"

Eva and the Technician glanced at each other, as if unsure of how to proceed.

"You realize of course," Eva began tentatively, "that I wasn't referring to a chiropractic adjustment. That was *your* interpretation of what I told you. I just hope you won't think I deceived you when you learn what's really involved."

"Well," said Eunice, "I've already learned that I can't trust my eyes here. I suppose I shouldn't be surprised that the same is true of my ears!"

"Plucky, isn't she," the Technician said to Eva, beaming. "Let me do the honors." He turned back to Eunice. "Mrs. Sackler," he began politely, "I hope you'll forgive me if some of what I have to say seems shocking. But the truth is that Calvary Baptist Church did little to prepare you for the Afterlife, despite your minister's good intentions."

"Doesn't surprise me," Eunice said. "He always did talk more about Hell than Heaven—if that's where this is." She eyed the machinery doubtfully.

"Your confusion is certainly understandable," the Technician continued. "Actually, where you are now is neither Heaven nor Hell. You could call this the *Redemption Zone*, if you wish. Its purpose is to purge you of, or redeem you from, any illusions you may have held while you were alive.

"This level of the Redemption Zone is where most good Christian folk such as yourself end up. Even the best of intentions to live a morally upright life can run afoul of several unfortunate weaknesses in the human character: lust, fear, and control. Now don't get me wrong. These are not sins in the sense that you'll be forever damned for allowing them to influence your thoughts or actions. But they do interfere with the soul's plans for your growth. Here in the Afterdeath Zone, you have an opportunity to review your life and see to what degree you remained true to or deviated from the soul's plans. But you'll be unable to accomplish this task without first stripping away the illusions that prevented you from seeing things from the soul's perspective while you were alive.

"Now if you'll look to your left, you'll see a bank of washing machines. That's the area where illusions based on lust are cleaned out. Those bundles of what look like soiled clothing are actually lust-distorted perspectives on life, oneself, and all persons one has been attracted to or romantically involved with—individuals who were perceived not as people but as sexual objects. Clothes were invented to protect people from this kind of lust, which is why you see washing machines in that area. The clothes aren't real clothes, but rather represent the soiled dignity of every individual one has perceived in a lustful way.

"The people at this level who need to free themselves from lust-distorted perspectives on life must go back through their memories of people soiled in this way and restore to them what lust had suppressed—the dignity of having a soul. Mostly men over there, as you can see.

"You managed to keep your own sexuality in proper perspective, and so we won't be visiting that area while you're here."

"I should say not," Eunice exclaimed, pursing her lips.

"To your left you'll see what looks like an auto repair shop. The cars in the mechanics' bays symbolize one's motivation. The Technicians over there are concerned with the extent to which one's motivation derived from a desire to gain control over other people. Trying to control others is terribly inefficient. It wastes energy in much the same way as a car that needs a tune-up."

"Wait a minute," Eunice began suspiciously. "Didn't you tell me, Betsy Mae—I mean Eva—that we were going to pick up my car at the shop?"

"Yes, Eunice. I'm afraid you haven't been entirely free of the motivation to control other people's lives."

"Like who?" said Eunice, suddenly petulant.

"Like Betsy Mae," Eva replied. "When your daughters moved out of town and you had to give up driving, you began working on Betsy Mae. You weren't above hinting about ungrateful daughters and your will for her benefit, and even promised her antiques and jewelry from your home, 'in gratitude for all you've done for me,' as you told her every time she helped you out."

Eunice's jaw quivered, as she tried to find some way to defend herself. "But who is there to help an old woman if her children abandon her?" she said defiantly.

"Now, Eunice. Your daughters didn't abandon you. Their husbands simply found jobs that took them elsewhere or their companies transferred them to other locations. Would you have wanted your daughters to choose you over their husbands? Would you have wanted to break up their marriages?"

"Of course not. I always wanted them to be happy."

"And after they moved, they never phoned, wrote, or visited, right?"

"That's not true at all! I saw each one, and all my grandchildren, at least once a year—sometimes twice if they asked me to come see them."

"So what's your definition of abandonment?"

"No one to take care of me in my old age. My son is a very busy man, you see. Vice president of his company. I certainly couldn't expect *him* to help me. So naturally I turned to his wife. Who wouldn't, under the circumstances?"

"Who you turned to is not the point. It's how you did it that's the problem. You wheedled and threatened and whined and tempted. You invented health difficulties because you believed that Betsy Mae would be more willing to take you shopping if you had a doctor's appointment as well. And you were always so depressed when you came out of the office that of course she *had* to do something nice to cheer you up, such as take you to lunch at a fine restaurant. It became a game— how many ways could you get another half an hour out of Betsy Mae."

"But I was lonely. It was frightening sometimes to be in that big house all day by myself."

"Didn't Betsy Mae and her husband offer to add an apartment onto their house so you could be right there with them any time that you needed something?"

"Yes, but I would never want to impose upon them that way. They had their own lives to lead, after all."

"Do you mean to tell me that calling Betsy Mae to say you were feeling dizzy and seeing spots in front of your eyes so she would take you shopping after you went to the doctor wasn't an imposition?"

"What am I supposed to say?" Eunice retorted angrily. "I'm starting to feel as if I'm on trial."

"I'm not trying to make you uncomfortable, Eunice. I'm merely trying to lead you to an important realization. Betsy Mae truly loved you and would have done anything you asked—if you had simply asked."

"That wasn't *my* impression. It seemed to me that she never stopped thinking about what a burden I was. I don't want to remember how many times I caught her rolling her eyes when I tried to explain what I wanted her to do. But she never complained—at least not to me. It wasn't hard, though, to imagine what she was saying to Jake all that time."

"Betsy Mae was no fool. She knew perfectly well that she was being manipulated. If you sensed any resentment from her, it was because of your attempts to control her life, not because she didn't love you."

Eunice began to sniffle. She reached into her pocketbook and took out a lace handkerchief, dabbing under her glasses. It was too late. The tears had already begun to smear the perfect circles of rouge on her cheeks. "You just don't know what it's like," she said, blowing her nose, "to be alone for so many years in such a big house."

"Eunice, your tears won't do any good here. We know life is hard. Everyone's got a reason to feel sorry for herself—sometimes more than one. The important thing is for you to realize that you could have made better use of your time, creativity, and energy than to lavish it on turning Betsy Mae into a personal slave."

Eunice stopped crying, shocked into silence.

"You let most of the last twenty years of your life be dominated by fear of loneliness and a desire to control Betsy Mae—not to mention your daughters, when you saw them. From the soul's perspective, that's a distortion of the way things should be. Our job is to point out that distortion and help you free yourself from it. Otherwise, you'll carry it with you into your next life."

"Next life? What do you mean? Reverend Peterson never said anything about coming back."

"I don't imagine he did. The idea of reincarnation is unpopular among Christians. It takes the punch out of eternal damnation, which makes it harder to keep the flock faithful. But even Christians have to go back. Almost everyone does. You go back until you get it right—which, among other things, means not wasting your energy on trying to control people."

Eunice was having a hard time taking in what Eva had said. She began to sway, muttering that she felt faint.

"Eunice," Eva said sternly. "I'm not Betsy Mae. You can hold your breath until you turn blue if you want, but that won't stop me from telling you what you need to know."

Eunice straightened up immediately, looking abashed and somewhat confused.

"That's better," Eva said mildly. "Besides, you don't really have a body here, so you can't make yourself sick."

"Mrs. Sackler," the Technician broke in. "If you'll excuse the interruption, I have something to say that might clarify things. Not about reincarnation. That's up to Eva to explain. But you see, when your husband died, you began to fear for your own survival. Not in financial terms, since he had left you with enough money to make your last years comfortable, even if you hadn't been as healthy as you were right up until the end. Rather, you were afraid for your survival in emotional terms, afraid of loneliness. That fear dominated your thoughts and led to attempts to control your daughter-in-law.

"Lust, fear, and control are often closely interrelated. Problems in one area can soon lead to problems in another. Perhaps you'll better understand how you let your life be dominated by the desire to control others if we address the fear of loneliness that was behind it first. That's the purpose of this bank of machines behind us.

"Fear is like a cancer that spreads through the mind and body and distorts how you view your life and how you make decisions. Fear is far more powerful and pervasive than lust or control. That's why most of this part of the Redemption Zone is taken up with equipment designed to reduce and release fear. There are so many types of fear, and they are often so intertwined with one another, that we need to monitor its release very carefully. Otherwise, we might damage the underlying belief structure we're trying to purge.

"In physical reality, fear for one's survival can be either the greatest block to one's growth, or, if used creatively, can become the greatest impetus behind one's growth. We often have to make subtle distinctions between fears in order to differentiate between those which have obstructed growth and those which have promoted it.

"The adjustment Eva told you about involves getting something like a CAT scan to see where fear has been stored in your belief system. We'll then apply a kind of radiation treatment to the belief system, bombarding it with the pure energy of love. That energy always causes fears that have obstructed one's growth to wither and die, leaving those which have promoted growth intact. After this adjustment, we'll take you over to the mechanics, who will show you exactly how your motivation was affected by the desire to control others. Once you're free of distortions in both areas, your Attendant will show you to the zone where the next phase of learning about the life you've just completed will take place.

"Are you ready to undergo the treatment?"

"I think so, yes," Eunice said between sniffles. "But I must look a mess. I hope the doctors won't mind."

"How would you like to look for the doctors, Eunice?" Eva said patiently.

"Well, I'm sure my makeup has smeared, and I would like to check my lipstick," Eunice said, digging around in her pocketbook.

Still unnoticed, our group smiled at each other as we realized what Eva was up to. As Eunice searched for her compact, her makeup remade itself exactly as she had imagined it. When she looked into the mirror, perplexed, Eva put her arm around her tenderly and whispered something in her ear.

"I just can't get used to it," Eunice muttered, shaking her head. Eva turned her gently toward the bank of machines, arm still around her. The Technician pointed the way, and the two of them vanished behind rows of monitors.

"Any questions?" Karin asked when Eunice and Eva were out of earshot. Everyone agreed that our eavesdropping had provided an excellent overview of the third level of the Redemption Zone. Still, there was one thing that bothered me.

"The guy in the lab coat said that fear can be one of the primary motivating factors behind a person's growth. I always thought that fear prevented growth—as, for example, when somebody's afraid to undertake a new project of some sort."

"It's certainly true that fear can prevent growth," Karin began. "Keep in mind that the Technician was referring specifically to fear for one's survival. The soul is the source of the life force that keeps every individual on Earth alive. When someone refuses to undertake a lesson that the soul requires of her, the amount of life force available to her diminishes. That makes her more susceptible to illness. If she persists in refusing to learn what the soul requires of her, she may have so little life force available to her that she'll be unable to fend off an illness serious enough that she could die from it.

"As she begins to realize that fact, she may be willing to change her life. If she allows herself to learn the lesson the soul requires of her, then her life force will return. She'll be healed of her illness. In such an instance, positive growth came from fear for one's survival. While fear for one's survival can distort her perspective on reality, as we saw with Eunice's fear of loneliness, the soul can equally well use it to encourage growth.

"Most people experience some degree of resistance to the lessons that the soul requires of them at some point in their lives. Various signals will let them know that the amount of life force available to them is diminishing. If the resistance is slight, they may experience distraction, restlessness, or boredom. If it's of average strength, they'll experience melancholy, depression, or neurotic obsessiveness. If the resistance is extreme, they'll experience colds, flu, chronic, or terminal illness. If it's total, they may experience death.

"In a certain sense, spiritual growth is a matter of giving up resistance. Resistance causes one to grow in misery and suffering. Letting go of resistance allows one to grow in joy and celebration. Only by letting go of resistance can one move beyond the level of spiritual evolution in which growth is determined by fear for one's physical well-being.

"It's possible to grow simply for the satisfaction of becoming who one truly is. Unfortunately, this doesn't happen very often. And you certainly won't find such persons at this level of the Redemption Zone. They'll have cleaned up illusions based on lust, fear, and control on their own, while alive."

24

The Choreographer

When the elevator doors opened on the next level, I was surprised to find that we were in what looked like a ruined airport terminal. Through a wall of windows, I could see an empty air-traffic control tower off in the distance, rising almost to the top of the high cave ceiling. Three runways crisscrossed the floor of the cave between the terminal and the tower, forming a triangular pattern. No one was manning the ticket counters. The conveyor belts in the baggage claim area were still running, though empty of luggage. The television monitors were on, but showed no arrivals or departures.

The terminal seemed unoccupied but for one middle-aged man sitting dejectedly on the floor near a window, surrounded by shards of broken glass. He seemed to be intent on fitting these shards back together, as if they were pieces of a jigsaw puzzle.

Our group approached him, but the man didn't look up. So absorbed was he in the project of fitting the pieces of glass together that we might as well have been invisible.

"Don't worry," our guide said. "He won't hear us, even if we talk about what he's doing. If he were alive, one could say that he's in an altered state of consciousness something like a hypnotic trance. Trance is simply an intense focus of attention on some task. In Otherwhere, this kind of focus can exclude all possible distractions—a state rarely achievable while one's alive."

On closer inspection, I could see that the man was lean and muscular, quite well-developed for someone who seemed to be approaching the age of fifty. His longish dark hair was streaked with gray. He had an unusual face, neither handsome nor ugly, but striking—monolithic in its determination. His brown eyes had a depth and clarity that I've rarely seen, except in highly spiritual people. His features reminded me of a portrait I'd once seen of the French Romantic composer Hector Berlioz. Despite his apparent physical strength, the man's shoulders were slumped, as if he were suffering from a deep grief.

A small movement on the floor caught my eye. At first I thought that I'd seen an insect moving across one of the glass fragments. But on closer inspection, I discovered that the movement seemed to be occurring *within* the piece of glass. I bent over to look more closely, startled to find that the piece of glass contained a miniature holographic drama. A man and woman seemed to be having an argument, even though their mouths never moved. The argument was being carried out in purely physical terms—not as a fight, but by means of a highly stylized set of gestures. When the man swept the woman into his arms and carried her from one side of the stage to the other, her legs made wild yet graceful motions of protest in the air. I realized that I was watching a dance.

In a nearby fragment, a different drama was being enacted: young men in sailor suits dragged heavy ropes across a stage as a beautiful ballerina ran from one to another, flirting outrageously, trying to distract them from their work. In a third fragment, I saw a younger version of the dejected man performing agile acrobatics in the costume of a troubadour—eager to please, yet reviled by his audience of peasants, spurned by the noblewoman he loved, and finally hanging himself in despair.

Puzzled, I looked up at Karin, who was smiling. "Yes," she said. "The man before you was a choreographer. Not a famous one, but relatively well-known in the dance circles of the large city in which he lived. He died of AIDS. What you see before you are his memories of every dance he choreographed during his lifetime, as well as ideas for dances that were never realized, fragments executed only in his mind.

"As you can see, this area of the Redemption Zone gets little use. Most people end up on one of the earlier levels, especially the previous one.

"It used to be that painters, sculptors, poets, novelists, playwrights, actors, composers, performers, choreographers, and dancers saw their respective art forms as a kind of spiritual vocation. They worked hard to perfect their technique in the service of God or some higher power, whatever they may have chosen to call it—the soul, the muse, an angel, nature, the universe, or what have you. Creativity became for them a kind of religion.

"They learned that in order to create anything of lasting value they had to master lust, fear, and control. Through their art, they struggled with these and other emotions, seeking to discover joy, or purge themselves of melancholy or anger. They sought to uplift their own spirits and those of others through catharsis or celebration. They pointed out the strengths and weaknesses of humanity, probed the depths of human suffering, criticized the evils of society—all with an eye toward educating and enlightening the populace.

"Art would become their teacher, freeing them from the religious dogmas and social conventions of their times, or helping them to understand the true emotional or spiritual meaning behind scenes from the Bible or the rituals of the church. It could be said that the greatest artists took over the role of being God's messengers, after the church declared that Jesus was the last of the Biblical prophets.

"Times have changed. Art is no longer seen as a vocation, but as a business. There's nothing wrong with making money as an artist. But nowadays people seem to put more energy into marketing their work or producing what will sell, either to the masses or to the boards who disseminate grant money, than into developing themselves or their message.

"Competition for jobs and opportunities to show or publish one's work have made it almost impossible to nurture a relationship with the soul long enough for one to find his or her unique contribution to the arts and to humanity. Style is everything, content almost nothing. 'God is dead', the philosophers say—and when the arts are linked with growth, it's usually in psychological rather than spiritual terms. The word *soul* is anathema in intellectual circles. And artists who call themselves religious or spiritual are, more often than not, repeating messages the Masters said better, or that are no longer relevant, or they are dressing up their images in the latest new-age fashions.

"Occasionally, an artist stumbles on the soul's master plan for his growth and begins to realize it through his art, ignoring the critics, and eventually saying something that quenches the spiritual thirst of his audience. He may even become widely known because the depth behind his work is glaringly apparent when measured against the glitz and glitter of that of his peers.

"If he can remain true to himself, letting go of the fear of survival that would make him sensitive to the pressure of critics or of his audience to deviate from his chosen course into repeating himself or pandering to the masses, if he can avoid the temptation to use his fame to take advantage of others or to seduce his fans, then he has no need to spend any time at all in these lower levels of the Redemption Zone. His exemplary life *is* his redemption.

"It does sometimes happen, however, that an artist will have become a messenger of God, as it were, while falling prey to one or more of the magnified and distorted primate instincts. Yet everything he needs to know about his relationship to the soul or to God is contained within his work. He'll end up on this level, like the choreographer before you.

"This is the only one of the Redemption Zone's lower levels in which the individual needs no assistance in freeing himself of the illusions fostered by lust, fear, and control. He can't help but express his struggle with these illusions in his art. Here he'll have the opportunity to consider the entirety of his output, in order to better understand what he was learning, in spiritual terms, from the production of each work. When this process is complete, he'll be free of the illusions that distracted him from the fulfillment of his life purpose. He can then move on to other lessons within the Afterdeath Zone.

"The man before you had reached an age when it became necessary for him to consider the possibility of retiring from active performing—though not, of course, from choreographing. He'd put so much of himself into his dance that the thought of no longer performing frightened him. He would have to face the yearning for a lifelong companion that he had ignored throughout most of his career and sublimated through overwork. He was afraid that no one wanted him because, though lean and muscular, he did not have the pretty-boy face that he believed was the only thing that would make him attractive to another gay man.

"Actually, no one was interested in becoming his companion, not because he was unattractive, but because in relationships he tended to act out the role of the 'great artist,' as he conceived it—violent mood swings, melodramatic confrontations, nervous prostration, excessive world-weariness. In short, he viewed his vocation as artist in the most Romantic of terms, which is to say that he believed he had to be neurotic in order to create great art.

"He exhausted potential lovers with his intensity, acquired a reputation for being imbalanced and difficult, and was avoided by anyone he found attractive. This, of course, was in keeping with his tragic view of life, and his belief that love and happiness would eviscerate his art.

"As he grew older, he began to equate age with ugliness, which meant that, in his mind, each year that passed without his settling down with a lover considerably reduced his chances of ever being able to do so. He became obsessed with proving his attractiveness by bedding as many young men as he could find—outside of the dance community, and generally from poverty-stricken Black and Latino families. He thought that if he couldn't find an intellectual or artistic peer, perhaps he could rescue a young man from the slums and give him culture, a richer and more varied lifestyle, in return for companionship. What he was really trying to do was buy affection.

"None of these relationships lasted very long. The young men he encouraged to enact the 'great artist drama' with him didn't understand that cultural archetype, and ended up taking as much emotional abuse from him as they ever had from their often difficult families. Finally, he would throw them out on the street. They would be thoroughly disoriented and confused, unable to return home now that their homosexuality was known to their families. More than one of them became hustlers, for lack of other alternatives—and in hopes of finding another seemingly wealthy patron who would take them back off the streets.

"It was through an attempted reconciliation with one of these young men that the choreographer contracted AIDS. By this time, he'd wasted so much energy on the illusions caused by fear of loneliness, sexual desperation, and his attempts to reshape and therefore control the lives of his 'charges,' as he thought of them, that very little was left over for his art. Ironically, had he actually finished some of the dances he imagined, he may have come to realize the damage that the 'great artist drama' was doing to his life and could perhaps have freed himself from it, not to mention the 'age equals ugliness' belief."

"Will only artistic types end up at this level?" one of the tourists asked.

"That depends," Karin responded. "It's part of most people's master plans for them to develop the human capacity for creativity in some way. The soul would be just as happy for them to put that energy into cooking or carpentry as into any of the fine arts. The problem is that only art that bears a message, art that is more than an expression of creativity or of the individual's feelings or sensual experiences, can lead him beyond the social or religious conventions of his times. It's that freedom from convention that causes people to end up at this level.

"Artists are more likely to free themselves of convention than nonartists, although there are established conventions of bohemian behavior within the art world that can also limit the soul's growth. The key to ending up on this level is understanding how to battle and eventually dismantle the illusions based on lust, fear, and control. An artist may achieve this understanding unconsciously, through the practice of his art. He'll end up here, even if he's applied next to nothing of what he understands to his own life. Why?

"Because he doesn't need any help, once here, in seeing how he should have applied to his life what he understood unconsciously through his art. A deeply religious person who has tried to live a morally upstanding life within the dogmas of the church will most likely end up on the previous level—because the church never taught him how to dismantle some of these illusions.

"Being a slave to convention indicates that someone is desperately afraid of being ostracized for being different. Chances are that this fear will distort his understanding of and willingness to live from his life purpose.

"Occasionally, we'll get a philosopher, a student of comparative religion or mythology, or a psychologist at this level, but only if his study of any of these disciplines has moved him beyond convention and dogma. Once again, if the understandings are in place, it doesn't matter how successful he may have been in freeing himself from lust, fear, and control—he'll end up here, because he won't need any help applying what he learned to the process of dismantling his illusions in these areas.

"It's also possible that an individual might end up here if he has been exposed to spiritual teachings with an extraordinarily high truth content. Some of the material that has been channeled through mediums of the nineteenth and twentieth centuries has the potential to enlighten people about the need to free themselves from lust, fear, and control, and may even provide techniques of doing so.

"If an individual has succeeded in dismantling at least some of his illusions through the application of this material while he was alive, he may find himself at the previous level of the Redemption Zone. If he has been so successful that by inference, and upon close consideration of his life, he can easily see here in the Redemption Zone what he was unable to see on Earth, then he'll end up on the current level. It's not necessary to be an artist to end up here. The only requirement is that most of one's illusions based on lust, fear, and control were dismantled while he was still alive."

I had a question about the choreographer—I wondered why he ended up on this level, since it seemed to me that he had done a better job of mastering his capacity for illusion earlier in his life, when he absorbed himself totally in his work, than toward the end.

"Your question seems fairly straightforward," Karin replied. "However, it's debatable whether he was cleaner of illusion when he was younger than when he died. The 'great artist drama' was a compensation for his fear of inadequacy, a survival-inspired fear. Yet this fear contributed to his growth, since it caused him to believe in himself enough that he was willing to work as hard as he could to make his desire to become a great artist come true.

"The 'great artist drama' was also related to the fear of being unlovable, another survival-based fear. While it gave him the strength to become different from others, the necessary first step in discovering and fulfilling one's life purpose, it also made him so neurotic that he did, in fact, become unlovable.

"Here we have an example of intertwined fears, some of which contributed to, and others of which obstructed, growth. At this level the individual will free himself only of those fears that obstruct growth. In other areas of the Afterdeath Zone, he'll have opportunities to look into the question of whether his belief system allowed for the most efficacious use of his time and energy. It's not at all uncommon for a belief system that has its uses earlier in one's life—just as the choreographer's adopting the one associated with the 'great artist drama' convinced him that he could and should master the art of dance—to become destructive if it's sustained indefinitely.

"There have been instances in which someone had managed to free himself from most of the illusions inspired by the magnified and distorted primate instincts early in life and was overcome by one or more of them later on. Such a person would still end up on the present level of the Redemption Zone. Anything learned while one is alive advances the soul's growth, even if it seems to have been forgotten at some point."

I was confused. It seemed completely arbitrary which level of the Redemption Zone someone ended up on. Artists seemed to be given preferential treatment over good people who had tried to live righteously. I just couldn't accept that a kind and self-effacing woman like my grandmother might end up on the previous level, while someone like Picasso, who was notoriously brutish with women, could end up on the present one. Karin answered my question before I could put it into words.

"First of all, these levels aren't hierarchical in the way you think. It's not better to be on one level than another, not even the lowest. Each level indicates that the individual has a different set of lessons to learn in the Afterdeath Zone. From the soul's perspective, all lessons are equal in their need to be learned. Second, the amount of illusion one experiences has nothing to do with the level one ends up on. Placement is determined entirely on the basis of how much someone has realized the soul's master plan for his growth: at the lowest level, next to nothing; at the one we're on now, almost all of it.

"The highest level of the Redemption Zone is the City of Christendom itself. Only an individual who has not only realized the entirety of the soul's plans for his growth but who has also freed himself from all illusion will start off there. Realization of the soul's plans and freedom from illusion go hand in hand. It's impossible to achieve either goal without having concurrently achieved the other.

"Very few people start off their stay in the Afterdeath Zone in the City of Christendom. But everyone who has been exposed to the Christian belief system ends up there eventually. So it's not as if beginning on one of the lower levels of the Redemption Zone denies anything to anyone. It just takes a little longer to get through the processing of one's recently completed lifetime. But even the idea of 'taking longer' is problematic, since time doesn't function here in the way that you understand it. Which level one ends up on may have some bearing on the kind of lifetime he'll experience next, but not in the sense of reward or punishment. Lessons on freeing oneself from illusion will simply resume wherever they left off in the previous lifetime.

"Finally, you should understand that from the soul's perspective, to be a victim or a victimizer in the areas of lust, fear, and control are the same. Each is a choice. Each is equal in its potential for generating illusion. Each can block the realization of the soul's master plan. Social convention and religious dogma can severely limit one's growth—even your grandmother's.

"It just happens that in your society, artists are given license to free themselves from such conformity, and so are more likely in some respects to discover and fulfill their life purpose, or to provide themselves with the tools that will help them free themselves from lust, fear, and control.

"In your society there's such an emphasis on making money, on pursuing success in financial terms through activities that provide no real satisfaction, that many people never discover their life purpose. Creating illusions based on lust, fear, and control—high dramas of the victim and the victimizer—becomes the primary way in which they entertain themselves to make up for the spiritual emptiness they would otherwise experience.

"Every human being is immensely creative. But unless that creativity is channeled into some art or craft, it will be used instead to generate illusion. It could be said, therefore, that every human being is an artist, at least in potential. Developing this creativity is an essential part of every person's life purpose, even if it isn't the main focus of one's career. From the soul's perspective, the arts are a form of spiritual exercise, as basic to the process of enlightenment as meditation or religious devotion might be. That's why music, drama, and painting, for example, have been a part of religious ritual since time immemorial."

"I'm curious to know," I asked, "why I see this level of the Redemption Zone as an abandoned airport terminal." After I described the terminal to her, Karin explained what I saw as follows:

"The air-traffic control tower that you see off in the distance represents the ego's perspective on life—higher, in the case of someone on this level, than on the previous ones. This means that the individual has at least the potential to see his life in terms of larger patterns and lessons, a potential exercised whenever he considers his art in purely formal terms. The three runways symbolize lust, fear, and control. The purpose of this level is to gain an overview of how lust, fear, and control affected the individual's ability to rise beyond the ego's perspective, like an airplane taking off, in order to see things from the soul's perspective.

"The baggage claim indicates the necessity of claiming the spiritual baggage of one's illusions about life in order to release them. The monitors are there to let one know when he arrived at a destination intended by the soul, and when he departed from the course the soul intended. The many windows point out how each art form or spiritual discipline provides a different perspective on life, but all for the same purpose: to help strip away illusion in any form. The broken window in front of the choreographer symbolizes the perspective on life offered by the making of dances. Its fragments represent the life work of this particular artist. He didn't see the connection between the events of his life and his dances, so the window needs to be put together like a jigsaw puzzle. It was never really broken—it just wasn't properly assembled while he was alive.

"There's no one at the ticket counters because people who have made it to this level don't need any help in figuring out how to free themselves of illusion. Attendants and Technicians aren't as necessary here as on the previous levels. However, when the choreographer has figured out what he learned about lust, fear, and control—the three take-off runways—from his dances, that's his ticket out of here. An Attendant will come along to show him to the area of the Afterdeath Zone where his next set of lessons may be learned."

25

The Weighing of the Heart

"Now, if there are no further questions, let's proceed to the first level of the Redemption Zone, which, as I mentioned a moment ago, is the City of Christendom."

We boarded the elevator and after a brief journey found ourselves in the lobby area from which we'd begun our tour of the Redemption Zone's lower levels. During the ride, I thought of another question for Karin.

"Why do you refer sometimes to the VA and at others to the Redemption Zone?"

"Good question," she replied. "Remember what I said when we were standing in the central plaza—that on a tour such as this one you may perceive things from several different perspectives. The Facilitators see this area as one of healing for those who've done battle with the magnified and distorted primate instincts—thus the VA. The Shades who undergo this healing, however, are still very much involved with the Christian belief system. Thus they see things in terms of redemption. Their souls are being redeemed from the illusions fostered by lust, fear, and control—words which help them understand what we mean by the term 'magnified and distorted primate instincts.'"

"In a moment," Karin addressed the group as a whole, "we'll visit the upper levels of the VA, where the purification process continues. Now that illusions based on lust, fear, and control have been purged from the individual's belief system, he needs to go through every moment of his life and release himself of the distortions that such illusions engendered. Any so-called negative emotion such as anger, jealousy, hatred, frustration, or self-pity manifests itself because of illusions based on lust, fear, or control, or some combination of these primate instincts. The presence of such an emotion in association with an event one experienced while alive acts as a kind of place marker, indicating that the lessons the individual was to learn from that event were left incomplete.

"From the soul's perspective, every negative emotion is a precise indication of how, where, and when a growth process was abandoned, and what needs to be done to complete it properly. It may be too late to complete that process in physical terms, but seeing what should have been instead of what was actually done, can be helpful in preparing the individual for his next lifetime, in which it's not at all unlikely he'll confront a similar set of circumstances.

"There are four upper levels in the VA, corresponding with the four types of Shades I mentioned earlier: those whose lives were dedicated to self-actualization, and who largely succeeded; those who were aware of the need to self-actualize and went as far as they could, given the limitations of their too-conventional belief system; those who made attempts to satisfy the need for self-actualization but encountered obstructions that they were in some way unable to overcome; and those who were unaware of the need to self-actualize and made no attempts to do so.

"Souls of the first type will have fewer emotional distortions to purge than souls of the last type. An individual who has been completely successful in actualizing himself rarely experiences negative emotions, or has learned how to process them while alive. He'll end up on the present level of the

Redemption Zone, as I've already mentioned, and will probably have no need for a stay in the VA.

"In the upper levels of the VA, the souls are kept in wooden drawers, as in a mausoleum. To any outsider, these souls appear to be asleep. Meanwhile, Technicians take samples of their energies from time to time to see how they're doing. These samples are run through a kind of distilling apparatus and brought to the next level of purity. When the purified samples are added back to the drawer, the soul will strive to purge itself of emotion until its entire being has achieved that same level of purity.

"Now, if you'll step this way," Karin said, moving to a bank of elevators on the wall opposite the one we'd just emerged from, "we'll continue our tour of the VA."

As the others boarded the elevator, I lagged behind. I'd already toured the upper levels of the VA on an earlier adventure in Otherwhere. Now might be the time to do some exploring on my own.

The elevators we had just left seemed capable of going to levels higher than the one we were on. Yet Karin had chosen a different bank. Those elevators too had up and down arrows. But there had been only one bank of elevators on each level of the Redemption Zone. Unable to decide which bank of elevators to use, I pressed the up button for those we had just left, and the down button for the ones the group was now using. I would take the one that arrived first.

The down-arrow light clicked off as one of the elevators on the side the group was using opened. I got on. Now I had to decide which of the numerous buttons to press. When Karin was running the elevator for the tour, I'd assumed that it operated in much the same way as those in physical reality. I hadn't noticed that there were several buttons for each level. Each button was embossed with an acronym, evidently designating the destination. The central column was marked *CC*, probably for *City of Christendom*. The level I was on must be the *CCVAL*, in the exact center of the panel, short for *City of*

Christendom Veterans Administration Lobby. At least I would know how to get back.

Unable to make up my mind, I pressed a button at random. It was the farthest left button on the lowest level, marked *AEU*. The door closed and the elevator began moving. The trip took much longer than the rides between levels of the Redemption Zone. At one point I was no longer moving downward on a vertical plane, but horizontally. At long last, the elevator doors opened.

I found myself in a small, nondescript antechamber with perfectly white, featureless walls. To my right, as I exited the elevator, was a heavy metal door with a small glass window. I looked through the window but could see nothing. I was afraid that the door might be locked. As I reached for the bar that would allow me to push it open, I heard a sound behind me. Whirling around, afraid that someone might have come after me, I saw only that the elevator doors were gently closing.

I returned to the metal door and slowly put pressure on the bar. It gave, and the door began to swing open.

The area beyond the door was dark, but seemed to be quite spacious. Perhaps it was another cave, I thought, waiting for my eyes to adjust. I took a few hesitant steps forward, wondering if I could find some way to prop the door open. Would I be able to get out quickly if I had to? I was in the Land of the Dead, after all. There was no telling what I might encounter. Suddenly, I wished that I hadn't left the safety of the tour, or that somehow Karin could have been by my side. Her reassuring presence would have provided the perfect antidote for the dread that was beginning to build within me.

Before letting go of the door, I tested the latch. It seemed to function smoothly enough. I let go of the door and watched it glide closed. The light in the antechamber glowed wanly through the door's small window. Since the door opened again when I tried it, I turned to face the darkness.

After a while, I began to make out the shape of the space I was in. It seemed to be a large room with a high ceiling, like the interior of a warehouse. Furniture—chairs, boxes, wooden trunks—was stacked from floor to ceiling in some areas. Other areas were dominated by larger than life-size sculptures that bulked in the gloom. A narrow aisle ran down the middle of the room, just barely dividing the jumble into halves.

I took a few steps down the aisle, noticing that other, shorter aisles branched off from it at right angles, giving access to the items stored near the walls. I passed models of gondola-like boats the length of my forearm, and small jars carved from stone and topped with the heads of animals—cats and birds, an ape. Turning right down the first cross-aisle, I stopped in front of a statue that was pushed against the wall.

Three times higher than myself, the statue depicted a man seated on a throne, his arms outstretched authoritatively, if somewhat rigidly, on the armrests. The body seemed to be draped in the flowing folds of a tunic carved from stone. It was surmounted by the head of a god, crowned and inhuman—the hawk-face of Horus, Egyptian god of the Sun.

At once I understood the mass of furniture surrounding me. I'd seen reproductions of pharaonic tombs in museums and books. They were usually jammed to capacity with items from daily life in order to make the great king comfortable in the Land of the Dead. The boats I'd passed helped him on his journey to the Afterlife. The animal-headed jars were intended to contain and preserve the king's viscera, which were removed during the mummification process. The long wooden trunks must have been sarcophagi or mummy cases.

I tried to remember everything I could about ancient Egyptian funerary practices. There was a time in grade school when I'd wanted to be an archaeologist and had read several books on the subject. Was I in some kind of temple? Or was this the as-yet-undiscovered tomb of a pharaoh? It seemed more like a museum storage room to me, spooky in the dim light from the exit door's window.

I'd always been fascinated by the Egyptian Book of the Dead, a collection of spells, charms, and prayers to be used by the deceased under any of the circumstances he might encounter in the Afterlife. I remembered a scene painted on one of the pages of that ancient papyrus manuscript: the weighing of the heart. If the feather in one of the scale's pans was heavier than the heart in the other, the judge Anubis took the deceased to meet Osiris, god of the Dead. If the heart was heavier, then it was devoured by a terrible monster. I was struck by the similarity between this scene and the one I had witnessed at the lowest level of the Redemption Zone. In both cases, a terrible monster had devoured some part of a dead man's soul.

I wondered if I might find a copy of the Egyptian Book of the Dead somewhere in the jumble surrounding me. But where would I look? I didn't dare go deeper into the storage room, since I didn't have a flashlight or a candle. The light from the doorway was too dim.

As I considered what to do next, a movement along the wall caught my eye. Could there be rats down here? Not likely, if I were still in nonphysical reality. But what if I were in a tomb on Earth? I comforted myself with the thought that I would still be out of body and therefore immune to their predations. But what if there were other spiritual dangers of which I was unaware lurking in dark and unexplored areas of Otherwhere such as this—how would I deal with *them*?

Again I began to wonder about the wisdom of having gone exploring on my own. I had just decided to turn around and head back to the elevator when the movement came again. This time it was accompanied by a low grinding noise, as of stone against stone. I became aware of a gentle tremor in the floor and remembered the earthquake that had accompanied the dragon's appearance in the Redemption Zone. I wasn't about to wait around for such a creature to surprise me here!

Furniture began to tumble down around me as the tremors increased, blocking my way to the exit. As I looked around for another way out, I saw that the wall with its statue of Horus was sliding backward and turning, like the entrance to a secret passage. I began to panic as I sensed a presence in the room.

I saw no one else, but the movements around me seemed purposeful. None of the furniture simply fell. Each chair or casket may have toppled from its pile, but it always landed right-side up, sometimes scooting away, as if under the influence of a poltergeist. Other walls turned or moved outward. The furniture continued to rearrange itself, as if placed in precise positions by unseen hands.

A life-size wooden statue of Thoth, the god of wisdom, began to roll toward me, as if on wheels. I dodged past it and saw my way out between a chest and a divan that had previously been buried beneath a mound of clutter. The aisles were gone, replaced by an orderly pattern that was emerging evermore quickly from the chaotic jumble. I had to find a new path back to the door, while constantly on the lookout for statues and urns that might suddenly decide that they wanted to position themselves directly in front of me—or in the space I was occupying—as I tried to decide what direction to move in.

My sense that some powerful yet invisible presence was behind this flurry of activity grew, keeping pace with my panic. Yet that force didn't seem to be intentionally blocking my passage out, even though its activities sometimes drove me farther back into the room as I tried to avoid being run down by the stone columns and careening sarcophagi that could easily have crushed me.

I made it to the door, desperately afraid that it would be locked—that the presence in the room only seemed to be ignoring me, and that once it was through arranging its toys it would turn its full attention upon me. But the door yielded easily to my touch. Once again, I found myself in the empty antechamber with its single elevator door. It opened immediately after I pressed the up button.

I tried to calm myself on the long journey back to the VA lobby. Had I done something wrong? Would there be unpleasant consequences for my having left the tour group? Would I be able to find them? Had I been missed?

When at last the elevator door opened on the lobby, I found Karin waiting for me.

"Looks like you've been doing a little exploring," she said, smiling pleasantly.

I didn't know what to say. Was she being sarcastic? I felt weak in the knees and must have looked terrified. Her expression immediately changed to one of concern. She led me to a nearby couch and sat down next to me.

"Where's the group?" I stuttered.

"They've dispersed," Karin replied. "Some may still be hanging out in the city. But most have gone back to their dimensions and planets of origin. We finished the tour while you were gone."

"Why did you wait for me?"

"When I realized you were no longer with us, I figured you'd probably gone exploring on your own. Most of the Afterdeath Zone can be confusing without a Guide, especially for someone who's not dead yet. I thought you might have a few questions."

"Understatement of the eon," I replied, laughing weakly.

"Why don't you start by telling me where you went."

"Actually, I'm not sure. The elevator button said *AEU*."

"That stands for *Ancient Egyptian Underworld*," Karin said brightly. "So you're a comparative religion buff."

"Not exactly. I picked that button at random."

"You should know better than that," Karin chided me gently. "If you believe there are no accidents in physical reality, that goes double for Otherwhere. No matter where you go or how you get there, it's your need to learn that guides you."

"Well, one thing I learned was not to go wandering off by myself!"

"I doubt if that was the only thing. There are no rules against exploring Otherwhere without a Guide. We're here for your convenience, not your safety or protection. Nothing in Otherwhere can harm you, except something you create from your own fear. Fear often accompanies a confrontation with the unknown. Having a Guide who can explain what you're experiencing may reduce or eliminate that fear. Our only concern, aside from education, is that you don't become so frightened by what you don't understand that you'll never come back—until you have to.

"Now why don't you tell me exactly what you experienced, from the moment you got off the elevator."

After I had told Karin my story, she said, "I can certainly understand why you might find such an experience frightening. You thought that the force that was moving things around was out to get you. Nothing could be further from the truth.

"As you know, in Otherwhere your thoughts manifest themselves more or less instantly as experience. The same thing is true for all other human beings who find their way here, whether through death or some other means—dreams, drugs, out-of-body experiences, or what-have-you. As you yourself have found to be true, the more frequently you visit Otherwhere, the clearer your adventures become. Your ability to translate the energies experienced here into quasiphysical terms improves.

"This improvement occurs not only because of an increased understanding of the laws or concepts behind these energies and their interactions with one another, but also because your repertoire of symbols for describing them continues to grow. With each new set of symbols, you've conquered that much more of the unknown. This makes it possible to experience subtler energies and more sophisticated concepts.

"If you were a member of the ancient Egyptian culture, you might be perceived as a kind of prophet. You would bring back your stories of what goes on in the Afterdeath Zone and others would try to understand, perhaps even to spread the word through stories, writings, songs, sculptures, or paintings. Through such interpretations, not to mention your own further adventures, the number of symbols used to explain the concepts you'd experienced in Otherwhere would multiply.

"That set of symbols would eventually become what you call a public translation table. Later explorers of Otherwhere might carry that translation table with them. And because thought creates experience over here, the symbol set that makes your translation table would take on a kind of reality. When the earthly tomb of a pharaoh is arranged according to ancient Egyptian beliefs about what is needed or to be found in the Afterdeath Zone, the Afterdeath Zone begins to resemble the interior of a pharaoh's tomb.

"Any symbol encountered in the Afterdeath Zone is sustained by people's belief in it. Once energy has been invested in a symbol, it can't be retracted, except by a conscious act of will. If the people who believe in a certain set of symbols die out, the symbols will continue to exist in some area of nonphysical reality. After millennia of being fed by a people's beliefs, these symbols are so powerful that no one alive could dissipate the energy contained in them. Only one of the Overseers could do that. But the Overseers usually don't choose to do so.

"As long as some reference to the beliefs and symbols in question remains in physical reality, there's always a chance someone will encounter them, there or here. Through comparison of this ancient belief system with his own, he may arrive at a deeper understanding of life, death, God, and his function within the universe.

"The ancient belief system may have once taken up a whole plane or subzone of Otherwhere. But when it's no longer in use, it automatically contracts, just as a once-rolled-up map spread out before you will roll up again when you stop holding it down. During the heyday of the system in question, there were as many points of entry as there were people who believed in that system. When those people were gone, the system was less accessible. Now there's only one point of entry—the mind of the individual who wishes to visit it. Thus, it could be said that the system is no longer a plane or subzone but a single point.

"Please keep in mind, however, that because there's no space as you understand it in nonphysical reality, the idea of planes and points is merely an analogy. Over here, the closest thing to the concept of space is *psychological* distance, which is a function of understanding. The more easily you comprehend something, the closer you'll find it in nonphysical reality.

"The Ancient Egyptian Underworld was accessible to you because you were aware of some of the symbols associated with it through your study of archaeology. You have much less understanding of what lies behind that belief system, however, than you do of the Christian belief system you were brought up with. Thus it was a long journey between Christendom and the Ancient Egyptian Underworld.

"There was only one elevator door when you got there, instead of the three you had seen in the lobby. This fact indicated that there was only one point of access to that area of the Afterdeath Zone—your unconscious desire to visit it.

"The three elevators in Christendom served different functions. One was for Shades, one for Facilitators and Overseers, and one for Rangers, which is to say tourists such as ourselves. Yet this doesn't imply any kind of class structure, such as the old practice of separate bathrooms for whites and colored people. It means only that each of these three types of beings has a different way of, or purpose for, traveling in the Afterdeath Zone.

"Once in the Ancient Egyptian Underworld, you translated the compression of that belief structure into a storage room stacked high with symbols you were familiar with from your reading. The lack of light indicated that you were carrying with you only a limited potential to understand the AEU. To travel more deeply into it, you would have needed the illumination of a Guide.

"At the point when you remembered the scene from the Egyptian Book of the Dead, the weighing of the heart, your understanding of that concept and your belief in the fundamental truth behind it began to reinvest energy in that ancient belief system. Thus you triggered the expansion of that belief system from a point to a plane. All of its concepts and symbols began to rearrange themselves into their proper relationships.

"The force you felt behind this process of rearrangement

was not a personality, as you understand the term. In non-physical reality, energy harnessed for any purpose becomes distinct from all other investments of energy and is perceived as an entity. Its function *is* its identity, whether or not it has a personality as you or I do. So you could say that you became aware of the energy harnessed by the ancient Egyptians to describe their experience of the Afterdeath Zone—an impersonal entity whose function is to maintain the proper relationships between the symbols and beliefs used to represent that experience.

"As to the question of why you ended up in the AEU, I suspect that you'd made a not fully conscious connection between the ancient Egyptians' notion of weighing the heart and what happened with the dragon on the lowest level of the Redemption Zone. Some part of you wanted to explore this connection further.

"An Egyptian scholar would say that the feather against which the heart was weighed represented truth or moral rectitude. But on your tour today, you learned that moral rectitude has nothing to do with how faithfully one obeys religious law. Rather, it's a function of how close one has come to the fulfillment of the soul's master plan for his growth and the extent to which his relationship with the soul has been distorted by illusion in the areas of lust, fear, and control. That was as true for the ancient Egyptians as it is for the society in which you now live."

As Karin spoke these words, her face began to waver. The VA lobby slipped out of focus and I awoke.

26

Gateways to Nonphysical Reality

So far I've written much about the kinds of things one might encounter in nonphysical reality, but nothing about how to get there. Over the centuries, humankind has developed an enormous battery of techniques for altering consciousness, including meditation, hypnosis, drugs, out-of-body experiences, and lucid dreaming. Many of these techniques may be used as gateways into nonphysical reality, or at least as exercises in developing the flexibility of consciousness necessary to gain such access. I've tried some of these techniques, with varying success. Others I know of only by reputation.

In our society, meditation has been most frequently touted as a means of reducing stress. More serious practitioners see it as a tool for spiritual advancement. Many meditation traditions encourage quieting the mind and developing a calm detachment from the affairs of the world. Although some spiritual teachers acknowledge that meditation can lead to the development of paranormal abilities, they usually discourage studying it specifically for this purpose. Even so, a friend of mine who practices transcendental meditation once told me of several encounters with unusual beings which he experienced while meditating.

There are countless books on meditation and many people who teach it, from the lady next door to Indian gurus. If you wish to try this means of gaining access into nonphysical reality, be advised that meditation is rarely taught without reference to a spiritual belief system that could affect the way you translate and interpret your experiences.

Techniques of self-hypnosis bear a strong resemblance to meditation techniques and may be used for similar purposes, including gaining access to nonphysical reality. Hypnosis is usually conducted, however, by a trained hypnotist in a therapeutic setting. Some hypnotists are interested in exploring the consciousness-altering aspects of the technique and might be persuaded to experiment with it as a means of gaining access to nonphysical reality. Hypnotism has two potential drawbacks. The first is that not everyone can be hypnotized. The second is that hypnotized subjects are so highly suggestible that a hypnotist's line of questioning may influence the subject's responses, even unintentionally.

Many reports of extraterrestrial encounters involve hypnotism, which was used as a means of reclaiming experiences thought to be so traumatic that the individual had blocked them from memory. I don't entirely trust these accounts. The fact that the hypnotists are operating from the assumption that their subjects may have been abducted by aliens could cause them unwittingly to supply the imagery into which their subjects translate their experiences. Those experiences may not have involved aliens at all, but beings similar to the ones described in this field guide.

From time immemorial, drugs have been used as one of the most common means of entering nonphysical reality: wine and opium in Europe and the Orient; tobacco, marijuana, ayahuasca, peyote, and psilocybin in the New World. More recently, synthetic hallucinogens such as LSD or ketamine have been added to the list, as well as anesthetics such as nitrous oxide (laughing gas). The advantage of drugs is that they more or less guarantee the production of an altered state of consciousness. The disadvantages are that many of them are illegal and addictive—and if abused can cause physical deterioration, even death.

I've never used drugs as a means of gaining access to nonphysical reality. Yet there are reports of drug-induced hallucinations that bear strong resemblances to my own adventures. I suspect that some of the bizarre imagery associated with hallucinogens is nothing more than a representation of the body's metabolization process, which is actively seeking to purge itself of the drug. This purging process can take hours.

For me, the most frightening aspect of using drugs as a gateway into nonphysical reality would be that, in return for the guarantee of an altered state, I'd have to give up conscious control of both body and mind until the drug had been wholly metabolized. Most of the other means of getting into nonphysical reality can be terminated at will if one's experience there becomes too intense.

In ancient tribal societies, the shaman was a specialist in using altered states to travel into other realities. Sickness was believed to be caused by the soul's wandering away from the body, and shamans were often employed to retrieve it. Frequently, this required a visit to the Land of the Dead. Although shamans throughout the world have used alcohol or hallucinogenic drugs to alter their consciousness prior to such a journey, it was more usual for them to use a certain monotonous style of drumming, rattling, and singing to achieve that end. Recent proponents of shamanism, especially Michael Harner, have revived the drumming technique for altering consciousness.

The shamanic universe is divided into three worlds—lower, middle, and upper. The middle world is our earthly reality. Shamans traveling there are able to see or hear what's happening miles away from their physical bodies. Journeys into the lower world are used to gather information on healing, and journeys into the upper world for gathering information on other topics. Beings who provide help or instruction are commonly encountered in the lower or upper worlds.

Shamanism is not just a means of altering consciousness. It also provides its own translation tables. So, for example, illness in the body may be perceived as infestations of insects or poisonous reptiles, healing entities as benevolent animals, teachers as ancient gods. In a workshop taught by Michael Harner, I once encountered an Aztec god—Huitzilopochtli, the Left-Handed Hummingbird Wizard—on a journey in which I was searching for a spiritual teacher. I'd seen a picture of this god when studying the Aztecs in grade school. That picture formed the basis of my representation of the teaching entity I encountered. This incident illustrates one of the drawbacks of employing shamanism as a means of exploring nonphysical reality: the translation tables that go along with it can unduly influence one's perceptions. On the other hand, the advantage of the drumming technique is that it seems to work for almost everyone.

Michael Harner's book, *The Way of the Shaman: A Guide to Power and Healing*, provides an excellent introduction to shamanism. He and the staff of his Institute for Shamanic Studies teach workshops in which participants learn traditional shamanic journeying techniques. For a schedule of such workshops, contact:

The Foundation for Shamanic Studies
P.O. Box 1939
Mill Valley, CA 94942
Phone: 415-380-8282
Website: www.shamanism.org

Many books on out-of-body experiences and astral projection are full of abstruse metaphysics and bizarre ritualistic techniques. One book that successfully avoids such hocus-pocus is Rick Stack's *Out-of-Body Adventures: Thirty Days to the Most Exciting Experience of Your Life*. Stack's position, which my own experiences confirm, is that certain commonly held beliefs about life, death, the body, and the nature of consciousness can prevent out-of-body experiences from occurring. His approach is to identify these beliefs and replace them with others more conducive to such experiences. Stack also provides a number of techniques for inducing out-of-body experiences and some suggestions for what to do once one has succeeded in getting out.

Robert Peterson's *Out-of-Body Experiences: How to Have Them and What to Expect* is another excellent introduction to the subject. It provides one of the most complete rosters of possible ways to get out of body that I've yet come across, as well as an extensive bibliography.

There seem to be two basic kinds of out-of-body adventures: those that involve visits to actual locations on Earth, and those that involve visits to the various regions of nonphysical reality. In *Journeys Out of the Body*, the late Robert Monroe describes both types, with an emphasis on the first. In *Far Journeys* and *Ultimate Journey*, he deals mainly with the second type. I suspect that the function of the earth-based out-of-body experiences is to provide a not-too-jarring orientation within the unfamiliar state of consciousness that produces them. Such an orientation can function as a prelude to exploring the unfamiliar surroundings of nonphysical reality. That seems to have been Monroe's experience, and my own followed a similar pattern.

I believe that Monroe's books provide the best available introduction to the phenomena of out-of-body experiences and the characteristics of the nonphysical environment. All three books provide suggestions and exercises that I've found invaluable in developing my own ability to go out of body. In addition, The Monroe Institute provides seminars and tape programs designed to prepare people for exploring altered states of consciousness and out-of-body experiences. For more information, contact:

The Monroe Institute
62 Roberts Mountain Road
Faber, VA 22938-2317
Phone: 434-361-1252
FAX: 434-361-1237
Website: www.monroeinstitute.org

Some near-death experiences bear a resemblance to the out-of-body experiences described in Monroe's three books. But the only way to produce a near-death experience intentionally, it seems, is to attempt suicide.

In *Reflections on Life After Life*, Dr. Raymond Moody points out that near-death experiences caused by attempted suicide are rarely pleasant. There's some evidence, however, that people who have had near-death experiences as a result of natural or accidental causes may develop paranormal abilities afterwards, including the ability to leave the body at will. This was the case with the mother of my trumpet-playing friend in college.

P. M. H. Atwater's book *Coming Back to Life: The After-Effects of the Near-Death Experience,* or her more recent *Beyond the Light: The Mysteries and Revelations of the Near-Death Experience,* reports on this and other social, psychological, and spiritual consequences of near-death experiences.

An important resource for anyone interested in the near-death experience is the International Association for Near-Death Studies (IANDS). In addition to bringing out a newsletter called *Vital Signs* and a scholarly publication called *The Journal of Near-Death Studies,* the organization holds annual conferences and sponsors chapter meetings in many parts of the country. It may be reached as follows:

IANDS
P.O. Box 502
East Windsor, CT 06028
Phone: 860-644-5216
FAX: 860-644-5759
website: IANDS.org

A yearning to return to the regions of nonphysical reality visited during a near-death experience is mentioned by nearly everyone who has had one. If the ability to get out of body is one of the after-effects of the near-death experience, and if out-of-body experiences are one of the ways of gaining access to nonphysical reality, then it seems reasonable to assume that near-death experiencers would have little trouble returning to nonphysical reality. I suspect, however, that they rarely make the effort because they nearly died the first time!

If you've had a near-death experience, you may find it easier than most people to get out of body. If you wish to make other visits to nonphysical reality, perhaps the fact that I've been there many times *without* dying will inspire you to make the attempt. If your intention is to escape from the real world into that seemingly more perfect environment, you may not be successful. Chances are that you've got important work to do here on Earth, and you may not be able to afford the distraction of wanting to go back and preferring to stay. On the other hand, if your intention is to explore and map nonphysical reality, the Overseers might establish a contract with you, in which case you could come and go more or less as you pleased.

Lucid dreams may be one of the most readily accessible means to gain access to nonphysical reality. Some researchers claim that out-of-body experiences are really nothing more than extraordinarily lucid dreams. Monroe refutes this position by pointing out that many earth-based out-of-body experiences can be verified by checking what one has seen in a distant location against accounts by anyone who was physically there—or, as in my case, by visiting those distant locations, if they can be found, to see how they correspond with one's out-of-body-gleaned memory of them.

Many of my earth-based out-of-body adventures began as dreams in which I was leaving my body. I suspect that the same thing has been true for others, and that this is why dream researchers classify out-of-body experiences as lucid dreams. It seems to me that the question of whether or not an out-of-body experience is a lucid dream is really one of semantics. Where do we go when we sleep? It's obvious that the dream world isn't the same as the waking world. So where is it? One could equally well ask where the mind is in relation to the brain.

I believe that dreams originate in visits to the Dream Zone of nonphysical reality. One doesn't necessarily have to leave one's body to get to the Dream Zone. All one has to do is shift the focus of one's consciousness away from physical reality, which is precisely what happens during sleep. Just as there are degrees of awareness of one's surroundings while awake, so are there degrees of lucidity in dreams, as we have seen. It seems to me that if one recognizes that he's dreaming and can take control of the dream, he could also consciously make the decision to pass through what I've called the Otherwhere Gate into other areas of nonphysical reality.

Most of my adventures in nonphysical reality have occurred while I was asleep. I've never been able to predict when they would occur, nor have I been able to produce them at will. Currently, I'm engaged in teaching myself how to become lucid in dreams so that I'll be able to produce such experiences whenever I wish. Two books have been useful in this process: *Lucid Dreaming*, by Stephen LaBerge, and *Exploring the World of Lucid Dreaming*, by Stephen LaBerge and Howard Rheingold.

During the adventure in which I achieved full lucidity for the first time, the Instructor who resembled David Carradine had a few things to tell me after we'd walked together through the open iron door. His words may be useful for anyone who wishes to explore nonphysical reality.

"Now you're in Otherwhere," he said. "It's essential for you to maintain an awareness that everything you perceive is a translation of energy patterns. Now *you* are responsible for everything you perceive. My colleague and I are no longer controlling the imagery of your experience. What do you see?"

"We seem to be in a courtyard," I said. "It has a gate at one end, high stone walls, and tiers of many-colored flowers in full bloom. There are three or four tables besides ours. At the one closest to the gate, I see an old man with a long beard. He wears a gray robe. He's resting his head on his hands and staring off into space with a forlorn expression. He looks so thin and frail that I can practically see through him."

259

"So where do you think we are?" the Instructor asked, testing me.

"Well, I see a gate, so we must not actually be in Otherwhere yet, even though we've passed through the door you said would lead us there. My guess is that the old man is a Gatekeeper."

"That's correct." The Instructor smiled. "You could say that we're in the Garden of the Gatehouse."

"But the last time I encountered a Gatekeeper in Otherwhere, the Gate was surrounded by a desert."

"That desert was your representation of the Barrier Zone. You tried to force your way through the Gate, and because you were not yet sufficiently clear of negative emotions, a force prevented you from continuing. Had you been properly prepared to use that Gate, you would have come into a field of energy that expresses the Overseers' great understanding of and compassion for human suffering. Within that energy field is not only compassion, but also the assurance that no matter how difficult life on Earth seems to be, the Overseers have no other desire than to help you grow and realize yourselves, like the flowers in full bloom.

"You may have noticed that there are five tiers of flowers. These represent five possible reactions to the human condition. The first is disbelief that the Overseers—or the gods, or the one God—exist. The second is a passive and unquestioning acceptance of life's difficulties as a punishment for sin—however *sin* may be defined. The third is anger and resentment at the apparent unfairness and injustice of the world, in which horrible things seem to happen to good people and the villains go unpunished. The fourth is depression—a deep empathy for and understanding of human suffering, combined with a sense of the futility of trying to do anything about it. The fifth is ennui, a feeling that life has no purpose, that all action is pointless.

"People may succeed in cleaning up the negative emotions that bar them from Otherwhere, but still may not be allowed to pass through the Gate. They have to meet five conditions first. They have to *believe* that there's an intrinsic order to the universe, and that certain highly developed consciousnesses—call them what they will—originated and continue to maintain that order.

"They have to *perceive* themselves as masters of their fate, not as victims of the gods, the world, or the universe. They have to *recognize* that every experience, even a horrible one, is chosen by the person who undergoes it. They must also *realize* that the apparent magnitude of human suffering does not excuse them from finding a way to ameliorate it, no matter how small—and if nowhere else, then in themselves. And they must be willing to *accept* that every experience on Earth is a lesson. Learning is neither good nor bad. It just *is*. Either you learn through joy or you learn through suffering. Resistance to learning is the source of all human suffering.

"We have here a belief, a perception, a recognition, a realization, and an acceptance. While the Overseers extend their compassion to all equally, even those who lack one or more of these understandings, only those with all five in place are permitted to pass into Otherwhere."

"Am I lacking in any of these understandings? Is that why I haven't gotten any farther this time than the Gate?"

"Of course not. You've been to Otherwhere and back many times. After your recent journey to the Shadow Worlds, you wondered how you could help other people gain access to Otherwhere. So we've taken you through the entire process, as much for the education of others as for your own benefit.

"The techniques of gaining entrance to Otherwhere were once a part of every religious tradition. This tradition has been lost to Christianity since the time of the Inquisition. People don't need a church if they can answer the eternal questions for themselves, through personal journeys into Otherwhere. Such practices threatened the church's power structure and were repressed. Secret societies carried on the tradition, but had to disguise it in symbolism to avoid detection by the

Church. Over the centuries, the true meanings and practices behind these symbolic systems were lost, leaving nothing but empty ritual.

"The Gatekeeper looks sad because he's aware of the depth of human suffering but can do nothing about it. He would be glad to tell prospective visitors to Otherwhere what they need to do before he'll allow them to pass. That's why he's here.

"The reason you can almost see through the Gatekeeper is that any image chosen to represent him is nourished and sustained by the people who believe in it. Few use this Gateway into Otherwhere anymore, and so the image of the Gatekeeper is fading away."

"If I were to pass through the Gate at the end of the courtyard, what would I see?" I asked.

"That's up to you. Because of the Old-World feel of this courtyard, you might conjure up a lane lined with gates into other people's back yards. If you were to pass through any of those gates, you might end up in one or another of the Nonhuman Zones of Otherwhere."

"But I thought I needed to take a trolley to get to those zones—the NZ Line, if I remember correctly. What about the nonphysical subway system?"

"How you choose to represent to yourself the ways of gaining access to any zone of Otherwhere is up to you. The validity of such images lies in their usefulness, not in some kind of absolute truth. The only important thing is that you give yourself some way of identifying the zone into which you've traveled, so that you can return on future occasions. Whether this manner of identification is the name of a subway line or station, or the number on a gate in an alley, is your choice. The identifying function of such names or numbers is all that matters.

"Even though the Clear Light perceived by the Tibetan dream yogis provides a relatively undistorted experience of Otherwhere, it isn't terribly useful. In the Clear Light, no images are available to represent to oneself what happened in

Otherwhere. Consequently, nothing of the experience is recalled but the fact that it occurred. Even though images from physical reality inevitably distort what is perceived in Otherwhere, learning from your adventures there is far more important than not distorting them with physical imagery. A highly skilled translator can use such imagery in a way that little meaning is lost.

"Translation is like looking through a telescope at a galaxy that would otherwise be invisible to the naked eye. The telescope makes the galaxy visible, but doesn't show it as it truly is. The galaxy is much too large and far away for that. In the same way, Otherwhere is so large, and its psychological distance from what you're used to experiencing in physical reality is so great, that you would be unable to perceive it at all without the distorting instrument of language.

"As you map nonphysical reality, you provide a multitude of images that people may use, like telescopes, to help them translate what goes on over there for themselves, if they should ever make the journey. It doesn't matter whether you use gates, doors, hallways, alleys, or subway systems to describe how to enter Otherwhere. The differences between these images is like the differences between types of telescopes: the refractor, the reflector, the Newtonian, the Cassegrainian. And just as amateur astronomers have different tastes in telescopes, so may those readers who succeed in entering Otherwhere find certain images you've provided more useful than others in translating their own experiences.

"You may do your best to provide the map, but it's up to others to use or ignore any or all of it, as they see fit—or perhaps to improve it."

Sources Cited

Atwater, P. M. H. 1988. *Coming Back to Life: The After-Effects of the Near-Death Experience.* New York: Ballantine Books.

————. 1997. *Beyond the Light: Mysteries and Revelations of the Near-Death Experience.* New York: Avon.

Dante Alighieri. 1970. *The Paradiso: A Verse Rendering for the Modern Reader,* translated by John Ciardi. New York: New American Library.

Eliade, Mircea. 1964. *Shamanism: Archaic Techniques of Ecstasy.* Princeton, New Jersey: Princeton University Press.

Faraday, Ann, Ph.D. 1976. *The Dream Game.* New York: Perennial Library.

Fremantle, Francesca, and Chögyam Trungpa, transl. 1987. *The Tibetan Book of the Dead: The Great Liberation through Hearing in the Bardo.* Boston: Shambhala.

Grof, Stanislav, and Christina Grof. 1980. *Beyond Death: The Gates of Consciousness.* London: Thames and Hudson.

Harner, Michael J. 1980. *The Way of the Shaman: A Guide to Power and Healing*. San Francisco: Harper & Row.

LaBerge, Stephen. 1985. *Lucid Dreaming*. New York: Ballantine Books.

LaBerge, Stephen, and Howard Rheingold. 1990. *Exploring the World of Lucid Dreaming*. New York: Ballantine Books.

Monroe, Robert. 1977. *Journeys Out of the Body*. Garden City, New York: Doubleday.

———. 1985. *Far Journeys*. Garden City, New York: Doubleday.

———. 1994. *Ultimate Journey*. New York: Doubleday.

Moody, Raymond A., Jr. 1976. *Life After Life*. New York: Bantam.

———. 1978. *Reflections on Life After Life*. New York: Bantam.

Panchadasi, Swami. 1915. *The Astral Plane: Its Scenes, Dwellers, and Phenomena*. Chicago: Advanced Thought Publishing Co.

Peterson, Robert. 1997. *Out of Body Experiences: How to Have Them and What to Expect*. Charlottesville, Va.: Hampton Roads Publishing Co.

Stack, Rick. 1988. *Out-of-Body Adventures: Thirty Days to the Most Exciting Experience of Your Life*. Chicago: Contemporary Books.

Index

About the Author

Kurt Leland is an award-winning poet, composer, professional psychic, and author of *Menus for Impulsive Living: A Revolutionary Approach to Organizing and Energizing Your Life* (Doubleday, 1989). He received his master's degree in music composition from the University of Illinois. Since 1984, Leland has maintained a consulting practice in the Boston area called Spiritual Orienteering, whose purpose is to help people develop and maintain a soul-based approach to the challenges and opportunities of life. He is the winner of several poetry awards and was featured in 1996 in The Top 100 Psychics in America. He lives near Boston, Massachusetts.

Hampton Roads Publishing Company

. . . for the evolving human spirit

Hampton Roads Publishing Company
publishes books on a variety of subjects,
including metaphysics, health, integrative medicine,
visionary fiction, and other related topics.

For a copy of our latest catalog, call toll-free
(800) 766-8009, or send your name and address to:

Hampton Roads Publishing Company, Inc.
1125 Stoney Ridge Road
Charlottesville, VA 22902

hrpc@hrpub.com
www.hrpub.com